D0501526

The Prehistory of Sex

FOUR MILLION YEARS OF HUMAN SEXUAL CULTURE

Bantam Books

New York Toronto

London Sydney Auckland

THE
PREHISTORY
OF
SEX

TIMOTHY TAYLOR

THE PREHISTORY OF SEX
A Bantam Book / September 1996

BOOK DESIGN BY ELLEN CIPRIANO.

Library of Congress Cataloging-in-Publication Data

Taylor, Timothy, 1960–
    The prehistory of sex : four million years of human sexual
culture / Timothy Taylor.
        p.   cm.
    Includes bibliographical references and index.
    ISBN 0-553-09694-X
    1. Sex customs—History.   I. Title.
GN484.3.T39   1996
306.7—dc20   96-10803
                                                      CIP

Published simultaneously in the United States and Canada

Bantam Books are published by Bantam Books, a division of
Bantam Doubleday Dell Publishing Group, Inc. Its trademark,
consisting of the words "Bantam Books" and the portrayal of a
rooster, is Registered in U.S. Patent and Trademark Office and in
other countries. Marca Registrada. Bantam Books, 1540
Broadway, New York, New York 10036.

PRINTED IN THE UNITED STATES OF AMERICA
BVG   10 9 8 7 6 5 4 3 2 1

To Sarah

Contents

Illustrations

CHRISTOPHER ANTHONY MASTERS,
TH.D., Ph.D., J.D.
RANCHO SAN-DIEGO, CALIFORNIA

Acknowledgments

This book is based on a certain amount of firsthand archaeological experience and research, but it depends to a far greater degree on the work and opinions, published or otherwise, of others. The ideas and supporting research of Sarah Wright, my wife, have been crucial from beginning to end. Special thanks are also due to my research assistant, Alison Deegan, my colleagues Christopher Knüsel and Charlotte Roberts, and my former students David Lucy, Patrick Quinney, and Stuart Reevell, for all their contributions, criticisms, and support. Clive Gamble kindly read the text in one of its drafts and offered valuable corrections and comments; at a later stage Paul Bahn saved me from making some embarrassing errors in Chapter 5; neither of them necessarily agree with my views.

More generally, and in addition to the various acknowledgments implicit in the notes and bibliography at the end of the book, I would like to thank the following people: John Alexander, Sandra Assersohn, Douglass Bailey, Lynn Bevan, Richander Birkinshaw, Anthea Boyleston, David Brown, Aleksander Bursche, Christopher Chippindale, Sarah Colley, Joyce Connor, James Cox, Barry Cunliffe, Randy Donahue, Liz Dulaney, Peter Ellis, Rhîan Evans, Ginney Ferguson, Andrew Fitzpatrick, Rob Foley, Martin Foreman, Ken Hamilton, Richard Harrison, Gordon Hillman, Stephen Hobson, Ian Hodder, Barbara Hoddinott, Ralph Hoddinott, Veronika Holzer, Deborah Hughes, Chris Knight, Gicho Lazov, Yuri Lesman, Geoffrey Lloyd, Owen Lovejoy, Patty Stuart MacAdam, Leonie Madden, Alexander Marshack, Keith Matthews, Elizabeth McCann, Linda McClean, Leslie Meredith, Lynn Meskell, Peter Miller, Theya Molleson, Rodney Needham, Katharine Norman,

Christopher Pare, Nerys Patterson, Rachel Pilkington, Mark Pollard, Camilla Power, Mike Rowlands, Michael Ryder, Mick Sharp, Andrew Sherratt, Susan Sherratt, Mrs. Demitri Shimkin, Rachel Sholl, Janet Smithies, James Steele, Chris Stringer, George Taylor, Jill Thompson, Gerhard Tomedi, Bruce Trigger, Gerhard Trnka, Paul Vasey, Jenny Wagstaff, Nick Wetton, David Wilson, Alison Wylie, and Mrs. Rudy Zallinger.

My editors, Christopher Potter at Fourth Estate and Brian Tart at Bantam, provided consistent input and brought many new things to my attention. Janet Biehl's painstaking copyediting made my arguments clearer and more consistent. The book would not have been started without the inspired support of my agents, Katinka Matson and John Brockman, at Brockman, Inc. I would also like to thank my parents, Forbes and Mary Taylor, my godmother, Rosalind Moylan, and my parents-in-law, John and Joan Wright, for all their support.

Introduction

Beyond Nature

*"Eroticism, one may say, is
consenting to live."*

Pierrot-Le-Fou,
DIR. JEAN-LUC GODARD

In 1991 a corpse was found melting out of a glacier in the Ötztal Alps, on the mountain border between Italy and Austria. The mountaineer who first spotted the body, Erica Simon, thought from its delicate proportions that it was a woman's, perhaps that of an unfortunate skier from a recent season. But as the body was removed from the ice, it became clear that it was breastless, with what seemed to be male external genitalia, and that the remains of its clothing and equipment were strangely old-fashioned, not quite like anything ever seen before. The body became known as the Iceman and was nicknamed Ötzi.

Archaeologists believe that Ötzi died more than 5,000 years ago, around 3300 B.C., when the later Stone Age or Neolithic inhabitants of central Europe were beginning to use metals for the first time. He had been caught in a blizzard as he tried to make his way over a high pass from one valley to the next. He carried a number of items with

(Fig. 0.1)   The Iceman: emerging from a glacier on the Austro-Italian border,
September 20, 1991. Photograph courtesy of Gerhard Tomedi.

him, including a copper ax and what might have been magical talis-
mans. His body was well preserved. His general appearance and a
close study of his teeth suggest that he was between twenty-five and
forty years old when he died. Tattoos were still visible along either
side of his spine and on his legs. But what really grabbed public attention in the period between the initial discovery and the official
publication of the detailed and painstaking scientific investigations of
his body was the speculation about his sexuality and how it might
have been linked to his death.

Although the Iceman's scrotum was visible in the initial forensic
investigation, a mystery surrounded his penis or, more accurately, its
apparent absence. Bizarre stories began to circulate: his penis had
been eaten by a wild animal; it had snapped off as the body was being
removed from the ice; it had been removed and sold—for a six-figure
sum—to a collector of prehistoric sex organs. Someone informally accused the leader of the investigative team, Dr. Konrad Spindler, of
stealing it. A further theory, much favored in popular magazines, was
that the Iceman had been caught *in flagrante* and had been emasculated by the cuckolded husband before managing to escape up the
mountain, where he froze to death. Reports that the testicles had

mental qualities that our species has today have been chosen to some degree. Just as millions of years of sexual choice by peahens led, against the grain of natural selection, to the creation of peacocks with fantastic iridescent tail fans, so, I believe, the far more consciously directed sexual choices of our ancestors have led to a massive increase in brain size and to the establishment of a mental chasm between us and the rest of the animal kingdom. Our evolving consciousness now allows us, uniquely, to survey the remotest past and to investigate our own prehistoric origins.

This book tells a story in which biology is intertwined with culture. It is based on a vast body of archaeological evidence that is virtually unknown outside specialist circles: golden penis sheaths and graphic depictions of sex in prehistoric art, mammoth ivory phalluses, sculptures of women in childbirth, syphilitic skeletons, and the charred remains of aphrodisiac herbs. The story begins in the mists of evolutionary time, when the human form first emerged and sexual culture was invented. It ends by surveying the practices, prejudices, and confusions of the last five thousand years. It deals with sex in all its physical forms, as well as with reproduction, gender, and power—how societies have ordered themselves in relation to sex and sexuality.

Four million years ago in Africa, a small group of chimplike creatures began walking exclusively on their hind legs. The reason they did so is debated, but it marked a profound turning point, leading to the emergence of modern people. Our tree-swinging ancestors were very successful breeders. What they found erotic was probably quite varied: they may even have been as extreme as the pygmy chimps of today, who take their pleasure singly or in groups, often with no particular focus on reproduction, sometimes with members of their own sex or immediate family. However varied the behavior of our prehuman ancestors was, sex involved ideas of beauty, the physical basis of recognition and desire. Females had large clitorises and no breasts. Males had vanishingly small penises. Both sexes were covered with thick body hair. Then, somehow, what was considered beautiful altered dramatically. Upright walking hid the female genital

been "scraped out" of the scrotum also circulated and led to the out landish speculation that Ötzi was a castrated priest who had traveled from the Near East, a place where, it was thought, people sacrificed their genitals in order to be allowed to officiate in the temples of the "Great Mother." The fullest available autopsy report on the body, published in 1993, however, found that the Iceman's sexual organs were not missing after all—his uncircumcised penis and his testicles had indeed survived but were rather shrunk by cold and icy dryness.

A rumor that Ötzi's scrotal sac still contained viable sperm— quick-frozen, as in sperm banks—prompted a number of Austrian women to ask if they could be artificially inseminated and have his baby. Their motives—aside from the usual ones of novelty, publicity, or insanity—may have included a desire to breed with a "racially pure" individual, someone of ancient and impeccable Alpine stock. Modern clinical techniques would theoretically grant the women's re- quest, but certain ethical questions would arise. Because Ötzi may well have had children in his own lifetime, there is a fair chance that some of his direct descendants are alive in Alpine Europe today, two hun- dred or so generations later. Thus some of the women wanting insemi- nation with Ötzi's sperm might actually be his great-great-great . . . granddaughters. Perhaps all of them are. As physical anthropologist Torstein Sjøvold has pointed out, at a time depth of 5,000 years, the Iceman could theoretically be a direct ancestor of everyone on earth (although actual mating patterns among humans, along with geo- graphical barriers, make this virtually impossible in practice).

The possibility that the Iceman could be made to "live again," his sperm deployed in a macabre (and potentially incestuous) fash- ion, nevertheless reminds us that sex, in its rawest reproductive form, is a means by which humans can aspire to immortality, transcending material decay. Yet sex is also transcendent in itself, opening a door to a qualitatively different experience of being alive—ecstasy.

Nonetheless, the very ideas of eroticism, immortality, transcen- dence, and ecstasy are, on the billion-year timescale of sexual life on earth, strikingly new. People in their present form have been around for fewer than 150,000 years. Since higher animals usually select their reproductive partners carefully, it is likely that many of the

opening and encouraged the development of buttocks. The evolution of the first female breasts followed, along with the loss of most of the thick body hair in males and females alike. The clitoris reduced in size, while the penis grew dramatically larger.

Natural selection—"the survival of the fittest"—cannot explain all these transformations. In the process of natural selection, a species facing an environmental challenge either changes or dies out. In any species change occurs because there is some variation among the individual members, and only those best fitted to the new conditions survive to pass on their characteristics. Generation by generation, over millions and millions of years, changes accrue that turn not only sheeplike creatures into giraffes but fish into reptiles, and reptiles into birds. As a species changes, it sometimes divides into two different species. When it does, the criteria of mutual recognition between individual members must slowly alter: giraffes share a common ancestry with okapi, but they no longer try to mate with them. As Darwin himself pointed out, however, natural selection alone cannot account for the fantastic variety of life on earth. The peacock's tail, for example, makes the peacock an easy target for predators. The critical compensation for this vulnerability—and an important foundation for this book—is that peahens find it sexy.

Darwin recognized that certain characteristically human features, such as our lack of protective body hair (a stark contrast to our nearest primate relatives), make no sense in terms of basic survival. He proposed that "sexual selection" was the key to understanding them, arguing that the particular mate choices that individuals in a species make can be as crucial to evolution as pressures from the outside environment. In one form of sexual selection, brute force is used, almost always by males, to compete for the chance to mate with the opposite sex. A second, more important form of sexual selection is by the female, who usually makes the ultimate reproductive choice. Sometimes she may choose to conceive with a physically weaker but more astute and, in her eyes, more beautiful male while the brawny ones are still locked in battle.

Walking upright is another human feature that is hard to explain in survival terms, as it made getting around slow, hard work.

But it also shifted the focus of sexual attraction and contact from the back to the front of the body. Upright walking required a differently shaped pelvis, contorting the birth canal, with the result that child-birth became more painful and dangerous. Nevertheless, head size increased—the braincase tripled in volume over the last four million years. This remarkable enlargement cannot easily be explained in biological terms alone. But four million years ago our protohuman ancestors were not purely biological beings. Side by side with the—in evolutionary terms, rapid—changes in basic biology, an extraordinary new dimension was coming into being: culture.

Upright walking freed the hands, allowing protohumans to use as tools a wider range of naturally occurring objects than their knuckle-walking and tree-swinging ancestors had used. When they began to modify such found objects, they created the first artifacts. The oldest solid evidence for culture is the chipped stone artifacts—tools or weapons, made to a common pattern—that date to two-and-a-half million years ago. However, it is likely that many of the very earliest things that our remote ancestors invented to extend their powers over the outside world were made not of chipped stone but of less durable materials—grasses, skins, bark, and wood. Their perishability has meant that they have not survived for archaeologists to find. The first stone tools are usually considered to have been made by male hunters. They may well have been, but a large amount of evidence relating to sex, brain size, and changes in the mechanics of childbirth supports the idea that it was women who led the way in the creation of a distinctively human culture.

In an alternative universe we could have stayed on all fours, retaining a wide birth canal that would have presented no problems for a large head. But without free hands, it is unlikely that humanlike intelligence could have been selected for. Walking upright not only promoted tool using, it increased the possibilities for communication. The torso was given more freedom, independent of basic forward movement. The lungs and diaphragm were suddenly able to make more complex sounds. Around 1.6 million years ago, language emerged, and with it the first declarations of love, both sincere and insincere. It is probable that the first clothing was invented around this time too. Although we lack direct evidence, it is likely that clothing was initially used to conceal or enhance the genital region and therefore extend conscious control over bodily expressions.

Clothing, in turn, gave rise to the idea of gender—the extension of aspects of sex beyond obvious biological attributes. Clothing was from the outset "male" or "female." As such, the ability to interchange clothing gave rise to a new level of sexual awareness—the awareness of gender ambiguity. The bodies of prehistoric humans, denuded of their apeish hair, became material objects themselves. People could manipulate their own images through the use of cosmetics—applying body paints to their new expanses of naked skin. Sex itself became more tactile and prolonged. There are strong indications that prehistoric society utilized natural methods of birth control; I argue that for the past four million years the human line has been able to consciously separate sex from reproduction.

Culture provided sexual selection with massive new scope. Mate choice was no longer solely a matter of sizing up the relative merits of the basic inherited personality and appearance of a prospective partner. Now learned skills—singing, hunting, dancing, and painting— came to play an ever greater role in sexual attraction. The human brain continued to enlarge, from 1.6 million years to sometime just after 150,000 years ago, when "anatomically modern" humans first appeared. Since the period does not seem to have presented any obvious environmental challenge that only larger brains could meet, the enhanced cultural capacities of ever larger brains could have been a sexual fix. Love songs and nicely arranged bouquets may have been at least as important as aggression in the life of the species.

The implications of this new picture of human evolution are far-reaching. Much as Sigmund Freud once claimed that "anatomy is destiny," many geneticists and sociobiologists now make the claim that we are the slaves of our genes. They say that our sexual behavior, along with our sexual politics, is built-in, instinctive, and best understood in terms of animal behavior patterns. They have reached the conclusion that women have fundamentally different sexual and reproductive aims than men and, therefore, that certain imbalances in the modern world are biologically inevitable. For them, man is "Man the Hunter," a potentially promiscuous and inventive creature that women attempt—and fail—to keep in check. Although this view has been widely criticized, it is still popular. By contrast, some feminists have argued that women have a natural biological superiority and that the modern state of patriarchy, the oppression of women by men, is a passing interruption in the more natural state of matriarchy.

Matriarchy as an early phase in human development was first envisaged by Victorian ethnographers. These men were deeply impressed, not to say shocked, by encounters with certain native peoples of the British Empire who enjoyed what we might think of today as a degree of sexual equality. They concluded that women must be in control because the men were not and somebody had to be. (Freud thought that 1930s America was a matriarchy!) These supposedly matriarchal peoples were considered "primitive"—on a low rung of a universal ladder of social betterment. Further, their particular social organization was thought to have been true prehistorically of all peoples in the world.

The idea of a prehistoric society ruled by women remains popular to this day. The influential theories of the late Marija Gimbutas of UCLA suggest that, in prehistoric Europe, the supreme deity was a mother goddess, "The Great Earth Mother," and was represented during the last ice age, around 25,000 years ago, by little ivory and stone "Venus" figurines depicting fleshy naked women. But given that the widespread imagery of the Virgin Mary today does not demonstrate that the pope is a woman, the statuettes could be telling us something quite different. Indeed, in the light of other evidence from the Ice Age, I believe that they indicate that dominant males practiced polygyny—the taking of several wives.

Whatever the figurines actually represented, it is clear that "prehistoric society" was not uniform. Once culture was invented, cultural variation blossomed. Although humans may have had built-in reproductive aims in the remote past, their extraordinarily varied lives and experiences thereafter can be explained only by reference to culture. Although common biological drives and potentialities clearly play a part in every community, what humans do is not governed by any simple "human nature." Freud was wrong: anatomy is not destiny. Our behavior and achievements are at least as tied up with cultural and social expectations as with the inherited shapes of our bodies; further, our innovative technology continually alters the nature of the world we live and achieve in.

In a nutshell, humans have managed to pull ahead of the rest of the animal world by effectively opting out of Darwinian evolution. Instead, we now undergo a sort of Lamarckian evolution—the inheritance of learned information—not through genes but through culture. Instead of slowly, biologically adapting to different environments as we spread out from Africa across the globe, we used culture to adapt those environments to ourselves.

All modern humans share the same underlying biological drives and built-in physical potentialities, which to a degree are inescapable. Women can give birth, while men cannot. But, while the widespread oppression of women in the modern world may have its roots deep in prehistory, those roots are as likely to be cultural as biological. A major event in the development of sexual inequality occurred, I argue, when farming was invented, a system by which people could produce food when they wanted it rather than relying, like every other mammalian species, on natural availability. In the Near East and Europe this process began around 10,000 years ago, when people began to settle down in permanent villages—the "Neolithic revolution." Ironically, although women were central to its early development, farming quickly led to their general oppression. The domestication of animals and the availability of animal milk in addition to breast milk meant that women could raise children in quicker succession than before, becoming ever more tied to hearth and home in the process.

The choices humans make about sex and reproduction can alter or even deny biology. We have condom machines, breast implants, and penile augmentations, artificial insemination, purdah, surrogate pregnancies and cesarean births, drag queens and drag kings, circumcisions and clitoridectomies, telephone sex and cybersex, monasteries and brothels, erotic art, pornography, censorship, and a vast range of marriage types. All are part of our sexual culture. More precisely, they are individual components of the many different and often mutually exclusive sexual cultures in the world today. As anthropologist Ernest Gellner has noted, "What the human species does share genetically is an unbelievable degree of behavioural plasticity or volatility. . . . But possibly the most important sociological fact about mankind is that this plasticity is very seldom much in evidence *within* single on-going communities." Culture, a product of consciousness and free will, paradoxically involves elaborate systems of prohibition. Different societies have different codes of sexual conduct, but in every society individuals transgress. The idea that there is a sexual line that must not be crossed but in practice often is, is far older than the story of Eve's temptation by the serpent.

Only archaeology can take us back that far. The archaeological record—the totality of surviving material traces of the human past—can be divided into three or four broad types of evidence. First, there are *human remains*—skeletons or more fully preserved bodies. They are excavated from graves or salvaged by archaeologists from sites of ancient sacrifices, battles, or accidental deaths (as in the case of the Iceman). The second sort of evidence comprises things that people have made, be they small, portable, individual *artifacts*, or larger *sites*, the remains of houses or cemeteries, where lots of artifacts are found together. Some sites appear as discrete monuments, like Stonehenge, while others cover large areas and have no distinct focus, as in the case of the Val Camonica, an Alpine valley close to where the Iceman was found; its rocky walls are thickly covered with mysterious prehistoric engravings.

Prehistoric humans modified entire landscapes, producing a wide range of environmental effects. These landscapes constitute a third type of archaeological evidence, called *ecofacts*. The recently documented rise in atmospheric carbon dioxide levels is an ecofact, as is the continued felling and burning of the tropical rainforests, which contributes to it. Archaeologists can study such phenomena as they occurred in the past by a variety of means, such as by chemically testing lake sediments and analyzing the plant pollen found in peat bogs from different ages. By such means they have been able to prove that the arid, rocky landscape of much of modern Greece as well as the distinctive heather moorlands of England are ecofacts, both caused by prehistoric deforestation and soil degradation.

Somewhere in between artifacts and ecofacts are faunal and paleobotanical evidence—the traces of human use or human impact on animals and plants. By studying fragments of butchered and cooked bone, carbonized grains, preserved nutshells, and so on, from carefully excavated and dated units of soil (contexts), archaeologists are able to reconstruct many aspects of prehistoric diet. The jury is still out on whether the first humans in North America, who arrived around 13,000 years ago, were responsible for the subsequent and rapid mass extinction of the big game animals they hunted, but it seems likely that they were. Prehistoric people were as capable of grossly exploiting their world as we are today. How a society treats the natural environment and how it views food are both closely connected to its attitudes toward sex and to the particular quality of the relations between the sexes. The rapidly expanding agricultural populations of Neolithic Europe swamped the hunting and foraging peoples who had lived there before by sheer force of numbers. Farming set in motion a cycle of ecological devastation—intimately connected with human sexual and reproductive aims—that seems set to continue until the world's last surviving forests vanish under the plow.

The archaeological record is a mixture of the intentional and the unintentional. The felling of the rainforests today is deliberate, but the connected increase in carbon dioxide levels is not. Stonehenge was surely intentionally designed to impress, and it still impresses, whereas sites where food was processed were not usually consciously designed as "statements" and come to light only through careful excavation by archaeologists sifting small pieces of animal bones from the soil and painstakingly cataloging discarded oyster shells and nut kernels. The Iceman died by accident and was preserved where he fell, with his everyday clothes on—clothes he almost certainly would not have wanted to be seen dead in. More usually, archaeologists excavate bodies from graves that contain a careful selection of objects—grave goods—that were intended to convey a particular message about the deceased to the wider society and to its gods. The messages that such objects communicate in death may contrast greatly with the facts of the person's life.

Getting at the truth about prehistory is almost terminally difficult. Prehistoric art, much of which has explicit sexual content, obviously depicts things that people thought about, but it may not fairly reflect what they actually did. A Stone Age rock engraving made in eastern Siberia around the same time that the Iceman lived depicts a man on skis, attempting to sexually penetrate a moose (Figure 7.5). While the act probably *could* have been brought to a successful conclusion, the picture is more likely primarily symbolic. The man has a birdlike head, and the scene may illustrate the super-human prowess of a shaman. It could even be a visual joke. Actually, these interpretations are not mutually exclusive. Art often idealizes. The robust architectural curves of the Venus figurines may never have been fully attained by human females in life, but in living Ice Age women beauty was probably gauged against such models. The "unintentional" archaeological record provides a useful foil to the image dressing of our prehistoric ancestors: processed husks can tell us whether a prehistoric people used aphrodisiacs; traces of disease on a skeleton may indicate which sections of a community were most affected.

On the whole, however, very few material remains survive from prehistory. Human sexual culture is made up of both permanent material things (jewelry, penis sheaths, erotic imagery) and transient or immaterial things (songs, dances, romantic ideals). Archaeologists can directly study only the physical remains of past cultures, although careful interpretation may provide insights into other realms. Feet calloused in a particular way, for example, coupled with carefully manicured fingernails, may demonstrate that a male Egyptian mummy was a professional dancer in life; temple friezes may show the types of dances that he performed.

Although only firsthand accounts, which are absent in the archaeological record, can express the detail and inner emotions of people's sexual lives, archaeological methods do have a certain advantage in that archaeological evidence relates to real activities, free from the frequent dishonesty of words. In Tucson, Arizona, archaeologist Bill Rathje has been conducting a long-term project at the municipal rubbish dump. His students spend their time sorting fresh rubbish into categories and building up a picture of what people discard. Rathje's reconstruction of diet in the city is different from the picture that sociologists obtained through questionnaires. The questionnaire responses from one neighborhood, for example, suggest that only 15 percent of households consume beer, with none exceeding eight cans a week. The archaeological analysis, based on used beer containers and packaging, shows that 54 percent of households discard more than eight cans a week (the average being fifteen cans), while only 20 percent of households appeared "beer free."

One of the most sensitive areas of garbage work relates to sexual practices. The rubbish in any large municipal dump includes discarded contraceptives and their packaging, broken sex toys, punctured inflatables and worn clothing, medicines related to sexual diseases, and lots of pornography—some of it commercial, some privately created. Although Rathje works with Tucson's sanitation department, he needs the informal support of the people of the municipality as well. It is therefore not surprising that he has not produced any analysis of any sexual materials he may have found, comparing what people actually do with what they admit to. (The presence of Rathje's team of sorters has probably altered the way the people of Tucson dispose of sensitive or embarrassing items anyway.)

In modern Tucson most of the material evidence the researchers find can be quite easily identified. For prehistoric studies, however, there is a problem: it is not always possible to tell what something was used for. Very often what survives is a component of something bigger and more complex. It is a standing joke that the artifacts that archaeologists cannot easily identify get put in the wonderful, catchall category of "ritual objects." Nevertheless, new techniques are beginning to tell us more about the use of quite common objects. Gas chromatography, for example, makes it possible to analyze the chemical residues sometimes found inside prehistoric bowls and cups and thus to identify minute traces of milk, opium, olive oil, pine resin, and so on.

In modern Tucson it can be assumed that people have an idea of "sexuality," but this assumption cannot necessarily be made for prehistoric communities. Sex clearly has had an important place in all human societies. "Sex," as the anthropologist Bronislaw Malinowski wrote in 1929, "is not a mere physiological transaction . . . it implies love and love-making; it becomes the nucleus of such venerable institutions as marriage and the family; it pervades art and it produces its spells and magic. It dominates in fact almost every aspect of culture." But because of this ubiquity, studying sex objectively is not easy. Sexual culture is full of subtle and sometimes contradictory meanings. The French writer Michel Foucault in his *History of Sexuality* argued that "sexuality" is a modern idea. That is, the word conjures up a specifically Western, nineteenth- and twentieth-century idea of sexual identity—of sex as the psychological center of the individual. Nowadays it is widely believed that everyone has their own personal sexuality. One's "true" sexuality, or sexual orientation, may either be lived and celebrated or repressed and hidden; it can be searched for through introspection, through encounters with different sexual partners, and through sessions with a psychoanalyst. But people in Medieval Europe did not think about sex this way. Nor did the ancient Greeks or Babylonians. Nor do many people, both Western and non-Western, in the world today. It is thus effectively certain that prehistoric peoples—in all their variety—did not have ideas of sex corresponding to our current post-Freudian ones.

In this respect the idea of artificial insemination with 5,000-year-old sperm brings up some difficult questions, even beyond those of contemporary ethics, connected to what Ötzi himself might have thought about fathering children. Was he married? His belongings and tattoos could, like a wedding ring today, have expressed such a status, but it is impossible to tell at present. Indeed, it is not certain whether the institution of marriage even existed in European society when he lived or, if it did, whether it was monogamous, polygamous, polyandrous, or something else. Did Ötzi see any connection between sex and babies, and if so, what sort of connection? Perhaps he took no interest in heterosexual sex.

The Iceman has been sexually "claimed" not only by women as a prospective sperm donor but by homosexual men as a prehistoric role model. A Viennese gay magazine, *Lambda Nachrichten,* ran a story claiming that sperm were preserved not only in Ötzi's testicles but in his rectum: "Ötzi was the first known homosexual man. . . . Ötzi was the passive partner—of this there is absolutely no doubt . . . the sperm has been carbon dated." This story spread rapidly in popular newspapers and among gay communities on both sides of the Atlantic and was taken as proof that the gay lifestyle has a respectable prehistoric pedigree. One idea heard in British archaeological circles was that the odd mix of objects found with Ötzi indicated that he had been a shaman, whose alternative sexuality would have constituted just one part of his social "specialness." But in the end, as with the missing penis, the story turned out to be a fantasy. No semen was actually found in the Iceman's rectum.

It was not that semen was looked for and not identified, but that semen was not looked for. Still, even if investigation were to discover that Ötzi's rectum was clear of semen, that would not mean that it had never contained it. Further, if there were traces, it would not prove that Ötzi was a willing participant in getting it there. Indeed, it would have no necessary relevance to his sexual practices in life, since he could have had voluntary homosexual encounters and he could also have been homosexually raped. (Although it would have been unlikely in the blizzard conditions that led to his death, necrophilia might also have to be considered.)

That semen has not been looked for in the Iceman's rectum is partly because the rectum itself has not yet been found. As Konrad Spindler writes, "The anal region of the corpse, through to the bony pelvic area, was destroyed by the first [nonarchaeological] recovery team and their pneumatic chisel. No examinations were conducted on the soft tissue in the pelvis, nor were samples taken. The rectum has not even been identified in the computer tomograph of the body's internal organs, greatly shrunk as they were through dehydration." Nevertheless, although an analysis of Ötzi's rectum may turn out to be impossible to conduct, we have independent grounds for doubting that it is on the investigating team's agenda. As Spindler has written, he and his colleagues felt great pressure during the first months of analysis of the body in the face of "often absurd reports in the media."

In his book on the Iceman, Spindler gives a fairly detailed (although unillustrated) account of the Iceman's genital region. He felt compelled to do so, he says, in the face of press speculation. There would "normally have been no need," he writes, "to dwell at such length on the more intimate parts of the Iceman's body—but wild speculation must be refuted with scientifically corroborated facts . . . a Neolithic man is available as an object of research to us. . . . Nothing of the kind could have been expected by the man himself, and it probably would not have been compatible with his religious sentiments. . . . Thus, we are all the more obliged to apply the ethical and moral standards of our society to his dead body." Spindler goes on to say that a Jesuit theologian, Dr. Hans Rotter, has "urged us, notwithstanding the scientific interest of the case, not to overstep the limits of piety and to preserve the human dignity of the Iceman even beyond his death."

Spindler's point is a serious one, but it is nevertheless the product of confused thinking. He assumes that the Iceman's sexuality was an "intimate" matter, but no one can know if it was. And even if it was, how do we know which areas of his body were involved in his sexuality? Some societies consider the nape of the neck and the feet to be sexual and intimate. We do not know for certain which parts of Ötzi's body he considered sexual and/or intimate. Yet Spindler's research team has had no qualms about subjecting most of Ötzi's body and all of his belongings—perhaps sacred or even taboo belongings—to a wide variety of scans and tests.

In the light of Foucault's argument, we cannot assume that our modern way of thinking about sex—either biologically or sociocul-turally—is necessarily any more objective than any other way of thinking about sex. Even within the rather narrow Western tradition of thinking about sex, from Plato to Shere Hite, it is clear that no one has ever had a monopoly on the

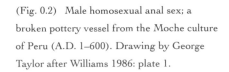

(Fig. 0.2)   Male homosexual anal sex; a broken pottery vessel from the Moche culture of Peru (A.D. 1–600). Drawing by George Taylor after Williams 1986: plate 1.

(Fig. 0.3) Male lovers; pottery vessel from the Vicús culture
of Peru (500–1 B.C.). Drawing by George Taylor after
Williams 1986: plate 2.

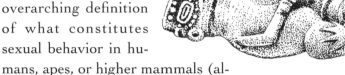

truth about our bodies. Nor
is there any single
overarching definition
of what constitutes
sexual behavior in hu-
mans, apes, or higher mammals (al-
though it seems to depend on a mixture of things learned, things
inherited, and things chanced).

It is easy to be judgmental about the sexual mores of other societies. The sixteenth-century Spanish were outraged by the widespread homosexuality and transvestism that they found among the
indigenous peoples they conquered in the Americas. They systematically destroyed sculptures, jewelry, and monuments that depicted and
celebrated such practices. Today some museum curators still keep archaeological material that they consider "indecent" or inappropriate
for public display under lock and key; several important collections
of Roman "brothel tokens," small coinlike objects that depict the sexual service that has been paid for, currently languish, unpublished, in
European museum basements. And where there is no information, invention takes over, as in the Ötzi case.

Because of the inaccessibility, for a variety of reasons, of data relating to prehistoric sexuality worldwide, I have focused in the latter
part of the book (which deals with the later prehistoric period) on
Europe, western Asia, and the former Soviet Union. These are areas
that I know well and where my colleagues and contacts have been
able to help me track down hidden or little-known material. Despite
this focus, many of the themes relevant to this material are of universal significance (or have now become so through the pervasive influence of Western ideology). Starting around 5,000 years ago, it is
possible to document great variation in human sexuality in Eurasia:
bestiality, homosexuality, prostitution (emphatically not the oldest

profession), transvestism (male and female), transsexuality, hormone treatments, sadomasochism, a vigorous interest in contraception, ideas about racially "pure" breeding, sex as an acrobatic and competitive pastime, and sex as a transcendental spiritual discipline. This variation went underground when Christian values were publicly adopted, whereupon the chivalric ideal of romantic, preferably unconsummated love gave rise to a view of physical sex as essentially sinful and forbidden, the legacy of which lingers on.

Despite these relatively recent influences on our experience of sex, the last few thousand years represent just a tiny part of the four-million-year saga of its prehistory. By taking a long view of the evolution of human sexual culture — by seeing what people actually did, rather than making claims about what they ought to have done — we will be better able to consider our options for the next four million years.

CHRISTOPHER ANTHONY MASTERS,
TH.D., Ph.D., J.D.
RANCHO SAN DIEGO, CALIFORNIA

Chapter 1

Making the Beast with Two Backs:

The Evolution of Human Sexual Culture

Brabantio: *What profane wretch art thou?*
Iago: *I am one, sir, that comes to tell you*
    your daughter and the Moor are now
    making the beast with two backs.

SHAKESPEARE,
OTHELLO

Iago's words conjure up ideas of love, lust, and jealousy, of sex as an intimate and a public act, of our fragile difference from animals, and of the potentially explosive differences between us as humans. "The beast with two backs" is the product of a prehistoric animal nature transformed by culture. Geneticists say that we share about 98 percent of our genetic code with chimpanzees, but between us and them is a yawning chasm of mutual incomprehension. That chasm did not always exist—eight million years ago we sprang from a common ancestor. But while chimps stayed relatively little changed, from four million years ago onward the human line began to evolve rapidly. Between then and now at least a dozen species of hominids came and went, some following on from previous ones, others developing in tandem. These intermediate creatures, known from their fragmentary fossilized bones and a few rudimentary stone tools, are difficult to flesh out. Yet they hold the key to understanding our unique humanity.

We did not reach our present incarnation because men were great hunters who needed to become naked to lose heat (the man-the-hunter theory), or because we evolved in the sea where large maternal breasts served as infant buoyancy aids (the aquatic theory), or because women and children were provided with meat by men who were provided with sex (the monogamy theory). Instead, I believe, our evolution was a complicated and chancy matter in which sexual attraction and the emergence of culture played crucial roles. Many of the most striking evolutionary changes in humans probably have to do with *sexual* selection, like the favoring of features such as nakedness that were deemed attractive rather than being of any great inherent or natural benefit.

It is often assumed that men made all the great cultural advances while women looked on, huddled with their babies at the back of the cave. But we have good reason to believe that some of the most crucial inventions enabling human development were made by women. The seemingly trivial invention of the papoose or baby-sling, around 1.8 million years ago, I argue, was critical in enabling a longer and more intense period of infant brain development, culminating in the emergence of language. Language marked a watershed in our reproductive and sexual lives, opening up a new world of deceptive possibilities.

The Missing Link's Missing Penis

If apes are hairy half-brained creatures that swing in trees, squeal, and mate promiscuously, while we humans cover our nakedness with clothes, walk erect, talk, marry our sweethearts, and regulate our sex lives in a civilized manner, then what would an evolutionarily intermediate creature be like? The popular answer is that "he" is a semi-hairy, stooped figure who dresses in a torn-fur loincloth, lives in a cave, and grunts out his words in a clumsy "me Tarzan, you Jane" manner. He takes his woman without consent and uses a club to frighten off any competition. This Apeman is popular with filmmakers and cartoonists, but their photo-fit portrait of him did not come out of nowhere. It came—sexism and all—from academic textbooks.

A familiar kind of image of human evolution, reproduced in Figure 1.1 from *From Ape to Adam*, a textbook from 1971, shows a series of fleshed-out individuals on the road to the present. The figure on the far left resembles a chimpanzee, stooped and shaggy. Next comes a simple missing-link type, who becomes progressively bigger and less hairy, stumbling as best he can, carrying a club or a rock. The penultimate figure on the right is Primitive Man, capable of fully erect walking and noticeably bearded; as yet he is too short to hold his head proudly, and he squints beneath dark jutting brows. Finally, Anatomically Modern Man appears, naked, with his head held high; he sports a fine forked beard and swept-back hair, and he totes a spear of his own manufacture. Biological evolution and cultural evolution are separated in these images, which suggest that uprightness, nakedness, and brain power all preceded the cultural ascent to clothing. Biological evolution is shown as a gradual affair, wherein our ancestors suffered hundreds of thousands of years of stiff necks and backaches in their struggle to become upright.

More recent artists' impressions, such as the one in Figure 1.2, are more realistic about the switch to walking upright. The chimpanzeelike creature on the far left does it in only one step and loses hair quickly in evolutionary terms. The disjunction between biology and culture is less marked than in Figure 1.1: the figures in the middle carry more than one thing—a burning brand and a flint tool, or a flint tool and a spear. Nevertheless, as in Figure 1.1, we are shown as hairless long before we invent clothing. Perhaps this is a reflection of the Garden of Eden myth—not until we left Africa did we discover, like Adam, our shame. Only modern man, in this case an archaeologist, is free to stride out, left leg forward this time, safe in the knowledge that his genitals are tucked away inside his pants.

(Fig. 1.1)   From Ape to Adam, frontispiece by Rudy Zallinger: estate of Rudy Zallinger.

The two pictures share many misleading features. Although convention bound both artists to show a sequence of lone individuals, the reality is that as far as we know, humans have always been sexual, social, and group-living. In both pictures the figures gradually become taller—a physical and symbolic ascent to full humanity. But this image is now known to be incorrect: 1.6 million years ago, around the time fire was first controlled, our ancestors were actually taller than the average person in most modern communities. In Figure 1.1, Anatomically Modern Man is clearly white, and in Figure 1.2 all the figures are pale-skinned; yet we know that human evolution took place in Africa, where people generally have dark skin.

Both pictures are male centered. Man, not Woman, is seen as the key figure in evolution, even though it is woman's womb and pelvis that must actually accommodate each evolutionary novelty. The male slant is reflected in the titles of the books: *From Ape to Adam* is unambiguous, while *The Evolution of Early Man* includes women only by virtue of the supposition that the word *man* can imply both "men *and* women" and "men *not* women" without confusion. So familiar is the doublethink that it is sometimes hard to see what the problem is, but phrases like "early man typically breast-fed for five years" and "man's clitoris became much reduced" may serve as a useful reminder. In fact, in these pictures it is impossible to tell what the apemen had between their legs. The coy leg-in-front reconstructions are symbolic of a wider unwillingness to acknowledge the centrality of sex to evolution.

Our sexual and reproductive lives are unlike those of any other

(Fig. 1.2) The Evolution of Early Man, frontispiece by Giovanni Caselli, with a text by Bernard Wood. Reproduced by kind permission of Giovanni Caselli.

animal. Our sex organs are highly unusual. Compared with other primates, human males have massive penises, which are visible even when flaccid. Our naked skin is also unique among primates; combined with distinct patches of pubic hair, it further emphasizes the genital region in men and sharply defines it in women, who otherwise lack the brightly colored and swollen sexual skin that marks primate females in estrus. Buttocks, which primates also lack, are a focus of sexual attention in both women and men. Additionally, women have distinct breasts, whose form cannot easily be explained functionally in terms of lactation (all other primates produce milk without them) but that are considered sexually attractive in all known human cultures.

Most likely, penis size was also gradually increasing among early hominids. Gorillas, orangutans, chimps, and bonobos all have vanishingly small penises, effectively invisible when flaccid. The most common explanation for big penises in humans is that we evolved them under conditions of furious "sperm competition." Sperm competition has been documented in many primates where females have numerous heterosexual liaisons. The male by whom a female becomes pregnant is thus not her exclusive mate; at any one time she may be carrying the sperm of several males—sperm that compete to reach and fertilize the ovum. A male's success in sperm competition relates to the amount of semen that he can produce. This does not have a simple swamping or displacing effect, but contains functionally different types of sperm, in varying proportions. Some sperm is geared at fertilization, some is geared to blocking the sperm of other males, and some is geared to attacking it.

For humans, the argument runs, the longer the penis is, the closer the sperm can be placed to the mouth of the cervix, and the more of a previous male's sperm will be physically displaced. But this argument makes no sense. The vagina is highly elastic, and it expands to accommodate virtually any size penis; the penis, for its part, ejaculates with force and direction that are independent of its size. The great apes, who have multiple partners and who evolved large testicles to produce copious quantities of sperm (chimps produce about three times more than humans, relative to body weight), do not have large penises.

What is important about the human penis is not its mechanical fertilizing capacity when erect but its flaccid visibility. Various methods of penis lengthening are used around the world, but none, not even modern surgical penile augmentation, has much effect on the size of the erection. In modern surveys looking at the reasons men undergo penile augmentation surgery, very few respondents cite pressure from a heterosexual partner, such as a wife. It is not so much sexual pleasure as prowess in the locker room that men buy when they undergo this procedure. Having a big one is part of male-male competition and, perhaps, bonding. Still, this is not to say that female preferences played no part in the evolution of bigger penises in humans.

Both upright walking and the evolution of nakedness made the penis more visible, so that flaccid size became an issue. Moreover, having a penis became an increasingly important visual signal of an individual's biological sex. Among gorillas, males and females are easily distinguished by their body size. The males are far larger, and they compete with one another through body size for control over harems; penis size, beyond basic functionality, seems irrelevant. Human males and females, on the other hand, are of similar body size. Although men are bigger on average, a significant proportion of adult females are actually bigger than some adult males. Features like genital appearance and the presence or absence of breasts or beards, consequently, take on a far greater importance in visually differentiating the sexes. Once the penis became a visual criterion of manhood, its evolutionary growth was guaranteed. In any generation there will always be *some* women who favor bigger penises, and few or none who positively favor smaller ones, so a trend toward greater length was established. The upper limit of penis size was set by considerations of physical comfort during intromissive sex, and by the basic mechanics of penile erection.

In a completely naked ape, however, the unruly nature of the male penis, coupled with its obvious visibility, could have made it a liability. Primate sexual and social behavior is very complex and is based on the evolution of Machiavellian intelligence—the ability to mask one's true emotions and feign others that may be strategically advantageous. Jane Goodall in particular has described this among the chimpanzees of Gombe. Having an erect penis clearly signals sexual interest, whether the mind wills it or not. Although pygmy chimps sit and lean back to deliberately display their erections when courting, their fur and their gait probably allow them to hide an erection better than a fully bipedal, upright walking primate can. Two questions, therefore, arise in relation to the development of large penises in humans. First, why did men become as denuded of hair as women, with their pubic hair and genitalia framed in the same stark manner against relatively bare skin? Second, did clothing—Adam's fig leaf—develop along with the evolution in penis size?

The answer to the first question has to do with pleiotropy—the process by which changes that evolutionary pressures bring about on one sex of a species are reflected to a degree in the other sex as well. Genetically, mammals are unlike birds in that particular features acquired by one sex are typically reflected to some degree in the other. Thus horns and antlers, developed for display and battle by billy goats and stags, are present to a lesser degree in nanny goats and does. It is likely that a sexual selection for nakedness in women would be reflected in men but would not become so strongly established. That is exactly how things stand with humans today.

The question of clothing depends on the degree of cultural development in different periods of hominid evolution. Unfortunately, the development of clothing is very difficult to follow, since soft, organic materials do not survive in the archaeological record from this remote period. Nevertheless, there are other, indirect ways by which we can hypothesize about cultural developments.

Man the Hunter?

A familiar and ingrained prejudice holds that men were at the forefront of developed culture, while women somehow stayed more natural. Prehistoric men, according to the mainly male academics who studied them, went off to the hunt, wielding their newly made stone weapons, while women sat nursing the babies back in the cave. Hunting was thought to have expanded men's minds, which explained their (claimed) greater intelligence.

Darwin thought that men were more intelligent than women (partly on the basis of a lifelong preponderance of wins in backgammon games against his wife). He believed that intelligence had arisen out of competition among men to win and subsequently provide for women. "Thus," Darwin wrote, "man has ultimately become superior to woman. It is indeed fortunate that the law of equal transmission of characters to both sexes prevails with mammals. Otherwise it is probable that man would have become as superior in mental endowment to woman as the peacock is in ornamental plumage to the pea hen."

Recently, the man-the-hunter theory of human origins has been roundly and justly criticized as sexist. It may be true that in prehistory, as in every known hunter-gatherer society today, hunting was mainly (but not necessarily exclusively) done by men and gathering was mainly (but not necessarily exclusively) done by women. In response to some female students who thought this assumption sexist, archaeologist Linda Hurcombe has written:

> Women breast-feeding children cannot leave offspring for long periods, children can more easily contribute to their own food-getting requirements if they collect static and usually non-threatening plant resources, on a hunt children

may not be able to be kept quiet, to move quickly enough, or may slow down an adult too much if they are carried. The age of children can affect a woman's role in the food-getting strategy; the children may be left in the care of elders of both sexes while the younger and fitter community members go off on longer trips. . . . To say that such ideas are sexist is to miss the point of sexual dimorphism as an evolutionary strategy and to be biased by our own cultural experience of the *status* of activities. The female students wanted women to be seen as hunters because this was the task *they* valued more.

Irrespective of whether or not hunting was a mainly male activity, the man-the-hunter theory certainly downgrades women's role in biocultural evolution. The theory holds that hunting formed the backdrop by which men developed language (in organizing the hunt) and made technological innovations (designing weapons), the benefits of which then trickled down to females, who were passive and biologically hampered. The evolution of nakedness has also been explained in relation to hunting, notably by zoologist Desmond Morris in his 1967 book *The Naked Ape*. Morris argued that nakedness was a cooling device (although he recognized that lions and cheetahs hunt well in their fur). Humans would have needed to lose their fur, he concluded, since the

essential difference between the hunting ape and his carnivore rivals was that he was not physically equipped to make lightning dashes after his prey. . . . But this is nevertheless precisely what he had to do. He succeeded because of his better brain, leading to more intelligent manoeuvring and more lethal weapons, but despite this such efforts must have put a huge strain on him. . . . By losing the heavy coat of hair and by increasing the number of sweat glands all over the body surface, considerable cooling could be achieved — not for minute-by-minute living, but for the supreme moment of the chase — with the production of a generous film of evaporating liquid over his air-exposed straining limbs and trunk.

The basic flaws in Morris's hunting-and-hair-loss theory are twofold. First, men were not compelled to make such extreme efforts. Early humans probably scavenged as much as they hunted, and when they did hunt, they probably used stealth, deception, ambush, and missiles more than speed on the ground in order to catch and kill prey. Second, as Darwin noted, despite great variations in the degree of hairiness of particular peoples, women are universally less hairy than their menfolk. Darwin concluded two things from this observation: that the loss of hair occurred at an early time, before people had dispersed out of Africa; and that the selection pressure must have operated primarily on women. If Morris is correct, women would be universally hairier than men — not having hunted, they would have retained more of their useful protective fur.

Buoyant Breasts: A Strange Aquatic Utopia

Morris has changed his mind since *The Naked Ape.* In his 1994 book, *The Human Animal,* however, he firmly adopted an even less defensible theory: that humans lost their hair because of an aquatic phase in their evolution. The "aquatic ape" hypothesis was developed in the 1970s by Elaine Morgan, from an original idea of marine biologist Sir Alister Hardy. Briefly stated, the hypothesis is that like dolphins and whales, humans have a naked skin with a warming layer of subcutaneous fat beneath it. The barely visible little body hairs grow in directions that follow the flow lines of water over a swimming mammal. And finally, unlike any other primate, we have partial webbing between our fingers and toes.

A gap in the fossil record appears between ten and five million years ago; Morgan argued that it is because humans lived in the sea during that period. The support of the water in the shallows helped us develop bipedalism, while our precise hand grip developed to help us dive for shellfish—marine protein crucial to the development of our larger brain. Living in the sea also explained, she thought, the development of human breasts, which the children could grab on to like a swimming float, while they were nursing in the surf. Women's long head hair was also available for children to grab in the water, while her buttocks were to provide some comfort if a woman decided to take time out and breast-feed sitting on the gravel. The hymen was to keep grit out—a benefit worth having even if only for one's virgin years, according to Morgan. Childbirth also could be accomplished better under water. Morgan cited evidence of some tropical islanders who sometimes get in the sea to give birth, and she connected her theory to the modern idea of water birth, first carried out in Moscow and later popularized by the great French obstetrician Michel Odent as part of a program of "natural" birth.

There are many things wrong with the aquatic theory, not least the absence of a single shred of positive evidence for it. The only skeletal evidence that places our early ancestors in a water environment consists of *Homo habilis* and *Paranthropus boisei* skulls that have been mauled by crocodiles. And if humans really are adapted to a marine life, why do they not still live one? The simple answer is that we are not, so we do not. It turns out that human subcutaneous fat is *not really* like that of marine mammals, and hypothermia is an ever-present danger for us in water. The Odent-style water birth, while quite outstanding as a technique, is "natural" only in that it generally avoids the need for drugs or surgical intervention. The pool equipment itself is cultural, not "natural," and the most critical aspect of it is control over water temperature, as tiny babies can lose or gain heat quickly and fatally.

Much else is left unexplained by the aquatic theory. Marine mammals of similar size to humans, such as seals, actually do have fur; only at a much larger size does the volume-to-surface-area ratio allow a sea mammal to shed this insulation. The slight webbing between our fingers could not really have helped us swim. A child cannot really grasp a naked breast in the surf (a hairy, chimpanzeelike one would actually be easier). Finally, there is the streamlined hair flow. Alister Hardy illustrated it for a human infant, making the claim—incorrectly, as it turns out—that such hair growth patterns are not found in nonhuman primates. Even if they were truly evidence for the aquatic theory, the theory singularly fails to explain why humans, having gone to the bother of evolving hair in a pattern suited to swimming, should have promptly lost it.

Lucy in the Tree with Apemen

Recent finds have confounded old notions of human evolution by demonstrating that walking upright came long before any significant growth in brain size. That a threefold increase in brain size followed on from bipedalism rather than preceded it is mysterious, as the pelvic changes that are needed to support and move a body in walking upright actually make it harder for females to bear large-headed young.

Reconstructing human evolution is like having a few thousand badly damaged pieces of jigsaw out of an original billion or so pieces, and the pieces may belong to an unknown number of different puzzles. For the period from four million to one million years ago, fossil remains of about five thousand prehuman apelike and humanlike individuals are known—an average of one per six-thousand-year period—but they are not evenly spread out in time. These five thousand individuals may come from a dozen or so different species, and only two skeletons are anywhere near complete. Many individuals are represented by as little as a single tooth or small piece of jawbone.

Still, over the past twenty-five years or so, huge advances have been made in understanding human evolution (though the field of human-origins research is fraught with controversies and bitter personal rivalries). For one thing, we now know that the old view of a single evolutionary line leading from apes to humans is wrong. Human evolution has been an explosion of variants—short ones, tall ones, clever ones, strong ones, meat eaters, and vegetarians. Some variants died out or were pushed out of the fold; some went their own

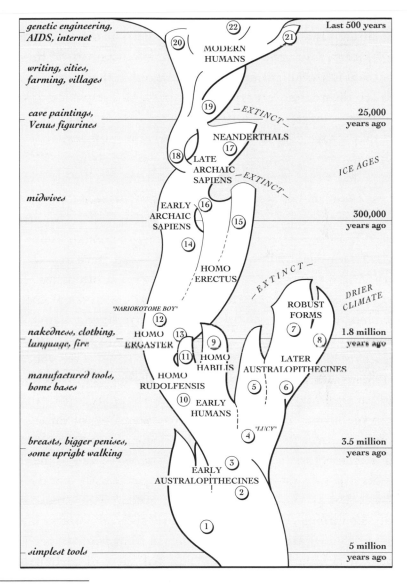

(Fig. 1.3) Human evolutionary tree (Genus abbreviations: A = *Australopithecus*, P = *Paranthropus*,
H = *Homo*): 1. *Ardipithecus ramidus*.   2. *A. anamensis*.   3. Laetoli footprints.   4. Lucy: *A. afarensis*.
5. Taung baby: *A. africanus*.   6. Black Skull: *P. aethopithecus*.   7. Swartkrans: *P. robustus*.
8. Zinj: *P. boisei*.   9. KMM-ER 1805: *H. habilis*.   10. *H. rudolfensis* (early).   11. KMM-ER 1470:
H. rudolfensis (late).   12. Nariokotome Boy: *H. ergaster*.   13. Mojokerto: *H. erectus*.   14. Bodo:
early archaic *H. sapiens*.   15. Asian *H. erectus* (late).   16. Petralona skull.   17. La Ferrassie:
Neanderthal.   18. Earliest Anatomically Modern *H. sapiens*.   19. Cro Magnon.
20. Pre-conquest Americans.   21. Tasmanians.   22. Contemporary humans.   Source: the author.

way for a while and then came back; some were runaway successes. The emerging pattern is hard to grasp at once. The diagram in Figure 1.3 serves as a rough guide. (Although some of the issues I raise may at first seem irrelevant to my theme, they are actually crucial to the emergence of breasts, buttocks, nakedness, larger penises, and the other quirks of the beast with two backs.)

Humans have labeled themselves primates. Primates are a group of mammals, the earliest of which first evolved around 37 million years ago and were small furry tree-living lemurs with big front-facing eyes. Eight million years ago in eastern Africa, violent tectonic changes created the Rift Valley with a mountain chain along its western edge. These mountains isolated the ancestors of chimps and gorillas in the moist rainforests of central and western Africa. The east became progressively drier; along the Rift Valley itself, around 4.5 million years ago, our ancestors walked upright for the first time.

Coming down from the trees may not have been so much choice as necessity—the forest was shrinking. In 1978 the prehistorian Mary Leakey made a dramatic discovery at Laetoli in northern Tanzania: three sets of fossil footprints, made by creatures that had walked upright along the shore of a prehistoric lake. Shortly after the tracks were made, they were sealed by ash from a great volcanic eruption. The creatures may have been fleeing from the volcano (although they were not running). The volcanic ash dates to 3.5 million years ago. The size of the Laetoli footprints and the distance between them indicates that they were made by creatures that were about five feet tall. Fossil bones found nearby are very fragmentary, but they are thought to belong to a species called *Australopithecus afarensis*, or *A. afarensis*. This early type of *Australopithecus* was named after the Afar region of Ethiopia where, in 1974, Don Johanson discovered one of the most famous fossils of all—the 40 percent complete skeleton AL 288-1, known as Lucy (number 4 in Figure 1.3).

Johanson claimed that Lucy, along with the less complete remains of fifty or so other individuals from the 3-million-year-old former lakeside site at Hadar, is ancestral to both later australopithecines and early humans. But the picture becomes more complex both with each season of fieldwork (two more species were named just during the writing of this book) and as the often very fragmentary bones are analyzed and reanalyzed. What is clear is that rather than just one "missing link," there are many. The pattern is pulselike. Several times in the evolution of early humanlike creatures, a burst of new variations can be observed, each time followed by a series of extinctions.

It is difficult to date fossils this old more precisely than to the nearest hundred thousand years, so it is also difficult to say which different humanlike forms were real contemporaries with one another and which represent different evolutionary stages of the same species. In a sense, it does not matter; the basic point is that hominids were evolving rapidly. By around 1.8 million years ago, around six different species of hominid were in existence within the same broad east African region. By one million years ago, however, the number was back down to one or two.

This pulselike pattern indicates that there was an intense amount of competition among the emergent species of hominid. They can be grouped into three basic types, represented in Figure 1.3 by the robust later australopithecines, also called *paranthropines* (on the right), the more gracile australopithecines and habilines (in the middle), and the early human, genus *Homo* group (on the left). The right-hand and middle groups retained relatively small brains, and although they could certainly walk upright, they never completely left the trees. But the left-hand group, which includes our direct ancestors, became fully savannah-living and, sometime between 2.5 and 1.8 million years ago, increased their brain size quite remarkably, to between a half and two-thirds of the modern human average. By one million years ago, only the large-brained species remained—*Homo erectus*—though with marked regional variations.

To claim that Lucy (number 4 in Figure 1.3) is ancestral to all later lines of hominids, Johanson had to make some controversial assumptions. First, in naming fossil skeleton AL 288-1 "Lucy" (after a famous line in a Beatles song), Johanson assumed that the skeleton was female. The first sex determination was made on the basis of pelvis shape and an overall height of around three and a half feet; he assumed that the five-footer who made the Laetoli prints was a male, and that there was thus a marked male-female size difference. If he is correct, then the "sexual dimorphism" of *A. afarensis* would have been about as dramatic as it is in gorillas—and not at all like the relatively small male-female size differences of modern humans.

But there is no compelling reason why the *A. afarensis* bones at Laetoli are necessarily those of the species that made the footprints close by. Russell Tuttle of the University of Chicago flatly disbelieves that Lucy's foot could have made the prints. He suspects that Lucy, along with others among the australopithecines, spent more time in the few trees that remained than on the savannah. Peter Wheeler, of John Moores University, Liverpool, sums up the debate simply: "If . . . Lucy-type australopithecines weren't good bipeds, then something else was out there, and something else made the Laetoli trackway." A recent reanalysis of Lucy's pelvis by Häusler and Schmid of Zurich University concludes that Lucy could not have given birth to an infant with anything like an expected average neonatal brain size for the species. It would be better to change the name to Lucifer, they suggest, "because with such a pelvis 'Lucy' would apparently have been the last of her species."

Breeding for Beauty

Heat regulation was important in human evolution—it is perhaps the key reason for bipedalism on the savannah, and a crucial element in the development of greater brain size. As we have seen, heat-loss equations show the aquatic theory to be nonsense. The equations do not predict, however, that we should have lost our body hair. While it is pleasant enough to be naked under a tropical sun, it is less than fun to shiver at night. It seems obvious that as hair was lost, clothing was developed to compensate for it. Contrary to the impression given by the picture in Figure 1.1, humans could never have been simply naked. As Darwin noted, "No one supposes that the nakedness of the skin is any direct advantage to man; his body cannot have been divested of hair through natural selection." How can it then be explained? Alfred Russel Wallace, who had developed a theory of evolution similar to Darwin's, specifically excluded humans from its implications; for Wallace, human nakedness had to have been an act of God. But Darwin, in *The Descent of Man, and Selection in Relation to Sex*, first published in 1871, proposed another mechanism—sexual selection.

According to Darwin, sexual selection depends "on the success of certain individuals over others of the same sex, in relation to the propagation of the species." By contrast, natural selection depends "on the success of both sexes, at all ages, in relation to the general conditions of life." Natural and sexual selection can apparently run in opposing directions. Sexual selection may spiral out of control, making an animal potentially more maladaptive. Darwin believed that the Irish elk became extinct because the massive size of the male's antlers, which had become ever bigger through competitive display and combat during the rut, left the species vulnerable to adverse living conditions—under pressure, the heavy unwieldy antlers became a fatal burden.

Hair loss happened relatively early in our evolution, Darwin argued. Women lost their hair, he believed, because men found hairlessness attractive, not because it was burdensome; women's loss of hair led to a concomitant but less marked loss in men. Sexual selection on men after we spread out from Africa resulted in very different patterns of beard growth worldwide. The old idea that sexual selection was responsible for human nakedness is more logical than either the man-the-hunter theory (which would have resulted in hairier women) or the aquatic theory (which would have ended in extinction from hypothermia and crocodiles), but it has not attracted much support in recent scholarship.

One reason for this lack of support may be the theory of the Specific Mate Recognition System, or SMRS, a sort of modern extension of Darwin's basic sexual selection idea. SMRS holds that species need to be different enough from one another to make correct mating decisions, irrespective of differences in appearance between the sexes within any one species. Among birds, the quickest and—in evolutionary terms—cheapest way to mark a different appearance is to change the plumage. In the sort of competitive, rapidly speciating

situation among early hominids in eastern Africa, the ability of individuals to identify their own emergent sort of hominid would have
been crucial. Hominids did not have feathers, but they did have hair,
with patches of sexual skin. Altering the distribution of these features
could, like semaphore, have been a very useful identifying tool.

One implication of our present nonhairy state is that the genus
Homo became the least hairy—extending the sexual skin over most of
the body. But SMRS theory does not explain why it was we, and not
the australopithecines, who played the nakedness card first. Was it
just chance? Could an alternative evolutionary path have seen naked
australopithecines go extinct and humans as hairy as gorillas survive?
I think not. To explain why, Darwin's original theory needs to be res-
urrected, but with a twist or two. Stated in brief, I believe that upright walking hid females' engorgable estrus skin between their legs;
walking itself both required buttock muscles and hid the female genital opening—an important focus of sexual signaling in primates; the
new buttock area became denuded of hair to compensate for the lost
sexual signal; and the bare buttocks were mimicked around the front,
in the form of bare breasts. That is, nakedness developed as a form of
sexual signaling to compensate for the disappearance of estrus skin,
which had formerly performed that function.

The emergence of nakedness was thus not a question of losing
hair but of extending areas of sexual skin. This process culminated
through sexual selection within a cultural environment—clothes and
cosmetics enhanced and selectively covered the areas from which
hair was lost, and encouraged it to be lost over yet wider areas. In my
view, therefore, we have never been truly naked apes. (My view will
take some arguing. This preview contains many assumptions that
need to be defended now, but the argument is not completed until the
beginning of Chapter 4. Moreover, it throws new light on an issue of
contemporary sexual morality that I discuss in the Conclusion.)

In *The Naked Ape* Desmond Morris interpreted breasts as sexual
signals that mimicked the buttocks. Females in several primate
species, including gelada baboons, have paired flashes of brightly colored skin around the nipples that mimic the shape and color of the
bright estrus skin on their rumps—the purpose seems to be to attract

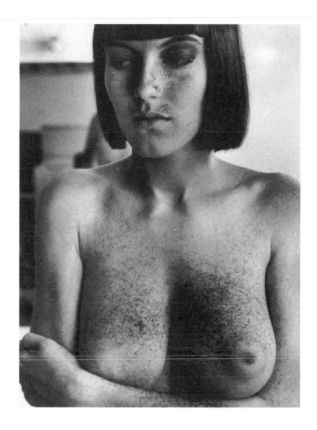

(Fig. 1.4) Naked breasts were probably sexually selected early in our evolution. But ideas of beauty can change. Some future culture may value hairy breasts and select mates accordingly: Arielle after a haircut, Paris, 1982. Photograph ©Helmut Newton.

sexual attention while remaining sitting down. Some primate males, such as mandrils, also have such skin patches, but in them it is the face that mimics the genital area (just as beards may do in men). The reason for locating this male-female distinction in front-of-body signaling seems clear: female nipples are a functional part of successful reproduction, whereas male primates often use facial appearance and expression as part of the status displays that regulate differential access to mates.

An upright primate could have evolved bare buttocks but stayed hairy over the rest of its body. But if Morris's idea that breasts evolved to mimic buttocks is correct, then breasts would have to be hairless too. This could have set a pattern for more general hair loss, with the round, fleshy aspects of buttocks and breasts becoming more important as particularly sexual areas. But Morris's theory has been criticized for failing to explain the initial evolution of naked buttocks.

Women's buttocks do not become engorged and signal estrus in the same way as the rump flashes of certain female primates do, and if buttocks cannot be explained as sexual signals, it is difficult to argue that breasts developed as sexual signals that mimicked them.

Walking upright alters the shape of the gluteus maximus muscles, so that hemispherical buttocks are formed. This configuration also creates an area where a lot of energy can be stored as fat, without interfering with basic movements. Neither muscular development nor any additionally fatty development requires the buttocks to be bare. But a sexual explanation does: once women became bipedal, the skin of the vulva that had formerly engorged during estrus became more hidden. Although swollen estrus skin could have been tactically exposed, it would have been uncomfortable to have it positioned between the legs. Instead, women's buttocks became denuded and fleshy, while at the front, a pubic triangle of hair developed against a bare background. Buttocks have never been engorgable, because it would interfere with their muscular and fat-storage functions, although as clothing developed, they could be "flashed." Nevertheless, fat deposits have their own sexual connotations: it is the level of stored fat in a woman's body that most usually limits her ability to conceive. On very low fat diets ovulation becomes irregular and may disappear altogether. But even when ovulation is regular, the successful implantation of a fertilized egg may be scuppered by body fat levels that are too low. (The fact that estrus is not signaled in humans with any display of reddened sexual skin has been considered behaviorally significant. This idea, along with the pervasive myth that primitive humans did not connect heterosexual sex with reproduction, is criticized in Chapter 4.)

Breasts evolved to mimic the now-sexualized buttocks by swelling, becoming hairless, and altering their form according to reproductive status. Judging by their pelvises, earlier australopithecines such as *A. afarensis* and *A. africanus* seem not to have had hemispherical buttocks. Thus, even if Lucy were not Lucifer, she would not have had breasts. Whether the thing-that-made-the-Laetoli-tracks had them is harder to judge, because we do not know quite what it was.

From Buttocks to Brains

Mary Leakey's Laetoli discovery remains crucial, however many new fossil species turn up. Peter Wheeler believes that the footprints represent the answer to the physiological problem of overheating. Fewer trees mean more sunshine, and a good way to avoid overheating is to present a smaller shape to the sun, which a primate in the tropics achieves very well by standing up. Most savannah animals cope without standing up, though, and Wheeler considers brain size important in the light of research carried out by anthropologist Dean Falk, of the State University of New York, Albany. Falk's "radiator theory" recognizes that special problems are involved in keeping a large hominid brain cooled. Their solution lies in allowing blood to flow in or out of the brain through valve-free veins that run through small holes or sinuses in the skull.

The number of such sinuses increases, Falk has found, as hominid brains grow bigger. When coupled with such a cooling mechanism, standing up may pave the way for a larger brain. Moving the head away from ground level places it in a significantly cooler air flow, while freeing the hands allows many more things to be done — using a wider range of tools, for example, which may provoke changes in brain organization and be reflected back in greater brain size. But there is a catch: walking upright also means a modified pelvis that makes childbirth difficult and imposes a limit on fetal head size. Because of this problem, bipedalism should not correlate with any increase in brain size. That it did suggests that more than just biology was involved.

Between three and two million years ago, the climate on the eastern side of Africa became cooler and drier. Hominids became more and more varied. The australopithecines and paranthropines ate a diet high in rough plant food, while habilines (*Homo habilis* and related species) seem to have had a much higher protein diet, emphasizing meat and perhaps fish. *Homo rudolfensis* lived on a broad spectrum of grains, nuts, fruits, and vegetables. Like nonhuman primates, all these hominids probably used naturally occurring objects as tools, but from around 2.7 million years onward, they used deliber-

ately shaped stone tools or artifacts. The bones of robust paranthropines, such as those found at Swartkrans in South Africa from
around 1.7 million years ago (number 7 in Figure 1.3) have been
found alongside stone tools. Their hands seem to have been fully capable of making them, but the presence of habilines at the same site
leaves open the question of whether they actually did.

Although we usually refer to early, deliberately shaped stone artifacts as "tools," it is quite possible that some of them were more specifically weapons. Most of the early hominid species seem to have been
markedly sexually dimorphic in terms of overall stature—the males
much bigger in relation to the females than they are today. This dimorphism would normally imply polygyny, that males competed with each
other to be selected by females, resulting in the strongest males having
sexual and reproductive relationships with several females, and the
smallest, weakest males losing out altogether. Significantly, however,
there is no marked difference between male and female canine teeth—
in stark contrast to gorillas and chimpanzees, where the males use
their large canines competitively in displays and fights with other
males for the control of harems.

The absence of big canines has been used to support the influential monogamy theory, promoted by Owen Lovejoy of Kent State
University. Lovejoy assumes that monogamy emerged as the primary
pattern for human sexual relationships. The only way our early ancestors could have survived, he believes, was if each woman and her
offspring were exclusively provided for by her hunter-mate. Among
the many curiosities about the monogamy theory, not least is the fact
that the current level of monogamy globally is largely the result of the
influence of Judeo-Christian values during the past five hundred
years. Although some of the largest population blocs have adopted
monogamy, a majority of individual societies worldwide still practice
some form of polygamy. There is thus no evidence for monogamy
ever having "evolved" in any species-wide sense among humans.

But the monogamy theory has other weaknesses too. For one
thing, competition among male hominids may typically have involved
the use of weapons instead of teeth. If large canines were neither useful in fighting nor particularly attractive to females, then they would

no longer have been actively selected for, and given the nutritional cost of growing them, they would tend to be reduced. Competition and aggression both within and between early human species would have been well served by weapons. This is a complex debate, and I put my view to Owen Lovejoy during a transatlantic telephone call. He responded by pointing out that *Australopithecus anamensis* (Figure 1.3, number 2) already shows canine reduction around four million years ago, while the very earliest stone tools or weapons date to 2.7 million, thus the canine reduction cannot be attributed to the emergence of an alternate mode of male combat. The problem for me with this is that I am sure that natural objects such as stones could have been used offensively for a million years or more without needing to be worked-up into artifacts that archaeologists can easily recognize. Indeed, supporters of the "throwing hypothesis," such as my Bradford colleague Chris Knüsel, believe that bipedalism emerged principally because of the mechanical advantages it provided in launching projectiles. In Knüsel's view *A. anamensis*'s degree of bipedalism is a direct index of the use of found objects as weapons in this species.

The First Words

The new sort of human that appeared around 1.8 million years ago quickly replaced all previously existing members of the genus *Homo* (late *rudolfensis* and the habilines). The new *Homo* spread outward from Africa to colonize Europe, the Caucasus, China, and Java. This rapid dispersion and subsequent regional variation have led Bernard Wood to divide the species into two forms, but with closely similar features and—presumably—capabilities: the African form, *Homo ergaster*, and the beyond-Africa form, *Homo erectus*. The earliest dated specimen of *Homo erectus* is the Mojokerto skull from Java (number 13 in Figure 1.3, dated to 1.81 million years), while the best preserved *Homo ergaster* is the almost complete skeleton of a boy, found by Kamoya Kimeu at Nariokotome in Kenya (number 12 in Figure 1.3). Richard Leakey and Alan Walker have dated the Nariokotome skeleton to 1.6 million years ago.

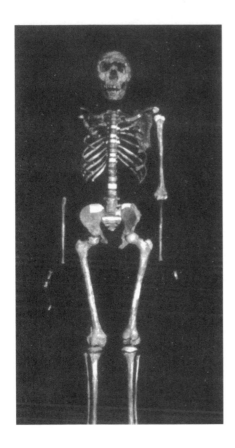

(Fig. 1.5) The Nariokotome Boy. A 1.6-million-year-old fossil. Photograph: National Museum of Kenya.

A cast made of the inside of the Nariokotome skull shows clear signs of lateralization—or specialization of the right and left hemispheres—which is associated with being able to make tools and to throw. Carefully fashioned stone missiles, discovered by the late Glynn Isaac at Olduvai Gorge, suggest that these humans may have hunted small game. Evidence from split marrow bones certainly suggests that the diet had a meat component, although it could have been scavenged. The Nariokotome boy's molars were still coming through, indicating that he was about ten years old when he died. (A dental abscess indicates that he may have died of blood poisoning.) Yet he was already 5 feet 3 inches tall and would probably have reached 6 feet 1 inch had he survived into adulthood. African *Homo ergaster* was more robust and taller than modern humans, although the brain capacity was smaller by about a third.

Despite some strongly argued doubts, the existence of Broca's area—the brain structure responsible for language in humans—convinces several scholars, including myself, that the Nariokotome boy could talk (although the musculature of his rib cage suggests that he may not have had as much breathing control as we have today). In *The Language Instinct* Steven Pinker quotes Lily Tomlin's guess for the first words: "What a hairy back!" From what I have said about the extension of sexual skin, this is less likely than it first appears. I want to return to the old Hollywood idea that the first words were actually grunts . . . but off-screen, and mock-orgasmic.

Language can be elaborated only where there is a conscious awareness of alternatives for action. Given the Machiavellian intelligence of the Gombe chimps, who use the "snake call" as a decoy to steal food, and given the sexual enthusiasm of our closest living relatives, the bonobos, it is plausible that the two came together in hominids to produce the mental ground conditions necessary for language.

The sexual embrace is a physical and social contact with possibilities for interpersonal closeness as well as for deception. It provided particularly good opportunities for developing what Nick Humphrey terms *introspection*—the ability to understand another's feelings by analogy with what one can monitor of one's own feelings under the same circumstances. It also provides ideal conditions under which to influence or exploit the other person by consciously projecting misleading information about one's own inner state. The presence of cognitive choices during sex creates a world in which effectively linguistic statements can be made. Faking orgasm, like developed language, is apparently unique to humans.

The overall pattern of cultural complexity around 1.8 million years ago supports the idea that a real social world existed. Glynn Isaac believed that the establishment of home bases, the organizing of hunting parties, and the elaboration of food-sharing behaviors would all have required language. The first systematic sexual division of labor, with males hunting and females gathering, might also date to this time.

Today, male-female brain differences are so slight that it requires the most sophisticated experiments to find even the slightest trace of them. The current consensus seems to be that while there are some minor brain differences, they are not of a sort by which male and female brains can be "ranked" in terms of overall ability. Nor is it clear whether these differences are genetically programmed or culturally learned (or arise as some interplay of genetic and cultural factors). Women seem marginally better at verbal skills and at hand-eye coordination, men at spatial tasks, such as orienting. On this basis, the originators of stone tool culture are more likely to have been women, but in practice the differences are too slight to determine anything. Still, the tasks that men and women performed in early prehistory were certainly not identical. Women must have taken the primary role in early infant care, a task that became far more demanding with the advent of bipedalism and even more so once body hair was lost. A chimpanzee baby clings to its mother's fur and hangs on around her body, leaving her limbs relatively free to move around. Standing upright ruins this arrangement; feet become modified for walking and can no longer grip. It becomes harder to hang from the torso, and with little body hair to cling to, it becomes virtually impossible.

The problem of infant carrying was addressed by Elaine Morgan, who is unusual among evolutionary theorists in having actually thought hard about this practical problem, even if her aquatic solution remains unconvincing. Owen Lovejoy believes that a principal reason that monogamy must have emerged among early humans is that females would not have been able to carry both babies and burdens. That is, they would have had to remain sedentary in order to reproduce successfully. On the front cover of Don Johanson's book about human evolution, *Lucy's Child*, artist David Bergen has solved this problem by putting a child up on the adult's shoulder, but this position seems precarious for food gathering and really leaves the adult with only one free hand (unless the infant clings hard to the head hair).

The Cradle of Culture

The logical conclusion is that women invented the first characteristically human artifact — the baby-sling. Until the recent invention of

(Fig. 1.6)   The Ovahimba sling: A Namibian woman transporting her children using both old and new methods. Photograph: The Hegenbart/Stern/SOA.

the wheeled baby carriage, the child-carrying sling was one of the most ubiquitous artifacts on earth. At its simplest, it is a length of animal skin, tied to form a pouch and hung from one shoulder. Animal tendons would have been useful for a range of binding and tying jobs, including baby-slings. Excavated material from hominid sites in the Olduvai Gorge, dating between 2 and 1.6 million B.P. (Before Present) shows that tendons were deliberately extracted from the carcasses of large savannah animals.

The sling should have been well within the conceptual reach of early humans who had the capacity to modify the shapes of stones. If the "throwing hypothesis" is correct, then humans who could throw better would have been at an advantage in hunting and combat. Throwing involves cradling a projectile in the hand or, more efficiently, in a loop of material—a sling—that extends the circumference of the arc through which the projectile can be accelerated. But hominids could have arrived at the principle of cradling from other activities too, notably transporting water and small objects in natural containers—a behavior observed among primates. The date of the in-

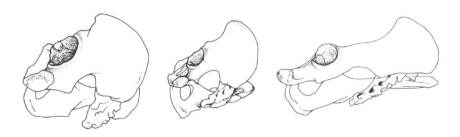

(Fig. 1.7)   Lucy's pelvis: Owen Lovejoy's reconstruction of the pelvis of "Lucy" (middle left),
compared with a modern human female (left) and a chimpanzee (right).
Photograph courtesy of Owen Lovejoy.

vention of the baby-sling is unknown, because soft organic materials
do not usually survive in the archaeological record. Nevertheless, we
have indirect evidence for it in terms of human mental development.

I believe that the invention of the baby-sling was the single most
crucial step in the evolutionary development toward larger brains.
This is because of a further condition that bipedalism imposes on evolution—the paradox, referred to at the beginning of this chapter, that
changes in the pelvic girdle restrict head size rather than encourage
it. There are marked differences between the pelvises of primates and
those of bipedal or semibipedal hominids. A side-on comparison of
Lucy's pelvis to a chimpanzee's and a human's makes this point well
(Figure 1.7). Looked at from above, however, they are very different
(Figure 1.8).

Comparing the pelvises of chimpanzees, australopithecines, and
humans, an increasing difficulty in giving birth can be observed. In
chimps, the inlet, midplane, and outlet of the pelvis have a virtually
identical cross-section, so that the head of the child does not move its
position in relation to its body as it moves down the birth canal. In
humans, however, the inlet, midplane, and outlet have markedly different cross-sections, so that the baby's head must actually rotate as it
passes down through the birth canal—a circumstance that makes
childbirth much more difficult. Reconstructing childbirth in australopithecines is difficult, but they probably rotated their heads through
the birth canal in a manner similar to modern humans.

CHIMPANZEE   "LUCY"   HUMAN

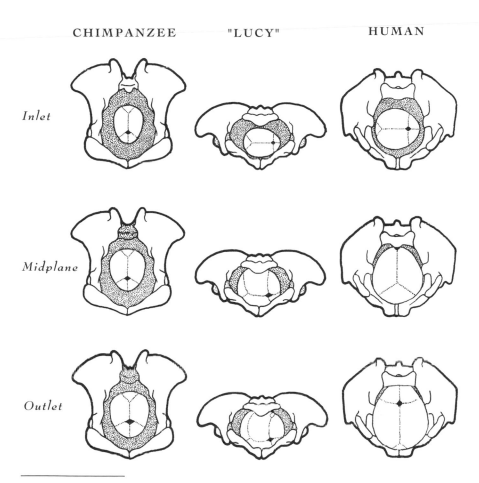

(Fig. 1.8) Australopithecine birth mechanics. The mechanics of birth in chimpanzees (left) and humans (right), showing cross-sections through the pelvis as the fetal head emerges. The central sequence shows how Lucy-like australopithecines may have given birth, as modeled on a reconstruction of the Lucy pelvis (assuming it to be female). Drawing by George Taylor following Tague and Budinoff's reconstruction in Bunney 1993.

The size limits for a baby's head are quite marked in australopithecines. Everything is a much tighter fit than for chimps. How did hominids overcome this problem to evolve larger brains? The simplest means was to give birth while the baby's head is still small, then let the head and brain develop outside the womb during a period of intensive neonatal care. This is in fact the solution that humans developed. Whereas the newborn brain weight of a nonhuman primate is already around 42 percent of its adult weight, a human child's is a mere 29 percent. The human infant continues its basic cerebral development for eighteen months after birth, during which time the rapidly growing brain is not held in by a firm case. Fusion of the cranial sutures is greatly delayed. The downside is that the human baby is far less physically and mentally autonomous than a chimpanzee baby at every stage and needs far greater cranial protection. Having an underdeveloped brain at birth retards the development of everything else. Thus a human baby is not only mentally but physically underdeveloped.

The australopithecines never managed to develop brains much larger than chimpanzees'. Their young, born with some difficulty, probably clung to mothers who had retained a fair amount of body hair. The powerful plant-processing jaws of australopithecines could also have pulled the infant skull apart if the cranial plates were not well fused. As the genus *Homo* developed, however, brain size grew rapidly.

In practice, the development of the baby-sling removed the crucial factor limiting the efficiency of postnatal care and allowed hominid females to bear underdeveloped babies that, with postnatal brain growth, could subsequently catch up and—crucially—overtake australopithecines in brain development. Hominid mothering, far from being a passive, essentially biological function that incapacitated early human females and made them dependent on male "providers," was a challenge to which females rose with an innovative solution. Not only would the sling have facilitated the evolution of an extended period of physical helplessness, it would also have freed the baby's brain to take in information about the outside world. As William Sears has argued, "carrying humanizes a baby." The mother's walking movement maintains what the child was used to in the womb, stimulating the balance organs behind the ear, "organizing" and calming the infant. In a calm state the baby is free to thrive, with its energy directed into physical and behavioral development. The calm state is the most interactive one; modern researchers have reported enhanced visual and auditory alertness in carried babies.

Sometime between 200,000 and 100,000 years ago, among late

archaic *sapiens* and Neanderthals, brain size increased to such an extent that birth must certainly have involved rotation of the baby's head, as it does today. By this time, Karen Rosenberg believes, a woman might often have required help to give birth safely, in the form of a midwife who could guide her through labor and manipulate the position of the baby as it emerged through the birth canal.

Mind Games

It is not clear what specific advantages a larger brain gave to humans. Its drawbacks, however, are evident. As Leslie Aiello has pointed out, a larger brain required a much higher food energy input from the mother, and it made childbirth more difficult. The timing of the development was clearly significant in making it advantageous. The crucial jump occurred between 2.5 and 1.6 million years ago, at a time when there was considerable competition between several different species of hominid. The ability to use a grammatical language, to forward plan, and to organize a social division of labor, may have emerged together and within a short space of time as brain size increased above some crucial threshold. Such abilities would have given the ancestral human line the edge over their close rivals. But the human brain continued to increase in size during later evolution too, when those rivals had already become extinct.

Why this brain-size increase should have continued in the absence of interspecies competition and after the emergence of speech is unclear. The growth may have been driven by competition *between* human groups, but larger brains may also have been sexually selected. Darwin implied they were when he compared the human brain to the peacock's fan, and others have recently suggested that a sort of "runaway" sexual selection could have been involved. Nor need we assume—as Darwin did—that sexual selection operated on just one sex (the male) and was more weakly reflected in the other (the female). Both males and females may have found larger brains "sexier"; the development of spoken language cannot be divorced from the development of song, and both are important elements in modern courtship. Whatever drove the increase in human mental capacity, it effectively operated on both sexes equally. In the end, what is so fascinating about human brain-sex differences is that they are virtually nonexistent in comparison with most other animal species, which have marked behavioral and cognitive differences between the sexes. These differences are particularly striking in birds and insects, where built-in genetic determinants of behavior—instincts—are of primary importance. In mammals learning plays a greater role in cognitive development than in birds and insects, and in humans the learned component is massive. It has given humans the great advantage of flexibility.

We became human not because men went hunting while women foraged for plants and carried children, but because when need arose, the two sexes could swap roles. (Several parts of this book were typed with my youngest daughter in a sling, across my lap, quietly sleeping.) Humans have effectively replaced an instinctive division of behavior along sexual lines with a learned or gendered division of labor that is based on but not limited by differences in basic biological function.

The invention of the sling was a turning point not just in brain development but in human sexual culture. It marked the origin of the idea of gender—the extension of human sexual categories into the realm of objects and ideas. Tool use among primates is not divided markedly along sexual lines—a mother may pass on a favorite hammer stone to either her son or her daughter. The sling is an altogether different item, representing an association with the close, continuous, mother-baby contact necessary for early demand-led breast-feeding. When men use it, it still carries these female connotations. The development of gendered clothing may have followed on from a functional yet sex-related item like the sling.

The brain-size increase that the baby-sling helped facilitate may have pushed us over the brink to full language. The emergence of language must be connected to the birth of fantasy—the point where males and females could tell each other their imaginings and share their thought worlds. Out of this new quality, upon which the arts of poetry and sweet-talk are based, came a specifically human sort of love, in which the pleasure of sex is increased greatly by the empathy that the participants can have for each other. Sex ceased to be necessarily short and sharp and became an act of potentially ecstatic mutual contemplation. On the other hand, fantasy opened up the possibility that the participants could become almost completely *disengaged* from sex, allowing their minds to drift to other subjects, such as where the next meal would come from. It is this mixed blessing that we have inherited. It has led not only to widely varied individual experiences of sex but to the establishment of marked differences in what particular societies feel sex actually is, according to the sorts of learning, fantasies, or myths they share.

CHRISTOPHER ANTHONY MASTERS,
TH.D., Ph.D., J.D.
RANCHO SAN·DIEGO, CALIFORNIA

Chapter 2

Skull Sex
and Brain Sex

"Just how much sex is there in a skeleton?"

GERMAINE GREER,
THE FEMALE EUNUCH

In 1979, as a young student, I was excavating at Gars-Thunau, a large prehistoric settlement in Lower Austria, when a request for assistance came through to my group from the local police. A farmer who was digging a septic tank in the middle of his yard had come across the skeleton of a young woman at a depth of eight or nine feet. Herwig Friesinger of the University of Vienna drove over with a small crew, and it fell to me, as the most junior, to drop into the hole and fully expose the remains so that a proper record of the position of the body could be made.

While the police and Austrian archaeologists stood chatting in the yard, filling out forms, their voices muffled by the damp earth walls around my ears, I worked away on the mystery woman. Her bones were well preserved, but there were no grave goods, no fragments of a coffin or traces of clothing, nothing immediate to fix the date of her death at five, fifty, five hundred, or two thousand years ago.

She lay on her back in a relaxed position and had either been buried while still warm or much later, after rigor mortis had worn off: not in a churchyard, not close to any known pagan or prehistoric graveyard, but very deep. As I cleaned around her pelvis and lumbar vertebrae, the hairs on the back of my neck stood up, and I felt both sad and somehow close to her. Such isolated and unmarked burial meant that she had most likely been murdered, or else she had died under circumstances that someone had wanted kept secret. I was disturbing that secret, as I gently brushed back the soil from her forehead and brought her white bones into the harsh sunlight of a day she could not have imagined.

But *I* had imagined *her.* I had been told we were going to where a *woman's* skeleton had been found, and I did not question it. True, the relatively gracile jaw and broad pelvis suggested that the bones had once been a woman's, but it takes many measurements to be sure, and only in some cases, as we shall see, can we have complete certainty. I have excavated many bones since, among them those of a sixth-century Avar "princess," the burned remains of a fourth-century-B.C. Thracian "warrior," and the eggshell-like pieces of an unidentified infant skull. Each time I am moved, and I inevitably personify the remains in my mind.

But these skeletons may not be what they seem. What if the one in the Austrian farmyard were a man's? Or that of an intersex individual—someone, perhaps, with androgynous characteristics who had passed as a woman until his/her wedding night, when things finally came apart? Although unusual, such things *do* happen. The farmyard burial was not ordinary, but the police, the farmer, the Austrian archaeologists, and I were all in quiet agreement about the sex of the bones from the word go. An anonymous murdered woman connected well with our ideas of contemporary society. The evidence did not challenge us; the "evidence" was simply what we were prepared to see. If we never look any harder, then all we will find in the past is our own reflection. As Germaine Greer put it,

When archaeologists state categorically that half a femur comes from a twenty-year-old woman, we are impressed with their certainty, not the less so because the statement, being a guess, is utterly unverifiable. Such a guess is as much based in the archaeologists' assumptions about women as anything else. What they mean is that the bone is typically female, that is, that it *ought* to belong to a woman. Because it is impossible to escape from the stereotyped notions of womanhood as they prevail in one's own society, curious errors in ascription have been made and continue to be made.

This statement annoys many of my colleagues. In the twenty-five years that have passed since *The Female Eunuch* was first published, our ability to determine the sex of human skeletal remains has become much more sophisticated, and analysis of ancient DNA has become an established, though expensive, technique. (It is effective even on cremated bone.) Our best practice, however, is not particularly widespread, while the emotional responses of individual archaeologists are universal. Don Johanson's *Australopithecus afarensis* was so emphatically "Lucy" that it has taken us more than twenty years to be able to see the pelvis as potentially male. The Nariokotome "boy" is so much the young hunter that we scarcely wonder exactly what range of skeletal variation existed between males and females in that specific time and place. Often we are not open-minded about what division of labor between the sexes may (or may not) have existed in the remote past.

If the Austrian farmyard had been in modern-day Albania, the skeleton could have been biologically female but, in most respects, socially male. The reason is that there are two levels in human sexual culture: biological sex, and gender, or the social elaboration of observed biological differences. The Sworn Virgins of Albania are a class of biological women who decide to be men, usually before the age of ten. They take a vow of chastity, dress like men, work with men, and are accepted by men as men — except that unlike men, they cannot be killed, which is part of their advantage as household heads in a society riven by blood feuds. Some become village headmen.

This chapter investigates the emotional commitments we all make when we recognize others as "male" and "female," not just by their bones ("skull sex") but by their bodies and their behavior ("brain sex"), and how those commitments can color our interpretation of prehistoric society.

Mix-and-Match Bones

Possession of male or female genitalia is usually an either/or question (although "in-between" organs sometimes do occur), depending on the presence or absence of the shortened Y chromosome in the pair of sex chromosomes that most people possess. (Men usually code as XY, women as XX.) On the other hand, sexual dimorphism—the measurable differences in features, such as legs and arms, that both sexes possess—is a question of degree. Although men are taller than women on average in most societies, numerous individual women are taller than numerous individual men. People cannot be divided up into short and tall in the same way that they can be divided into male and female.

Adult female skeletons are, on average, shorter, less robust, broader in the pelvis, thinner in the chin, and smoother over the brows than are adult male skeletons, but these differences are only average; individual cases demonstrate overlaps for every feature. In every community men and women share a single basic genetic blueprint for the human skeleton, adapted to suit adult purposes by exposure to different mixtures of hormones. At puberty the shared blueprint indicates that the pelvis should widen. For women this makes the pelvis mechanically less efficient for walking and running; the payoff is in its increased efficiency as a birthing conduit. (The ultimate efficiency is reached only at the critical moment, when the hormone relaxin allows the pelvic outlet to expand by an extra half-inch or so.) For men, however, there is no payoff in side-to-side growth of the pelvis, and secretions of testosterone during puberty suppress it.

The skeleton is not a static frame from which the body hangs.

Rather, it grows and remodels itself continuously. Old bone gives way to new, while shapes and volumes constantly change from birth to death. Although the sex chromosomes control some of the hormones that act on the skeletal blueprint, other factors can act on the skeleton by altering the ratio of hormonal secretions. Both dietary and emotional stress can stunt growth in humans, and both leave telltale bands (Harris lines) in the teeth. So distinguishing male and female skeletons is not as easy as it seems. If men are systematically more stressed than women in a particular society, then their average height will draw closer to women's. In female athletes strenuous physical exercise during adolescence can keep androgen levels high, so that the pelvis stays narrow and malelike. (Some female athletes experience a late "skeletal puberty" on retirement.) In the prehistoric past we know far less about the usual activities of males and females. The prevalence of arthritis and injury among the Neanderthals suggests that they had a very tough physical existence. Their skeletons display little sexual dimorphism, perhaps as a result of high androgen levels in females as much as sexual selection.

How people do things affects their skeleton as much as the simple fact of doing them. In fact, as social anthropologist Tim Ingold has noted, there is no such thing as "simply" doing anything. New Yorkers walk in a different style from Siberian fur trappers, and men walk differently from women. The male swagger and female teeter, easily observable on a Saturday night in any large American or European city, can be seen in children long before their pelvises become markedly different. Children copy the adults around them, and walking "like a lady" or "like a man" is encouraged from an early age and aided by functional differences in footwear. (Finding my daughters shoes with properly gripping soles is a perennial problem.) Gendered walking styles are largely reversible (women who want to pass as men can successfully mimic a male walk, and vice versa), but the mechanical stresses on the skeleton produce measurable differences.

Despite these complexities, most physical anthropologists believe that they can identify the sex of a particular skeleton with certainty in nineteen out of twenty cases. But in view of the many dimensions of sex, what sort of certainty can they have? What type of sex is being measured? Beyond genetic and skeletal sex, there are other measures of sex: the sex of the fleshy body (the sexual characteristics it displays) and that body's reproductive potential as male (able to physically inseminate to cause pregnancy in another) or female (able to physically bear children). The physical body is a mere potentiality until it is coupled with sexual behavior, the roots of which are thought by some to be in the innate physiology of the brain, and by others to be principally connected to learning and culture.

Part and Counterpart

The common genetic blueprint for the human skeleton is actually part of a common genetic blueprint for the entire body. The plan for the flesh, as well as the bones, is basically female; maleness is created hormonally. Men have nipples because nipples are part of the original plan. Male human nipples very rarely produce milk (although males of some species, such as the goat, often produce it), but they are quite susceptible to erotic stimulation. Men also have an organ analogous to the womb situated at the base of the prostate gland, the utricle (or *uterus masculinus*). Its opening into the urethra is guarded by the delicate membranous circular fold of the male hymen, close to which the ejaculatory ducts open; it may be connected to the experience of anal orgasm in men.

In a famous essay called "The Spandrels of San Marco," Stephen Jay Gould and Richard Lewontin suggest that particular features of living things need not have been deliberately evolved but could have come into existence by virtue of something else that was constructively necessary. They drew an analogy with the small, flat, triangular areas of wall—spandrels—that occur high up inside some churches, such as San Marco in Venice. These spandrels, ideal spaces for paintings, simply come about by virtue of the angles at which the vaulted ceiling panels support the roof. For Gould and Lewontin, male nipples are somewhat like spandrels. Their erogenous qualities, like a frieze of paintings, represent a fringe benefit that was neither planned nor evolutionarily selected.

When it comes to the penis, many biologists have argued against the original-female-body-plan idea. Instead, they see the clitoris as like a spandrel, a spin-off from the body plan, which reserves a bud of embryonic cells for potential development into a penis. Gould believes that the female orgasm is functionless in the strict evolutionary sense, since conception can occur in its absence. This explains, for Gould, why female orgasm seems less reliable (more prone to dysfunction) than male orgasm.

The clitoris, however, is not a small bud of underdeveloped cells. It is actually no smaller than the penis, although in humans much of it is hidden. When flaccid, the glans is partly or wholly covered by a fold formed by the inner lips of the vagina. After the first inch or two, the clitoris divides, and the remainder of its erectile tissue (the "bulbs of the vestibule") run down for six or seven inches to either side of the vaginal opening. In female lemurs—primates with whom, going back twenty million years, we share a common ancestor—the urethra runs down through the clitoris, so that urination occurs in the same way as in males. In hyenas the clitoris in the female is long, like the male's penis, and the birth canal runs down through it. Such functions flatly contradict the idea that the clitoris is an evolutionarily functionless spin-off.

The Wisdom of the Ancients

The physiology of the female orgasm has been hotly debated over the past hundred years. Sigmund Freud maintained that in psychologically healthy women, the center of orgasm should shift from the clitoris to the vagina in adulthood. By contrast, Alfred Kinsey argued that vaginal orgasms were a "biological impossibility." Yet with appropriate training and focus, all sorts of different parts of the body can be stimulated to result in orgasm, so it seems strange to rule out the vagina. In fact, the whole female pubic area can be actively involved in sexual pleasure; it can also play a decisive part in conception.

One of the most detailed ancient descriptions of female sexual and reproductive physiology was written by the ancient Greek medic

Hippocrates of Cos and his followers. Hippocrates was born around 460 B.C., at a time when many oral traditions were being committed to writing for the first time. The Hippocratic medics were not a legally recognized profession, and they competed for business with many other healers and trainers. Hippocrates' knowledge was probably based not only on his own firsthand experiences in his practice but on the unwritten knowledge of midwives and wise women — women who, because of the evolutionary pattern of the human pelvis described in Chapter 1, were custodians of techniques and knowledge that had been continuously developed over the last 100,000 years or even longer. (If Hippocrates did rely on them, then his unacknowledged incorporation of their knowledge marks the earliest identifiable stage in the ongoing male takeover of the management of pregnancy and childbirth, the most extreme form of which — the outlawing of autonomous (female) midwives by (male) gynecologists — has so far been reached only in a few places, such as Sweden and some American states.)

Hippocrates saw female sexual physiology as active — so active that he envisioned the womb as able to move around the body in search of moisture, sometimes getting stuck and sometimes drying out and traveling to the liver. Such apparently bizarre beliefs have caused most modern scholars to reject Hippocratic gynecology as pure fantasy. Yet his basic facts were correct, even if his explanation was not. In the condition known as endometriosis, part of the uterine lining can detach itself and migrate to other parts of the abdomen and, more rarely, beyond, to the arms, lungs, head, and so on; there is no reason why it should not attach itself to the liver. Endometriosis is a painful condition (often causing monthly inflammation of the affected area) that ancient Greek healers could have attempted to treat surgically or herbally, and Hippocrates may well have examined the affected tissues postmortem.

Hippocrates described female orgasm in some detail:

It is my contention that when during intercourse the vagina is rubbed and the womb is disturbed, an irritation is set up in the womb which produces pleasure and heat in the rest of the body. A woman also releases something from her body, sometimes into the womb—which then becomes moist—and sometimes externally as well, if the womb is open wider than normal. Once intercourse has begun, she experiences pleasure throughout the whole time, until the man ejaculates. If her desire for intercourse is excited, she emits before the man, and for the remainder of the time does not feel pleasure to the same extent.

This last is a clear reference to female ejaculation, the existence of which has often been questioned in modern medicine (mostly by men), though it has always been real enough for those who experience it.

Hippocrates believed that a woman could work her cervix to regulate the uptake of sperm:

When a woman has intercourse, if she is not going to conceive, then it is her practice to expel the sperm produced by both partners whenever she wishes to do so. If however she is going to conceive, the sperm is not expelled, but remains in the womb. For when the womb has received the sperm it closes up and retains it. . . . If the woman is experienced in matters of childbirth, and takes note of when the sperm is retained, she will know the precise day on which she has conceived.

This process can be attested by modern experience. During orgasm the top of the vagina balloons out to form a kind of pool for the semen, into which the cervix dips, drawing it up into the uterus. This action is aided by the semen itself, which contains the fatty acid prostaglandin that causes vaginal spasming.

Hippocrates's description of women with active reproductive

anatomy fits with the findings of the Liverpool-based researchers Robin Baker and Mark Bellis, who have studied the way in which women can manipulate sperm within their bodies, rejecting it ("flow-back") when they do not want to conceive and sucking it up ("up-suck") when they do. Baker and Bellis are convinced that female masturbation plays an important part in the process, generating uterine contractions that help a woman to keep a particular man's sperm in play for several days after intercourse. The control of orgasm and up-suck also allows a woman with more than one partner to have a surprising measure of control over whom she conceives by.

The Hippocratic view, based as it was on a long tradition of female body knowledge, and Baker and Bellis's research both suggest that the clitoris has a functional dimension. Its situation, toward the top of the pubic area and a little away from the vaginal opening, allows comfortable masturbation without the risk of infection from the insertion of fingers or objects. Gould's idea of the clitoris and the female orgasm as functionless can in fact be reversed, so that *male* orgasm becomes the spandrel. While a penis seems necessary for normal insemination, it does not need to spasm to ejaculate; it could just produce a directed flow, as with urine. The characteristic spasming of male orgasm may therefore be a pale neuromuscular reflection of vaginal "up-suck." Nevertheless, the comparability of women's and men's sexual organs probably indicates a fair degree of overlap between their inner experiences of sex. Sex, after all, is mostly in the head. But are women's and men's minds the same?

Proper Girls and Boys

Many people believe that boys and girls are psychologically different from birth onward, but the evidence is controversial. Researchers claim to have found structural differences in the brains of adult men and women, but whether these differences are innate or come about in some complex interplay between genes, hormones, and socialization is not clear.

It is something of a modern Western habit to discount the impact of culture during the earliest moments of a child's life. Babies are thought of as completely natural beings from whose behavior general principles of sexual difference can be inferred. Matt Ridley, in *The Red Queen: Sex and the Evolution of Human Nature*, quotes from a letter written by a mother to a newspaper: "I would be interested to know if any of your more learned readers could tell me why, from the time my twins could reach for toys and were put on a rug together with a mixed selection of 'boys' and 'girls' toys, he would inevitably select the car/train items and she the doll/teddy ones." Ridley's answer is that, although there are no genes for liking guns or dolls, there are "genes for channeling male instincts" into imitating males and for channeling female instincts into imitating females.

But this notion is nonsensical. Male and female babies are often dealt with as male and female from birth on, and they can easily learn to imitate one or the other parent or activity sphere. In the case in point, we do not know whether the twins were placed among the toys completely at random, or whether their particular choices throughout the day were differently approved or recorded. What is certain is that many cultural factors were at work. By virtue of writing to a newspaper to challenge its "more learned readers," in fact, the mother shows a prejudice in favor of a particular answer. In a society that generally mocks boys who play with dolls and girls who tote guns, mothers of twins with the "wrong" preferences are much less likely to publish the fact.

Measures of sex differences in the brain do go beyond the anecdotal. They are thought to show up most clearly under laboratory test conditions, where particular forms of intelligence can be tested in isolation. Women appear to have (marginally) better verbal capacities, and men (marginally) better spatial ones. The way men and women mentally "map" the world seems systematically different. A surge of testosterone in the male fetus at around six weeks is crucial to the development of brain sex, some researchers think. Boys who do not get this surge, though testosterone may physically masculinize them at puberty in the usual way, apparently retain a femalelike brain pattern. On the other hand, Edelman has recently presented evidence suggesting that much of the nervous "wiring" of the human brain is actually fixed into place during the early years of life, under the influence of learning.

Degrees of Sex

Many of the hormones that guide the development of the human body are also found in animals and plants and have synthetic counterparts. Hormone levels can thus be artificially boosted, a fact that has led sports regulators to run genetic and hormonal checks on athletes. Biologically, female athletes can take androgen supplements to develop their skeletons in order to gain what is termed "unfair masculine advantage." (Most sports favor the male physique; activities where women naturally excel, such as long-distance ocean swimming, do not attract Olympic recognition.) But marked variation is a fact of life, both in individual hormone production and in the degree to which an athlete genetically conforms to typical maleness or femaleness.

Since 1968, the International Olympic Committee has required all women athletes to show an "XX" sex chromosome configuration as part of their "gender verification" procedure. In the 1985 World Student Games, Maria Martinez Patino, a Spanish athlete, was disqualified as a bona fide female competitor because, although she showed no physical signs of masculinization, she was genetically XY. In a landmark appeal case, she was reinstated. It is possible for someone to look female and be reproductively female but still have an XY coding—a fact that sports regulators will have to face. Conversely, genetically female (XX) fetuses with adreno-genital syndrome (AGS) react to androgens while they are in the womb, causing them to develop as men. They may often have competed in sport as men, although their position since genetic testing became widespread is unclear. By the strict genetic criterion, they should compete as women, despite being male in all other respects.

Many other body–sex variations are known. Where AGS is less marked, females may develop in a partially masculine fashion, with enlarged testiclelike labia, a penislike clitoris, and a generally robust skeleton. Many XY boys are born with their testes undescended; if they do not descend from their internal position before the onset of puberty, an adrenal failure results, causing femalelike bodily characteristics to develop. Differences may occur in the uniformity or number of sex chromosomes: some people's bodies have a mixture (or "mosaic") of XX and XY cells. In Turner's syndrome the presence of a single X chromosome leads to the development of a female body type, but without ovaries.

Sometimes three or more sex chromosomes are present, the most common variation being XXY—Kleinfelter's syndrome—which is usually manifested in the body as male external genitalia with a femalelike pelvis and hormonal pattern, and possible infertility. A rare inherited disorder called 5-alpha-reductase deficiency, known from thirty-eight cases reported in the Dominican Republic, causes XY fetuses to develop outwardly as girls, which is what they appear to be at birth. At puberty, however, they suddenly develop into men, with the labia developing into testicles and the clitoris into a penis. Still, the opening of the urethra remains below it, so that ejaculation is not well directed.

Some people are fully hermaphroditic, having the internal and external reproductive organs of both sexes. The overall birthrate of recognizably "intersex" individuals is surprisingly high, running at between one and two in every thousand. In industrialized societies, when intersex babies are born, doctors usually do a genetic test to determine the "real" sex, surgically conform the genitalia accordingly, and administer additional hormones as necessary. But in many non-Western societies a child is accepted as it is, and outside medical interference aimed at changing its basic identity may be viewed with extreme hostility.

The birthrates for intersex individuals probably vary from society to society. Odd genetic effects may often be quite local, and their retention in a fetus from conception to birth may depend on the degree of environmental stress that a population faces. In harsher conditions, evidence suggests, birth abnormalities of any sort are much rarer. Intersex animals are more common among domestic populations than in the wild, an effect that seems to be an accidental genetic side-effect of strongly selective breeding.

Most likely, intersex individuals were born at roughly the same rate in prehistory as they are today, although archaeologists have so far failed to definitely recognize a single example. In a prehistoric community, an intersex person would usually have been fairly obvious, as little could have been done surgically to "normalize" them, even if that were considered desirable. Community reactions probably varied widely. Positive reactions could have included normal integration into the community as either male or female (through tolerant "muting"); normal integration as a third catch-all ambiguous gender group (such as the *sag-ur-sag*—a recognized social group in Mesopotamia around 2000 B.C. that may have included castrated males, homosexual transvestites, and intersex individuals); or some special social treatment (hermaphrodites, for example, were thought of as semidivine in the ancient Greek world). Negative responses may have included infanticide (if the ambiguity was recognized at birth) or ostracism (if it developed later).

Mothers in the Men's Hut

One clear measure of sexual difference is between those people who can and do give birth (and those who look like them), and those who do not. Such people can often be identified by their skeletons. Pelvic scarring, especially of the preauricular groove, seems to indicate childbirth (although most experts now agree that its extent cannot accurately reveal the number of births). Sometimes archaeologists excavate burial sites where a fetal skeleton is preserved within the body cavity of an adult skeleton. A burial recently discovered at Beit Shamesh in Israel, dated to the fourth century A.D., contained the skeleton of an individual of around fourteen years of age, identified as female not because of her bone structure but because a full-term fetal skeleton was present in her pelvic area. They probably died because the baby's head could not fit through the girl's narrow pelvic girdle. Traces of burned cannabis found within the girl's skeletal void indicate that it

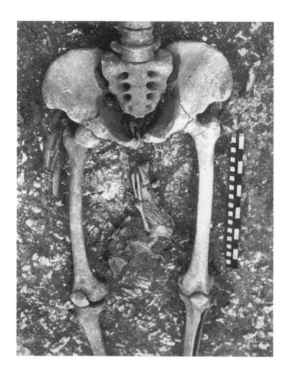

(Fig. 2.1)   Coffin birth. The fetus still has its legs within the birth canal. Anglo-Saxon cemetery at Worthy Park, Kingsworthy, Hampshire, England. Photograph: Calvin Wells Laboratory, University of Bradford.

was inhaled during the final fatal stages of the uncompleted labor. Cannabis is a pain-killer that is also known to increase the force of uterine contractions. (Its use in childbirth goes back at least to 1550 B.C., when it was mentioned in an Egyptian medical papyrus.)

Certain skeletal sexings are also possible in rare cases of "coffin birth." In the Anglo-Saxon cemetery at Worthy Park, Hampshire, England, one grave contained the skeleton of a woman who died with her unborn baby lodged in her birth canal. After burial, the relaxation of the traumatized tissues and buildup of putrefaction gases in the viscera caused the fetus to be pushed out, so that when the grave was excavated, it looked at first as if the child had been buried indecorously hanging from its mother's body, with only its feet still inside.

While motherhood is usually one of the characteristics used to define the social gender "female," it does not necessarily establish mothers as women in perpetuity. Among the Hua people of New Guinea, bearing children actually has a masculinizing effect. The Hua separate physical sex from social gender by reference to a substance called *nu*. *Nu* is thought of as a moist, life-giving essence, mainly produced by women but transmittable to men through sexual intercourse and food. *Figapa* people contain lots of *nu*, and *kakora* people have very little *nu*. The *figapa* include women in their child-bearing years, children of both sexes (because of their close contact with the former), postmenopausal women who have had fewer than three children, and old men who have had so much sex and *nu*-rich food that they are irrevocably permeated with *nu*. The *kakora* include males who have been initiated through a period of heterosexual absti-nence and avoidance of female foods, and postmenopausal women who have borne three or more children, a process that has so purged them of *nu* that they can be given male initiation and go to live in the men's house.

Because the basic anatomy of men and women is so similar, many societies culturally exaggerate physical sexual differences through tattooing, penis enlargement, or clitoridectomy. Among the Hazda of Ethiopia, older women conduct ritualized surgery on girls to make them into women, removing the visible part of the clitoris along with the outer (and sometimes inner) labia. These features are viewed as being uncomfortably like the male testicles and penis. As such practices show, gender is not a biological given but a cultural performance. It is based on real physical differences but, as the an-thropologists Penelope Brown and L. J. Jordanova say, what cul-tures make of these differences "is almost infinitely variable."

The skeleton in the Austrian farmyard was unusual in that it expressed no gender. In most funeral rites, the deceased is accompa-nied by artifacts, "grave goods," which express things about them. Archaeologists generally assume that these artifacts are gendered—swords being male and spindles being female, for instance, symboliz-ing a division of labor and activity in daily routine. In reality, things are not so simple. The perceived gender of artifacts typically alters according to context, as social anthropologists have observed. Since death may be seen as the opposite of life, it is possible that some pre-historic societies wholly inverted the genders of objects used in funer-ary rites, so that men were buried with "female" grave goods and women with "male."

Archaeologists' own biases often come to the fore in identifying the functions of things buried as grave goods. My research assistant, Alison Deegan, wrote to me from an excavation that "a classic example occurred a couple of weeks ago—a short sword was uncovered in the course of excavating a skeleton; however, as soon as it was discovered that the skeleton was female, the object became a weaving baton and has remained so ever since."

The Iceman and the Gay Gene

Ötzi, the Iceman, was found with a number of artifacts that archaeologists usually consider to be male: an ax and hunting equipment. But when Konrad Spindler concludes his discussion of the Iceman's sexuality with the words, "The anthropological sex diagnosis agrees with the archaeological one. There cannot be the slightest doubt that the Hauslabjoch corpse is that of a man," he is using the word *man* in two significantly different senses, only one of which is actually warranted by the evidence. Ötzi's bones and body tissues are clearly male, but we do not know whether the idea of "being a man" in modern society had any recognizable counterpart in Ötzi's society. (It is possible that Ötzi's idea of "being a man" has, via a chain of historical influence, contributed in some way to Western ideas of "maleness" today— 5,000 years later.)

At a superficial level, dress conventions were clearly different in Neolithic Europe. Ötzi's underclothes, made up of a leather crotchpiece, probably pulled tightly up between the buttocks and hooked over the equivalent of a leather garter belt (used to keep his leather leg coverings up), inspired the headline "Stone Age Leatherman Found in Alps" in the British magazine *Capital Gay*. More profoundly, we may legitimately ask whether Ötzi was a full man in the sense of belonging to something like a men's house. He might, like older genital males among the Hua, have become so saturated with some *nu*-like substance that he was no longer an initiated member.

The speculation about Ötzi's sexuality, while not based on any positive evidence, may prompt the thought that certain features of his brain might provide some indication of his sexual behavior in life. Recent work by Dick Swaab at the Netherlands Institute for Brain Research seems to demonstrate that a part of the brain directly involved in sexual behavior, known as BSTc, is smaller in women than in men, and is also smaller in male-to-female transsexuals—people born with a male external anatomy who have an awareness, from an early age, of being "a woman trapped in a man's body."

Some researchers in the United States have claimed to show that there is a "gay gene" that affects a particular area of brain development and hence sexual orientation. Simon LeVay has conducted autopsies on a small sample of men (some of whom had died of AIDS). Those thought to have been homosexual in life were claimed to have a smaller INAH3 cell area in their brains than those thought to have been exclusively heterosexual. But even assuming that measurements of relative cell-group sizes are reliable (which they may not be, since the length of time a brain spends in preservative on the way to a research lab affects the degree of shrinkage of its internal features), and assuming that the lifestyles of these men were well-enough known (they were not), and assuming that the correlation between the cell-group size and behavior is statistically valid (which it may not be), it is still not clear if the relative size of INAH3 depends on possession of the gene or is a result of having AIDS. Or whether, rather than causing certain behavior, INAH3 actually changes size under its influence. LeVay's findings have not yet been independently replicated.

Whatever its statistical and procedural integrity, the gay gene debate is, at another level, total nonsense. The Goodies—a British satirical comedy team—once imagined a regime that segregated short people ("Apart-Height"). Under this social system, a gene coding for tallness could statistically correlate with a feeling of superiority. But that would *not* mean that there was a "superiority-complex gene." Reverse the Apart-Height legislation to discriminate against tall people, and the tallness gene would become statistically correlated with a feeling of inferiority. That would no more make it an "inferiority-complex gene" than it was previously a "superiority-complex gene."

The same logic can be applied to the debate over the so-called

gay gene. No statistical correlation between a particular genetic endowment and homosexual behavior in modern America, even if
proven, would prove the existence, biologically speaking, of a gay
gene. It would simply mean that a particular gene appears to correlate, imperfectly of course, with behavior construed as homosexual
within a particular culture. Not everyone who identifies themselves as
homosexual in modern American culture would have the gene, and
not everyone who had the gene would identify themselves as homosexual. The simple truth about at least some identical twins (who
have identical genetic endowments) is that they can differ markedly
in their adult sexual orientation. If the hypothetical gay gene had existed in ancient Athens, where male-male sexual relations were *de
rigueur,* both in philosophical circles and in the army, its occurrence
might not have been connected to any particular behavior at all.

The controversy over the gay gene is part of a central problem
in the prehistory of sex: whether behavior is principally determined
by biology or by culture. In discussing sex today, many people are
concerned to distinguish the natural from the unnatural. Several
world religions stigmatize sexual activities that are not potentially reproductive, especially homosexual ones. It is against such a background that lesbian and male homosexual interest in the gay gene
debate must be viewed: "The gay gene made me like this" carries
more immediate power as a moral statement defending the right to
exist than "I choose to do this because I like it."

The interaction between biology and culture is unimaginably
complex in all aspects of life. Genetics, the intra-uterine hormonal environment, profound early learning experiences, and later, personal
and political factors can all play significant parts in the individual experience of sexual identity and the development of sexual preferences. Even at an apparently basic level, biology does not exist
independently of culture: biological sex as a distinct idea is actually
part of the modern Western system of gender, a system that includes
scientifically derived and evolving knowledge alongside many ingrained prejudices and unconscious assumptions.

I never found out if the skeleton in the Austrian farmyard was
that of a woman or a man. But even if evidence of pelvic pitting and

an XX DNA test had indicated that it was a woman and that she had once had a child, what would I really have known about the woman's *gender*, about her experience in her own society? Seen this way, the problem of gender in prehistoric archaeology seems daunting. Yet progress can be made. Once the extent of human variation and flexibility in the present is at least partly grasped, significant patterns can be more easily and securely recognized in the past—although recognition typically requires far more evidence than a single skeleton provides.

CHRISTOPHER ANTHONY MASTERS,
TH.D., Ph.D., J.D.
RANCHO SAN-DIEGO, CALIFORNIA

Chapter 3

Mysteries of the Organism

"We, alone on earth . . . are separate and independent enough from our genes to rebel against them . . . we do so in a small way every time we use contraception."

RICHARD DAWKINS,
THE SELFISH GENE

In William Gerhardie's novel *The Polyglots*, the hero-narrator lies in bed, having consummated his love for his cousin on the night of her wedding to someone else. He is deflated because he feels that for all its buildup, love ultimately reveals only that "concavities are concave, and convexities convex." Some societies find these concavities and convexities dangerous, disturbing, and obscene. Britain (along with Ireland, China, and Albania) currently censors nearly all visual representations of human sexual activity—erect penises, sexual penetration, ejaculation, erect clitorises, and so on. (The film from which this chapter takes its title, made by the Yugoslav director Dusan Makavejev, has not been shown in its entirety in Britain because of its erotic explicitness.)

The definition of sexual behavior varies from one society to another. Touching someone's arm in one culture may serve simply to attract their attention; the same action in another culture might be taken as an aggressive act or, alternatively, as a sexual advance. Some paraplegics have learned how to achieve orgasm through physical contact at the elbow—for them, a touch of outwardly similar type, following on others, could be the culmination of sexual activity.

This variation makes it extremely difficult to give a universal definition of what sex is. Advanced proponents of oriental tantric yoga, a sexually oriented physical and spiritual philosophy, claim to be able to achieve a whole-body orgasmic state and maintain it for several hours. But many people in modern industrial society view sex in mechanical terms, as a discrete and separable *function* of human bodies. This view was expressed in its most extreme form in the Soviet idea that performing the sexual act (and there was only one) was like drinking a glass of water—straightforward, hygienic, necessary, and brief (suggested optimum time two minutes).

Pleasurable self-stimulation of the genitals (not necessarily leading to orgasmic experience) begins early: recent ultrasound images show a baby boy masturbating in the womb. In the modern West the average age that children are observed to start masturbating is eighteen months. In Victorian England the idea that masturbation was an inappropriate and unhealthy activity, especially in children, led to the development of a range of restraining devices and methods, including female "circumcision"—the amputation of the external parts of the clitoris—an operation that was performed on girls in the United States as late as the 1950s and that continues in several parts of the world.

The end result of such repressive measures was that human sexual activity, hitherto private and unrecorded, came under medical, legal, and psychiatric scrutiny. Pioneers such as Richard Krafft-Ebing, Havelock Ellis, Sigmund Freud, and Wilhelm Reich recorded and theorized tirelessly, producing great lists of sexual activities that read like diseases—urolagnia, undinism, scotophilia, eonism, stuff-fetishism — and processes that were so obscure, they were often plausible — sublimation, transference, and the production of orgone energy. But activities that were originally thought to be "perversions" turned out to be so widespread that they were renamed "deviations" and, perhaps becoming still more popular as a result of the candid descriptions in sexological books, finally became "diversity." Some ideas have hung on way past their shelf life. One is the idea that women are less sexually motivated than men. Another is that, despite all the talk of diversity, monogamous heterosexuality is the natural norm. Neither idea holds for higher mammals, and patently not for our closest relatives among them.

After briefly summarizing what is known and what is conjectured about the emergence of sexual activity, I will show how, in higher animals, sex began to move beyond its primary, and evolutionarily significant, reproductive function to become a source both of pleasure and power as ends in themselves. The widespread bisexuality of the animal world culminates in the extraordinarily wide-ranging sexual behavior of our closest living relative, the pygmy chimpanzee, or bonobo. Sexual pleasure has been taken yet further by humans — and so has sex as an aspect of power. Effective plant-based contraception was available to our prehistoric ancestors, freeing sex from any necessary reproductive shackles. This must have speeded up the process of sex-selected evolution, as people, especially women, gained more control not only over whom they had sex with but whom they bred with.

Women and the Sex War

In his 1992 book *Sex and Reason* the eminent American jurist Richard Posner attempted to provide a thoroughly argued basis for laws that regulate sexuality in all its forms: marriage and adultery, birth control, homosexuality in civil and military society, rape, erotic art, pornography, nudity, coercive sex among adults and with children, and the complicated issues surrounding adoption, surrogacy, artificial insemination, and eugenics (selectivist or racially motivated breeding, discussed further in Chapter 9). For the bases of his arguments he turned to the history of sexuality and the various current theories of it. He presented the following description of women's sexuality as biologically correct:

> A woman who wants to maximize her reproductive success must be charier of her sexual favors than a man. She must try to make every pregnancy count. . . . in the evolutionary period, when life was precarious, a woman had to be intensely concerned about the quality of her mate as a potential father. . . . Since a powerful sex drive would probably stimulate a taste for sexual variety, or at least make it more difficult to adhere to a strategy of being choosy about one's sexual partners, it is plausible to expect natural selection against a powerful sex drive in women.

This argument is completely speculative and runs against virtually all we know of sexuality among primates. In practice, female primates do not have unlimited choice, and they have substantial sex drives. But Posner continues, claiming that:

> There is much evidence that women do in fact have (on average, of course, not in every case) a weaker sex drive than men. For example, lesbian couples have intercourse less frequently, on average, than heterosexual couples do, while male homosexual couples have intercourse more frequently than heterosexual couples do.

Posner supports this conclusion with statistics, but they are statistics relating to intercourse rather than to sexual behavior in its broader sense. His focus is on quantity, how many times a person does "it," rather than quality. Women's greater ability to have multiple orgasms, and their more whole-body approach to sexuality (in Western culture at least), could actually lead one to the conclusion that women have a higher sexual potential.

Statistical data generally do support the idea of lower sex *drives* among women in the Western world, agreeing with evidence presented by Nancy Friday (among others) for the childhood suppression of female sexuality. Friday adopts the term "cloaca concept" to describe the current of repression, passing from mother to daughter, that ensures that girls are not familiar with their sexual anatomy in the same way that little boys are. They may remain ignorant of the fact that they possess a clitoris, and even if they are not they have no word for it. They are subjected, in Friday's terms, to a "mental clitoridectomy." You cannot easily value what you have no words for, as it is quite literally "nothing."

Outward anatomical differences between men and women are thought to reflect yet greater existential ones. In humans, where the fertilized egg develops inside the female body, the female's principal reproductive concern after conception is to make sure that the embryo develops properly and survives to reproduce in its turn. The male's reproductive concern ought, on the face of it, to be the same as the female's—that is, it is as much in the male's interest as in the female's that offspring are well nurtured. But there is—supposedly—a crucial difference. Whereas a woman is thought to instinctively know that the baby developing within her carries half of her own genes, a man—unless he guards his mate day and night—cannot be quite as certain that his genes are being passed on. He may therefore attempt to make a number of females pregnant, and he may be encouraged to do so if other males around him are following the same strategy—if they have sex with lots of different partners, then they will increase the likelihood that at least some of the next generation will carry their genes, but if they are faithfully monogamous they may be cuckolded and never reproduce.

Such strategic differences are claimed to lie at the heart of the so-called war between the sexes, indicating why competition within species—between males or females—is as important a force in evolution as competition between species. Marx and Engels considered that "the first division of labour is that between man and woman for child breeding," and Engels went on to state that "the first class antagonism which appears in history coincides with the development of the antagonism between man and woman in monogamous marriage, and the first class oppression with that of the female sex by the male."

When it comes to a conscious strategy for passing on genes, people have — for the vast majority of their time on earth — been entirely ignorant. The very concept of a gene has been around only for about the last hundred years, so it can hardly have explicitly informed human mating patterns before then. Practicalities seem far more important: a woman is reproductively committed by pregnancy and childbirth for nine months at the very least, but a man is not. It is actually possible for him to go and get other women pregnant in this period, irrespective of whether he knows anything of genetics.

Sperm Competitions

Marriage and mating patterns in humans differ widely, and to a degree independently of each other. In a marriage of whatever sort — monogamous (two people, generally of different biological sex), polygynous (a man with several wives), or polyandrous (a woman with several husbands) — the prescription and proscription of various sexual and reproductive relationships and practices are not necessarily adhered to in practice. In tests of genetic paternity recently conducted by Robin Baker and Mark Bellis, they found that around 10 percent of children had been sired by someone other than their ostensible fathers — although the fathers consciously believed these children to be their own.

Baker and Bellis believe that male biological mechanisms are geared to the expectation of cuckoldry. Human males have relatively large testicles and produce far more sperm than they seem to need. In normal conception a single egg is fertilized by a single sperm. So what are the other 2,249,999 sperm from an average 2.25-million-sperm ejaculation up to? Humans (along with other species such as chimpanzees and lions), Baker and Bellis argue, have evolved a system of sperm competition in which the majority of sperm actually make no attempt to find the egg. Rather, these sperm are on anti-cuckolding duty. Some wait around ready to attack alien sperm, while others—whose tails seem deliberately deformed—knot together to form a passive tangled barrier against any intruders. If a man spends an entire day with his female partner, then has sexual intercourse with her, he ejaculates far fewer sperm than he would have had he spent the day apart from her—a period with opportunities for her to be unfaithful. Nevertheless, although the man's sperm may battle it out, it may ultimately be the woman's internal manipulation of sperm via orgasm during intercourse and subsequent masturbation that most influences whose baby she will have (see Chapter 2).

What motivation could the women in Baker and Bellis's study have for cuckolding their husbands at a rate of one in ten? Matt Ridley interprets their case in stark sociobiological terms, citing the work of Anders Møller. Møller, a zoologist, has found that the more physically attractive a male swallow is, the less parental investment he makes in his offspring; female swallows are thus encouraged to find a mediocre-looking but caring partner and to cuckold him. Humans may do this too, Ridley suggests—a woman may marry a rich but ugly man but take a handsome lover. But what he does not explain is why a woman would wish to conceive by her handsome lover. Surely her children would be better off, in a society that ultimately values wealth, having the genes of the rich man. It may be that people and society are unclear about what they value most; nevertheless, it seems unlikely that Baker and Bellis's one-in-ten cuckoo-in-the-nest children can be explained in purely sociobiological terms.

Liverpool, where Baker and Bellis conducted their survey, is an international seaport that, since the industrial revolution, has seen hordes of seamen and laborers come and go. Whether Liverpudlian traditions of marital fidelity and uncertain paternity closely mirror those of say, Salt Lake City or Stockholm or even many other parts of Britain, is debatable. But even accepting the statistics at face value, the researchers' conclusions are not foolproof. A woman's chances of conceiving with a lover whom she has actually chosen purely for sexual pleasure are rather high for a set of rather mundane and practical reasons: cheating lovers do not want to be caught carrying condoms or diaphragms, or the sex might be opportunistic or a chance, drunken encounter.

Embarrassing Relatives

The possibility of pure sexual pleasure brings us to a major problem with sociobiological explanations of human sexual and reproductive behavior, as well as that of many animals. In many higher animals the evolutionary development of sensuous and sexual pleasure has led to the partial separation of sex and reproduction. Although reproduction requires sex, sex need not always be aimed at reproduction. This is clear from observing the sexual behavior of animals, both wild and domestic. Among cattle, pigs, and rabbits, for example, sexually receptive females regularly respond to other females in heat by mounting them in a masculine fashion and making pelvic movements like the male's copulatory thrusts, although most will choose to mate with a male when that option presents itself. Similarly, males may mount one another, and some mounted males may respond with a display of female mating reflexes, although at other times they may mount receptive females. Observation suggests that female mammals experience orgasm much as males do. Female rhesus monkeys who were clitorally stimulated with specially adapted electric toothbrushes under laboratory conditions showed similar brain activity to that of males.

On the basis of such observations, zoologists long ago concluded that "the behavior of male and female animals . . . reveals that the inherited neuro-muscular constitution of both sexes includes mechanisms capable of mediating many of the responses which make up the mating pattern of the opposite sex." Given that animals cannot reproduce all the time, there is no natural disadvantage in such mediation. Recent research shows that both male and female homosexual activity is commonplace in more than two hundred species of mammals, birds, reptiles, amphibians, fishes, and insects, although exclusive homosexual subgroups do not occur.

The sexual behavior of the great apes has often been examined to provide clues about the sexual behavior of our earliest direct ancestors—to define the essential sexual nature of humans. Unfortunately, these other hominoids have very different sexual patterns from one another as species, and they themselves vary from community to community. It is possible to believe whatever one likes about human sexuality's "true" nature, depending on which of these apes one chooses to describe and which studies one refers to. But some generalizations are warranted. In most species early learning appears to be crucial. A male chimpanzee who before the age of six is denied all sexual knowledge, whether through watching sexual acts or through a degree of participation and experimentation, will never be able to have intercourse with a female, irrespective of how receptive and helpful she is or how physically excited he himself may become. He simply has no idea what to do, as his responses were not developed during a crucial phase of his life.

In captivity, primates such as rhesus macaques show a wide variety of sexual behaviors that are apparently nonfunctional in the genetic sense—masturbation, same-sex behavior, even heterosexual avoidance—and that have not been seen at all or to the same degree in the wild. These behaviors may be due to the animals' boredom in captivity; thus it has been said that they cannot be used as any guide to the true nature of sex. In reality, however, such behavior in captivity only confirms that apparently "set" biological predispositions can be socially modified in species of primate similar to those that already existed twenty million years ago.

Observations of sexual behavior in the wild confirm the idea that animal sexuality is flexible. Perhaps the most interesting of the great apes are the bonobos of central Zaire. Little was said about them until recently, apparently because their behavior challenges the fondly held view that male dominance is natural and universal in both primate and human society. Observers have often sought to compare humans with chimpanzees and gorillas. We are clearly evolutionarily related to these two apes, but genetically they are more similar to each other than either of them is to us. There is more than one type of chimp, however. The bonobos, which are also called *pygmy chimps* (though they are no smaller than others), actually form a separate species, characterized by a more upright gait and a less "specialized" skeleton. In fact, they are the closest living analogue to the early australopithecines of four million years ago.

A more significant reason evolutionary science has ignored the bonobos for so long — according to Alison Jolly and other researchers — is our sexual puritanism. "The sexual promiscuity of pygmy chimpanzees makes Sodom and Gomorrah look like a Vicar's tea party." Bonobos have sex most of the time. Aside from adult heterosexual activities, females indulge in a lot of genital rubbing with each other (*GG*, which is called *tribadism* in humans). Males indulge in "penis fencing" and rub their swollen rumps together, back to back. Most shockingly to human eyes, adults and children have a lot of sex. In fact, infants are often initiated by their mothers — the only observed taboo is on sex between mothers and any sons over six years of age. Sex is a natural part of childhood for bonobos, researchers believe, and it mingles imperceptibly with care, play, all the other elements of growing up. Sex for bonobos appears to be a fairly quick, perfunctory, and relaxed activity that functions as a social cement.

I am not saying that bonobos provide a model for what human sexuality *ought* to be like — that, but for cultural constraints, we would all behave more like bonobos. They challenge us to think more openly about the range of sexual behaviors that were potentially open to our remote ancestors. In physical terms, there is actually nothing that bonobos do that some humans do not sometimes do.

But how human observers interpret bonobo behavior is tricky. What one sees depends very much on what glasses one is wearing. A classic example is the "food for sex" scenario. In wild bonobos a male will approach a female carrying a food item to share. The two will share the food, then have sex. Most observers interpret this sequence as a transaction, and some draw conclusions about human evolution and even modern human behavior based on it. Robert Jay Russell has termed it the "lemur's legacy," as it is a behavior apparently shared by lemurs, one of our most remote direct mammalian ancestors. Yet such interpretations have as much to do with the observer as the observed. This is like saying of human society (and some people do say it) that any woman who has dinner bought for her at a fancy restaurant by a prospective male partner and has sex with him afterward is a prostitute. It is a sexist interpretation in that it denies the possibility that the female may enjoy sex as well. The assumption is that she "gives" sex to the male but he does not "give" sex back (having already given food). But looking again at the bonobo pair, we could equally well conclude that the male suggests sharing some food, which is nice, and then sharing some sex, which is nice.

Invisible Sex

One of the most striking differences between the sexual behavior of contemporary humans and that of the great apes is privacy. Although primates do seek privacy for sex on occasion, much of their sexual activity goes on within eye- and earshot of the rest of the group. But human sexuality is often hidden—so hidden, in fact, that privacy becomes an obstacle for those who study it. In an article entitled "Sex the Invisible," Ernestine Friedl surveyed the worldwide ethnographic literature and concluded that "hidden coitus may safely be declared a near universal." She went on to discuss various sociobiological explanations for its hiddenness. But her initial premise remains unproven, since the potential problem is actually the ethnographic literature itself. From A.D. 1400 onward, when Catholic merchants set out to explore the seaways of the world, the very earliest accounts of "natives" that they wrote often contain descriptions of or oblique references to open sexuality.

Many peoples of the world, prior to European colonization and its attendant Christian missions, seem to have openly celebrated their sexuality, at least on occasion. Days of sexual license, where adults had sex with as many partners as they wished quite publicly, seem to have occurred among North American Indian groups like the Huron. Jesuit missionaries were eager to crack down on such activity, so that by the time trained anthropologists arrived to study these communities in detail, from the nineteenth century onward, they found a very different culture from what the Jesuits had encountered. Sexual behavior had changed, and where it had not, we can surmise that it was well hidden from the Europeans. But Friedl is wrong to think that coitus is entirely hidden even in modern Western society. Although it is not an everyday public act, it is regularly performed in small private groups as well as for larger paying audiences at live shows and for the video market.

In many societies children observe adult sexual activity. Jean Liedloff, in *The Continuum Concept*, writes that the Yequana Indians of Amazonia consider the presence of infants during lovemaking a matter of course, and she claims that children who do not witness it miss out on an "important psycho-biological link" with their parents. These same Amazonian parents also teach their children head hunting, however. Clearly practices that are acceptable in one culture may be quite unacceptable in another and may have very different effects. In Viennese apartments, Sigmund Freud assumed, it was effectively inevitable that children would at times be able to observe their parents' sexual activities, but this did not tend to make them into well-balanced people.

Power Play

Despite the evidence that sex is a largely learned behavior among primates, and despite the documentation of homosexual activities and instances of obvious "sex-as-pleasure" among many higher animals, sociobiologists still contend that reproductive success ultimately determines sexual behavior. They would explain male homosexuality in chimps, for example, primarily in terms of male-male bonding or the subordination of one male by another—that is, as part of a process of forming alliances and pecking orders whose ultimate goal is to gain access to females for reproduction, and to protect the genetic legacy embodied in one's offspring. But beyond sex-as-pleasure, the idea of sex-as-power raises further problems for sociobiologists. A cherished notion among sociobiologists is that men are naturally promiscuous, while women are naturally monogamous.

Robin Baker says in *Sperm Wars* that most male readers of his book will have sex with around a dozen women in their lifetime, while female readers will average eight male sex partners. But this is illogical; statistically, for heterosexual pairings, the numbers simply have to even out. The discrepancy in Baker's survey data arises from men's tendency to exaggerate and women's fear of derogatory labeling. Still, these very tendencies betray real imbalances in modern Western society — not in the relative amounts of sex but in the power relations associated with it.

When men rape women, according to sociobiology, they could be pursuing a strategy — albeit a violent, criminal one — of genetic maximization. The ethologist Robin Dunbar has recently argued that rape is an evolutionarily sensible policy for unattractive men who would not otherwise get a partner; by contrast, Robin Baker argues that women, following the genetic imperative, should seek out men with above-average reproductive success. His argument is so incredible, it is worth presenting in some detail.

Since rapists "do indeed have an above-average [reproductive] potential," argues Baker, "it should be no surprise to find that when a woman's body has a one-off opportunity to collect a rapist's genes, it often does so." But Baker does not want one of Dunbar's losers. "On the contrary, it is reproductively important to the woman that her body collect genes from only the most successful of rapists. If she conceives to an inept rapist, doomed quickly to be caught . . . her male descendants would inherit unsuccessful characteristics." Thus a woman should "do everything possible to avoid being raped"; that way, she "is unlikely to fall victim to any but the most cunning, determined and competent of rapists. The result is that only a minority of women are ever raped, but those who are may then respond by conceiving."

The absurdity, not to say bad taste (though that never bothers sociobiologists), of this argument is patent. Only by a long stretch of the imagination could a tendency to rape — were it inheritable — ever be seen in cultural terms as a more "successful" characteristic than, say, courage (and culture is ultimately where success gets judged). Moreover, the "minority" of raped women to whom Baker refers are known because their attackers were subsequently *convicted* (at a rate, estimated by the London-based Rape Crisis Centre, of around one in every thousand actual rapes committed). Some of the victims may conceive, but many of them will abort the fetus. Studies of the connection between rape and reproductive success leave out the very obvious point that rape is used to express power and to give the rapist pleasure. It is rarely used to pass on genes.

One social situation where rape is definitely directed at generating pregnancy is in some types of war. In the recent war in Bosnia, the systematic rape of Muslim women has been geared to breaking up communities, as the rape victim is traditionally ostracized. But it cannot be said that the Serbian rapists have any great reproductive interest in the offspring so created, as they are prepared to shell the areas where mother and child might well be staying. In war, and perhaps outside it, rape, by whatever mechanism, involves forced sex under circumstances that seem unconducive to the subsequent birth survival and success of offspring.

Despite the fact that it is possible to support theories of sex-as-pleasure and sex-as-power, sociobiologists may still turn around and say that underlying reproductive strategies, however circuitous, ultimately determine observed human behavior.

Bucking Biology

The factor that completely derails the sociobiological bandwagon is contraception. The human ability to learn presupposes a mind that can be changed, a mind that can make certain choices. The development of such a mind, to be sure, may have been enabled by the development of particular genes. (One could, if one were naive enough, postulate a "free will" gene to set alongside the "gay gene.") But the emergence of that mind put an end to most of the determinism of the other genes. That is, although one may have "an instinct" to do one thing, one may choose to do the opposite. People may choose to "rebel" against their genes by using contraception; they may choose to be celibate; or they may choose to be sexual but never have children. Contraception is not some recent invention involving vulcanized rubber and packages of tinfoil-wrapped pills. The body has its own contraceptive mechanisms that can be culturally enhanced, while further means of contraception are commonly available in nature.

Breast-feeding suppresses menstruation in women. The reason is now thought to be that suckling increases the activity of opiates in the hypothalamus, which in turn suppresses production of the hormones involved in ovulation. Menstruation may recommence as early as six months after birth, but if breast-feeding is kept up, then both ovulation and the successful implantation of any new fertilized egg may be delayed for much longer. One of the benefits of not menstruating is that the iron that a woman would otherwise lose is channeled into the breast milk; another obviously good reason for a woman not to get pregnant again right away is the intensiveness of early infant care. On a global scale, lactational fertility control is the most efficient contraceptive known. (Women do not forget to breast-feed, and it is free.) The ancients were aware of it, and exploited it more widely. Thus, Hippocratic Aphorism V. 50 says: "To restrain a woman's menstruation, apply the largest possible cupping glass to the nipples," while Aphorism V. 39 notes, "If a woman who is neither pregnant nor has given birth produces milk, her menstruation has stopped." A woman's sex-work as a prostitute might in this way be neatly combined with employment as a wet nurse, a dual occupation referred to in Flaubert's novel *Madame Bovary*.

Knowledge of the role of the cervix in mediating sperm, of fetal development and the circumstances and techniques of mechanical abortion, and of the control of menstruation through lactation could all have been employed in prehistoric fertility control. Caustic or blocking vaginal pessaries were known and used. The ancient Egyptian Kahun gynecological papyrus of around 1900 B.C. prescribes natron (hydrated sodium carbonate) mixed with crocodile droppings—a recipe, one imagines, that could have been an aphrodisiac as well as spermicidal! Other pessaries contained acacia gum, mentioned in the Ebers papyrus of 1550–1500 B.C. Modern tests on acacia gum show it to have spermicidal properties. Inserting half a lemon into the vagina was a popular contraceptive device in ancient Rome. (The fruit was first widely available in Greece from the fifth century B.C.)

Forgotten Fruits

Many plants can have a direct hormonal effect on human reproductive function and can be used as oral contraceptives and short-term aborti-facients ("morning-after" drugs that prevent the fertilized egg from implanting). So widespread and effective are these plants that I believe that they must have been used in prehistory and possibly throughout our evolutionary emergence. This controversial belief can, as yet, be substantiated only from indirect kinds of evidence. There are four such sources: the hormone chemistry of the plants themselves; the extent of their use among present-day societies; their well-established and wide-spread use in ancient Greece and Rome; and finally, their possible use by animals, including primates, in the wild.

At first glance the fact that plants produce sex hormones that can affect animals and humans is surprising. It did not begin to be scientifically accepted until 1933, when Boleslaw Skarzynski found a substance in willow, trihydroxyoestrin, that resembled estrogen. In the same year, Adolf Butenandt and H. Jacobi isolated female hormones from date palm and pomegranate. It is clear that plants contain many complex chemicals that can affect humans. They can bring menstruation to a halt (menses prohibitors) or, conversely, bring it on (emmenagogues); they can act hormonally to alleviate premenstrual syndrome (PMS) and function as contraceptives or abortifacients; and they can be aphrodisiac.

Ethical considerations, prejudices, and moral scruples on the part of Western scholars have meant that they have grossly underestimated the true extent of knowledge about and use of natural reproductive controls among traditional societies worldwide past and present. Modern Western herbals and pharmacopeias do not generally list effects of plants on sexual function beyond the formulaic standard warning "should not be used in pregnancy." One of the most effective early-term abortifacients, Queen Anne's lace, has not appeared in any official medical record since the sixteenth century, although it has been recently reported to be in regular, everyday use in parts of western North Carolina, western Virginia, Tennessee, and Indiana.

Only rarely have botanists, social anthropologists, and ethnographers thought to ask local peoples about the day-to-day realities of their sex lives. Most of these travelers have been male, whereas most of the relevant knowledge concerns women's bodies and lives; herbalism is part of the magical tradition of midwives and medicine women and is often kept secret. The ethnobotanist Edward Anderson, who has worked for many years among the hill tribes of northern Thailand, writes in relation to the "immense arsenal of medicines related to fertility, pregnancy, parturition, and the critical few weeks immediately following birth" that:

> Most women were unwilling to discuss this subject with me and my male interpreters. Although men know some of the plants used by women during this period, the subject seems to be almost totally in the domain of women. My Thai colleague from Payap University, Duangduen Poocharoen, a woman who speaks excellent northern Thai, and my daughter, Erica, who also speaks Thai and who served as my assistant for a period of time, were able to gain considerable knowledge of this subject which I could not.

The most clearly systematized bodies of herbal knowledge are found on the Indian subcontinent. The Ayurvedic system of medicine uses around seventy-five plants, twenty-eight of which are said to be effective for aborting pregnancy. Listing their names gives a feel for the extent of the known natural pharmacopeia of a single region: prickly chaff flower, custard apple, celery, betel-nut palm, worm-killer, Indian birthwort, common bamboo, giant milkweed and swallow wart, papaya, ringworm shrub, purging croton, lesser cardamom, cotton plant, common cress, horseradish tree, oleander, black cumin, syrian rue, black pepper, rosy leadwort, Ceylon leadwort, bushy gardenia, Indian madder, sandalwood, marking-nut tree, sesame, and bala. Ten of the herbs on this list are also used as emmenagogues—serving to bring on menstruation; along with a further forty-eight species listed as commonly used to stimulate menstruation, they are likely to work as early-term abortifacients, either of a "morning-after" type or at the point when the period is first missed.

The preparation of these plants for consumption is complex, involving variously the seed, fruit, oil, root, bark, flower, or—in the case of bamboo—the stem joint. They are sometimes applied in the form of a vaginal suppository or douche, sometimes decocted in order to be drunk, and sometimes the two methods are combined. In all cases both the dosage of the plant and the reproductive state of the individual are critical. Many of the same plants, in differing strengths, are used by women to stimulate milk production (galactogogues), to clamp down the uterus after childbirth, to alleviate morning sickness, and so on, as well as by men as cures for impotence and other sexual disorders, and by both sexes as aphrodisiacs. Saffron (*Crocus sativus*), for example, contains the substance picrocrocin, which promotes menstruation and soothes menstrual pain in small doses, while in large doses it is said to be both an aphrodisiac and an abortifacient. But in general, few of these plants have been clinically tested in the West, and their possible active ingredients remain unidentified.

Similar numbers of plant species are used by peoples living in the world's other tropical belts—the rainforests of South America, Africa, and the Malay Peninsula—as well as in colder climes. A type of fennel, *Ferula moschata*, is used as an abortifacient by folk practitioners on the Central Asian steppe—a region where artemisia (which has similar properties) also grows. In Hispanic New Mexico, rue is used as a traditional abortifacient. Among the Saami people of the European Arctic, a tree bark lichen is reputedly used as a female contraceptive. But the most comprehensive evidence for plant-based contraceptives in a temperate region is contained in classical European writings, especially those of Hippocrates and Soranus.

Hippocrates was aware that the seed of Queen Anne's lace or wild carrot, when taken orally, both prevented and terminated pregnancy, as did an infusion of pennyroyal (also mentioned by Aristophanes in 421 B.C.). Tests in 1986 showed Queen Anne's lace to contain compounds that block the production of progesterone, the hormone that prepares the uterus for the fertilized egg; it can thus be used as a powerful "morning-after" remedy. Perhaps the most potent herb was a variety of silphium or giant fennel, genus *Ferula,* discovered by Greeks on the coast of northern Africa in the seventh century B.C. So sought after was it as a contraceptive and such a high price did it command that, by the third or fourth century A.D., it was driven to extinction. The active ingredient in silphium was probably the substance ferujol, which has been shown in clinical tests to prevent pregnancy in rats up to three days after coitus. Myrrh, artemisia, and rue were also known and used as abortifacients.

These plants commanded high prices when they reached the city, but they were much cheaper than having more children. Polybius, writing in the second century B.C., said that Greek families were limiting themselves to one or two children. They could have achieved this by widespread infanticide, but we have no evidence in the medical literature that they did. Nor is there demographic evidence, in the form of a skewed sex-ratio—in all known societies where infanticide is practiced, more girls than boys are killed, leading to an obvious imbalance between the sexes in adult life. Archaeologically, infanticide sometimes shows up in the form of separate neonatal cemeteries, but these are not common. It seems ancient Greeks employed a variety of other methods of contraception. Soranus's early-second-century-A.D. treatise *Gynecology* distinguished between contraception and abortion and listed several methods for each; eight out of the ten plants that he listed have been shown in modern tests to have distinct effects.

While we know that women both in antiquity and in traditional societies worldwide used an extensive range of reproductive controls, far less is known about precautions taken by men. Male contraceptives are not mentioned in the Hippocratic corpus, although we may surmise that materials and technology for condoms were available. In visualizing a scientific experiment, Hippocrates says, "Suppose you were to tie a bladder onto the end of a pipe"; the bladder is then filled via the pipe—a simple process from which the principle of the condom may easily be deduced. That male contraception was desired at times is indicated by the first-century medical writer Dioscorides, who says that men could make themselves barren if they drank a preparation of the plant called *periklymenon* for thirty-seven days. We do not know for certain what the plant is, but it could be honeysuckle, which Linnaeus later named after it *(Lonicera periclymenum)*. Modern ethnography records male oral contraception among the Deni Indians of Amazonia. A single dose of a plant closely related to curare is taken by both men and women as a contraceptive. It seems, however, to actually work only on the men, in whom it can produce temporary infertility for around six months.

Pro-Choice Prehistory

A veritable chestnut in the prehistory of sex is the claim that early humans did not know that sex and babies were in any way connected. Reay Tannahill, on the first page of her book *Sex in History,* states that in prehistory, before the relatively recent development of farming, "there is nothing to suggest that man was even remotely aware of his own physical role in the production of children." The eminent British scientist Sir James Biment has recently claimed that "Stone Age man probably didn't associate sex with something that came along nine months later," adding "I doubt he could count up to nine." Many people think that prehistoric life was a struggle for existence that neither required deliberate population control nor was conducive to providing any rational understanding of its possibility.

"The struggle for existence" is a phrase coined by Thomas Malthus, who in 1798 published the first edition of his influential *Essay on Population.* Human populations increase naturally, Malthus argued, and are checked only by war, famine, and pestilence, as well as misery

and vice. The second edition stressed an additional factor in population control: "moral restraint," or the postponement of the age of marriage and strict sexual continence. Malthus lived some three hundred
years after the first systematic witch-hunts, at a time when women
were formally excluded from the medical academy and their long-
established plant-based contraceptive knowledge had been destroyed,
forgotten, or gone underground. At a loss to explain why the size of
simple hunting groups did not rise in the way that his theory predicted,
Malthus supposed that such people felt less "passion" for one another.

But passion was clearly not absent from hunter-gatherer societies. The indigenous peoples that Western colonialists met in the
South Seas seemed in fact to celebrate sex—a fact that made their
relatively stable population levels all the more puzzling, even though
the explanation lay clearly in view. For example, the British anthropologist George Pitt-Rivers noted in 1927,

> European observers, such as missionaries and government
> officials, have often supposed that some mysterious contra-
> ceptive drug was used by the unmarried girls. Native herbs
> and roots, mixed together with all manner of magical sub-
> stances, such as spider's eggs, skins of snakes, etc., are as a
> matter of fact made into concoctions and drunk by girls
> with this idea. I have myself collected such recipes from
> Melanesian and Papuan sorcerers and old women, but
> there is no reason to suppose they have any physical effect.

The most influential anthropological view was that of Bronislaw Malinowski, who argued in his 1929 book *The Sexual Life of Savages in
North-Western Melanesia* that infertile premarital promiscuity among
the Trobriand Islanders could not be explained by reference to deliberate birth-control measures: "any suggestion of neo-Malthusian ap-
pliances makes them shudder or laugh. . . . They never practise *coitus
interruptus,* and still less have any notion about chemical or mechanical preventives."

Malinowski's views were disputed by other Europeans resident in Melanesia, who believed that the natives used herbal remedies. One magistrate wrote that he had "been informed by many independent and intelligent natives that the female of the species is specially endowed or gifted with ejaculatory powers, which may be called upon after an act of coition *to expel the male seed*. It is understandable that such powers might be increased by use and practice, and I am satisfied that such a method does exist." This description is almost identical to the description of volitional control described by Hippocrates.

Malinowski maintained that Trobriand and Andaman Islanders were ignorant of the physiology of conception because of their belief that children were the result of a divine spirit entering the womb, and that semen was merely a nutrient for the growing fetus. Yet this belief does not reflect a denial of any connection between semen and the successful birth of babies, and it must have been a matter of general knowledge in this community—as it was, I believe, in every other human community that has ever existed—that women who remain virgin do not become pregnant. Male orgasm is everywhere implicated in the process of human reproduction, but it is everywhere seen as insufficient in itself. Pregnancy and subsequent childbirth do not result from male homosexual acts, or from lesbian ones, or from sex using inanimate objects, or from any sort of sex by any type of person with animals. Many people in the modern world, in both Eastern and Western philosophies, continue to hold the compatible belief that divine intervention is required for the initial implantation of a soul. Speaking for myself, I find the proposition that no spirit is involved in conception unpleasantly atheistic, although I do not deny the physical part that bodies play.

Proceeding from the assumption that male sexual activity and the production of offspring from it are connected acts, sociobiological reasoning assumes that male animals can recognize something of themselves (in modern parlance, their "genes") in their offspring through smell and other senses. Human fathers too can recognize their own by sense of smell, as well as by facial characteristics. Female animals are thought to make the connection, in behavioral if not conscious terms, between heterosexual intromissive sex during estrus and pregnancy. Human females who are in touch with their bodies are often able to consciously pinpoint the moment of conception — knowing both when they ovulated, when they have retained sperm from their partner, and when the hormonal effects of fertilization are beginning. Only by consciously obscuring this straightforward bodily knowledge (by placing an almost religious reliance on the comparatively clumsy machinations of modern medicine, for example) is it really possible to imagine that prehistoric women and men thought the creation of progeny was unrelated to sexual activity.

In reproductive terms, human beings are termed K-strategists: that is, they have few children, but they invest hugely in them. Contraception is not just a way to get sexual pleasure without having children; it can also be part and parcel of good K-strategy planning. To give children the greatest chance in life, everything from the timing of their birth to the number of competing siblings they have can be brought under conscious control. Such control is a hallmark of our species and is directly related, I believe, to our evolutionary success (thus far).

That people all over the world have recognized certain plants as having the potential to affect human reproduction is not surprising since, until the recent rise of urbanism, most people lived among plants. People in hunter-gatherer societies are exposed to tens of thousands of complex plant-based compounds; such societies typically utilize two hundred species of edible plant, *each* of which in turn contains around two hundred complex organic "secondary product" chemicals, many of them unique to that particular species. Plants from closely related species can therefore have very different effects. "The plant killing the life," *Aneilema lineolatum*, for example, is closely related to *Aneilema nudiflorum*, which is a staple vegetable. In some parts of the world 40 percent of plant species contain estrogenic compounds that have the potential to modify sexual functioning.

Just touching certain plants can produce marked effects on human sexual chemistry. Since Roman times, for example, hops (the flowers of *Humulus lupulus*) have been used in brewing; picking them was traditionally known to reduce men's sex drive, while women commonly suffered a disruption or cessation of menstruation. Both of these effects are now known to be caused by skin absorption of an oil containing a female sex hormone. One way that humans could have learned about the properties of plants was by observing their effects on animals. Farmers were often aware that the reproductive cycles of their livestock could be disrupted if they fed on particular plants, such as ivy—now known to contain estrogenic compounds.

Animals may at times seek such plants out deliberately. In some species of rodent, changes in diet trigger reproduction, while howler monkeys and other primates seem to use them more deliberately for this purpose. Chimpanzees use various plant species for self-medication, although not, apparently, to control fertility. But orangutans have been observed to deliberately eat the leaves, bark, and fruits of particular trees (*Melanochyla, Melanorrhoea,* and *Dispyros*) that have clear toxic effects, causing blackening of the lips and peeling skin. The primatologist Paul Vasey tentatively hypothesizes that the toxic effects may also extend internally, to the lining of the uterus; in view of the fact that forced copulation (rape) occurs among wild orangutans, Vasey believes it at least possible that females are using these plants to produce abortion (although this currently remains a speculation only).

On the basis of the available evidence, I think it is highly likely that most prehistoric communities were in control of their fertility and fully able to separate sex from reproduction. Egyptian and ancient Greek knowledge dates back several thousand years. Techniques recorded in the Bronze Age period in Europe and the Near East are presented as tried and tested—and there are a great number of them. The inevitable conclusion is that these techniques were already under development in yet earlier periods. But for this period itself, direct evidence is currently lacking. The processing of medicinal plants is known from as early as 40,000 years ago (discussed in Chapter 4), but so far we have no positive evidence for plants with contraceptive or abortifacient qualities.

Reproductive control was a crucial part of our evolution, causing sexual selection to proceed at a fast pace and facilitating greater cultural investment in children. Prehistoric communities must have been well aware of the facts of life. Most likely, awareness of the connection between certain forms of heterosexual sex and subsequent pregnancy was part and parcel of the evolution of consciousness itself. But prehistoric communities were not identical: it is always possible to "unlearn" or culturally obscure the facts, something that humans are rather good at. Societies that feel a need to censor the "mysteries of the organism" can erode the natural body knowledge of their constituent members and banish the age-old wisdom of medicine women to the realm of satanic superstition. Control over sexual knowledge and erotic imagery for social ends is nothing new. It began more than 30,000 years ago, during the last ice age.

Chapter 4

Meet the
Real Flintstones

*"If you believe in nothing else, believe that
sexual repression never sleeps."*

NANCY FRIDAY,
WOMEN ON TOP

When our prehistoric ancestors started to communicate with each other, they did so in a number of ways. Spoken language allowed subjective expression and the development of communally shared ideas, while the symmetry and standardization in objects such as stone tools expressed shared aesthetic ideas. The point at which subject and object met was the human body. At once personal and public, natural and cultural, a person could express inner states through the body, using gesture and appearance. As it became progressively more naked, the body became a potential canvas for art. Plant-based cosmetics, such as henna, could be applied directly to areas of skin and hair. Belladonna could be used to dilate the pupils. Mineral pigments, such as red ocher, were used to create dramatic temporary ef-

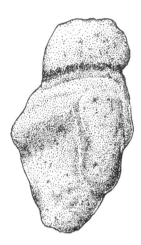

(Fig. 4.1)   A 230,000-year-old sculpture from
Berekhat Ram, Israel. Drawing by George
Taylor after Goren-Inbar 1986.

fects on the skin. Clothing and jewelry could mask or enhance particular body parts and express changing moods and intentions. More
permanent changes could be achieved through decorative scarifica-
tion and tattooing.

I believe that the evolution of nakedness and the development of
body decoration and clothing were interconnected processes. In this
chapter I argue that body art constituted a ceremonial language, one
used as a form of self-representation. It also marked the first rites of
passage and helped formulate ideas of status-appropriate behavior
and punishment for transgression.

The Dawn of Art

The very first time that we know of for certain that our ancestors
made representations of themselves is sometime between 800,000
and 233,000 years ago. The evidence is a tiny hand-worked figurine
sculpture that was discovered in 1981 in a deposit sealed between
two datable basalt floes, on a site called Berekhat Ram in the Golan
Heights, Israel. The excavator, Naama Goren-Inbar, believes that
the archaic human occupants of the site selected a pebble that bore
some resemblance to the female form, and enhanced it by cutting
grooves to delineate the head and arms. Depending how one looks

at it, the Berekhat Ram figurine seems to have some type of projecting breast, but it is hard to say more than that. Our capability for
appreciating artistic images dates back some three million years, to
an australopithecine-inhabited cave at Makapansgat in southern
Africa, where a pebble in an occupation deposit was found to look
like a human face.

The Makapansgat pebble is a small quirk of nature. Looking at
it, one cannot fail to see two eyes, a hairline, and a mouth, which is
presumably what the australopithecine who brought it back to the
cave also saw. Neither the Makapansgat pebble nor the Berekhat
Ram figurine tells us what early people looked like—the one because
it is a natural object possessing only the simplest features, the second
because it is so crudely made that it looks less like a person than the
natural pebble. But their importance should not be underestimated.
The first seems to suggest some gleam of self-awareness, while the
second tells us that people were actively sculpting each other. If the
Berekhat Ram sculpture represents what people could do with an in-
tractable bit of stone, tough enough to survive for more than a quar-
ter-million years, then what were they able to do in more forgiving
media, such as clay? Or on their own bodies?

That naked skin presented itself as a decorative field is a supposition that cannot be tested unless we can find the potential coloring materials in the archaeological record. At Middle Stone Age
sites in southern Africa dating from sometime after 300,000 B.P., red
ocher begins to be found. Archaeologist Ian Watts has documented
six certain and five possible instances of the deliberate use of ocher
in the following period, down to around 130,000–110,000 B.C., after
which its use suddenly becomes very widespread. The standard
archaeological interpretation of red ocher is that it was used for curing hides, since iron oxide (the coloring component of the ocher)
can stop the action of the enzyme collagenase, which starts the
decay process in leather. But among hunter-gatherer groups in the
savannah region, as Watts notes, the use-life of most hide items is
shorter than the time it takes for collagenase to render them unus-
able. He proposes instead that the ocher was used in the artful creation of "sham menstruation." This part of his work is closely

connected to a research group, led by Chris Knight of the University of East London, that have developed the "sex strike theory" of human cultural evolution.

The Sex Strike Theory

The sex strike theory, developed within a revolutionary Marxist framework and inspired by a rather idiosyncratic reading of Richard Dawkins's "selfish gene" theory, holds that reproductive conflict lies at the heart of human social relations. Marx and Engels believed that prehistoric communities lived in a state of primitive communism, but that it did not last very long. Classes emerged with cities and writing and set up a dialectical process of conflict and social contradiction whose ultimate resolution was envisaged as the communist ideal. Today, now that the immense timescale of human prehistory has been recognized, orthodox Marxists are left without any real theory for social change during some of the most significant periods of human development. The sex strike theory is an elaborate attempt to see men's and women's genes as the conflicting class-agents that powered the "human symbolic revolution"—the period in which art first emerged.

The sex strike theory has been well received by a number of sociobiologists and social anthropologists, although less so by archaeologists. The central belief is that among archaic *sapiens*, women, incapacitated by babies, needed the men to go off and hunt and bring back game animals that they could all eat. In such circumstances the women, according to the sex strike theorists, had two options. The first was to live in subservient polygyny of a type in which a dominant man had several wives and divided his time among them. The sex strike theorists feel that this option would have given women too little male support and have been bad for the group as a whole, as subservient males would have hung around on the margins of the community, contributing little. Therefore, they believe that the women organized things so that each of them could be provisioned by a single, faithful male—as in the Lovejoy scenario—in order to maximize the amount of nutrition and child care they got. According to the theory, they first had to synchronize their menstrual cycles, so that they all became fertile at the same time, thus apparently thwarting any incipient polygynists (although why this should actually work is not clear). Second, in order to obtain food, they periodically persuaded the men that sex was off. The obvious time they did this—according to sex strike theorists—was when they were all menstruating.

In order not to misrepresent the complexities and nuances of this theory, I present it here in the words of a sympathetic reviewer, Robin Dunbar of the University of Liverpool. As Dunbar puts it:

> As meat came to provide an increasingly important element in the diet of the ancestral hominids, the females, with their increasingly large brained offspring, came to be progressively more dependent on the hunting activities of the males. However, like the males of most primates, the hominid males were not especially interested in the females' problems in rearing offspring: their primary interest was simply in sex, and if meat offerings provided them with greater access to sex (the so-called "prostitution theory" of human social evolution), then they were prepared to trade meat for sex, but that was that.

But because "the females' heavy reproductive burden" required more meat, they came up with the "organized policy of sex strikes."

Red ocher has a place in this strange scenario, albeit slightly inconsistently. According to Camilla Power—a member of the East London group—menstruation, which signals a "sex strike," also signals impending fertility. Thus, men would wish to hang around menstruating women in order to get them pregnant (although they would also be prepared to disappear again, once their genetic seeds were sown). In Chris Knight and Charles Maisels's words, menstruation signals a female's imminent fertility — and hence by contrast the *infertility* of neighbouring females not displaying such blood. Logically in selfish gene terms, fitness-maximizing males ought to have been attracted by any such fertile female within the local area, competing to bond with her rather than with pregnant or breast-feeding females. Mothers with heavy childcare burdens, lacking the menstrual signal, would then have lost out at the very moment they needed help most.

To get around this,

When not really fertile, females signalled *as if* they were, acting within kin-coalitions of both fertile and non-fertile individuals even to the point of borrowing one another's blood or similar coloured pigments. Such strategies were designed to thwart male philanderers, not collude with dominant males.

Thus, conclude Knight and Maisels, "selfish genes in the case of our species have clearly led to the emergence of human solidarity."

One of the most obvious problems with the sex strike theory is that menstruation does not actually signal fertility; ovulation generally occurs in midcycle. The sham menstruation in the sex strike theory is the corollary of concealed ovulation — a feature that sociobiologists think emerged in humans naturally rather than culturally but for the same purpose — to keep men guessing. The idea of concealed ovulation is popular among animal behaviorists and sociobiologists. According to Richard Alexander and Katherine Noonan, concealed ovulation meant that females were able "to force" desirable males to stick around and not be promiscuous, as the males would not know when ovulation occurred; "thus concealment of ovulation could only evolve in a group-living situation in which the importance of parental care in offspring reproductive success was increasing . . . these two circumstances together describe a large part of the uniqueness of the social environment of humans during their divergence from other primates."

A second theory, developed by Nancy Burley, is that because human females had the intellectual capacity to practice contraception, they avoided the pains of childbirth as far as they could and stopped well short of having the maximum number of children that they were physically capable of producing. Because these women left fewer descendants, natural selection somehow, according to Burley, evolved a mechanism to thwart them by giving them a reproductive cycle recalcitrant to birth control—one in which the time of ovulation was not known.

Body Knowledge

Both the sex strike theory and Burley's theory have their problems. As Sarah Blaffer Hrdy has pointed out, what is termed concealed ovulation is not unique to humans, and plenty of nonreproductive, outside-estrus sexual activity goes on among many primates. Burley assumes that the only method of contraception available to early human females was the rhythm method, yet hunter-gatherer women today use a variety of methods to space births judiciously at a rate of around one every five years to an average of four or five live births per woman. This birthrate does not translate into a demographic explosion because of the high early mortality among hunter-gatherers. In short, it is simply not true that concealed ovulation causes more babies to be born. Human evolutionary success did not—in early prehistory, at least—depend on producing massive numbers of offspring but focused on intensive, high-quality infant care.

The main point against Burley's theory, however, has escaped most behavioral scientists: ovulation is not really concealed in humans at all. Many women know when they are ovulating. Some experience a specific pain that can be detected to the left or right, according to which ovary is releasing the egg; and some develop skin coloration—on the cheeks, for example—that is associated with ovulation. Ovulation is also signaled by fertile mucus; the changes in vaginal discharge may be noticeable both to a woman and to her partner. Further, a number of studies have shown that women are more sexually active at the time of ovulation. In small group-living communities, women menstruate and ovulate pretty much in synchrony (for reasons discussed in the next section). The mechanism by which they achieve this synchrony is pheromonal—women are able to smell each other's menstrual status and bring their bodies into line with one another accordingly. All of this suggests that reproductive cycles within early human groups would have been fairly well known by both females and males, consciously or unconsciously.

I proposed in Chapter 1 that the mechanical practicalities of upright walking undermined the signaling function of estrus skin. So-called concealed ovulation is nothing more than a result of that evolution. In the last chapter I argued that reproductive body knowledge and fertility control were part and parcel of human consciousness as it developed. There is thus no reason to suppose that men would not have known when women were reproductively receptive. Both the sex strike theory and Burley's theory also seem to assume that most women had a "heavy reproductive burden" to bear, yet this is not true of most primate females or human females in hunter-gatherer societies. Most crucially, the sex strike theory rests on the idea that a menstrual sex strike would be effective—that men would not wish to have sex with menstruating women, or with each other, or with postmenopausal women. If it really was sex alone that the men were after, why did they have to be forced to go hunting in order to get meat to trade for it? The theory assumes, of course, that it is not just sex that the men wanted, but reproductive sex with no follow-up commitment to child care.

The sex strike theory also assumes that a man would actually be fooled by red ocher into thinking that a woman had a period when she had not. Given menstrual synchrony, the women not having periods would either be premenarchic or postmenopausal, or they would be pregnant; only the pregnant women—according to the theory—critically needed the extra meat that could come only from a dedicated hunter who believed that he had yet to get her pregnant. Yet during the most crucial time span—late pregnancy and the first few months after childbirth—she would be in big trouble if she *did* persuade her man that she was still potentially fertile—because if he believed her, he would be demonstrating intelligence somewhat lower than that of a lemur! If men really were not interested in helping during this crucial time, then why could not the "female kin-coalitions" that Power postulates (and that exist among other primates) help supply her and so obviate the need for the whole ocher palaver?

Marginal Fertility and Menstrual Synchrony

Another weakness of the sex strike theory is that it does not deal with the perfectly well-established reason for menstrual synchrony. Menstrual synchrony keeps some women fertile who would not otherwise be. Female fertility is a delicate thing; it depends on the slow accumulation of sufficient fat reserves to see a pregnancy through. In hunter-gatherer communities this delicacy would be highly apparent. But in agricultural societies, as in the modern world, this delicacy is often ignored, and a more sedentary lifestyle and more constant food supply coupled with other factors (detailed in Chapter 3) mean that the intervals between births are much shorter. Menstrual and ovulatory synchrony is achieved quickly when women live together, using scent clues as a conscious or unconscious trigger. Women who live more isolated lives are less likely to have regular ovulations, and under conditions of nutritional stress they may lose them altogether for a while. Staying close to a group containing one or two strong menstruators keeps the more borderline women in the game. Menstrual synchrony indicates the existence of a "female kin-coalition," with its implied good outlook for child care.

That men should go off hunting at the time of women's menstruation—as they do in many traditional societies—is not actually at all odd. Most societies have a taboo on sex during menstruation, based on a variety of aversions, such as the symbolic association of blood and death and the idea that women's blood is ritually contagious. These taboos may be rationalizations for the facts that menstruation is a rather messy time, that the woman is unlikely to get pregnant (if that happens to be the aim), and that women themselves often do not feel sexy during their periods (although there are exceptions).

Alexander Marshack has conducted a series of analyses that seem to show that the regular incisions found on many small pieces of portable bone and antler found on Upper Paleolithic sites have a time-tracking significance. If this is true (and the marks are so varied that it is hard to know), then it would make sense in terms of people keeping track of the annual migrations, gestation periods, and so forth, of the big game animals that they hunted. Boris Frolov has suggested that one particularly complex plaque from Mal'ta in Siberia records a calendar year in which the gestation period of the reindeer is picked out. Women might also have wanted to keep track of moons. In many societies living in marginal conditions, there is a particular best time of year to have a baby. Indeed, the human gestation period of three-quarters of a year is adapted to such a system: a woman can fall pregnant at the end of the season of plenty, when her fat reserves are highest, and give birth the following year at the beginning of the next season of plenty.

A Cosmetic Advantage

The sex strike theory involves the same sexist assumption as the "sex-for-food" theory, namely that women did not want sex as much as men did. Nevertheless, if one focuses more narrowly on reproduction, the "sex-for-food" theory becomes rather more plausible, and may indicate a more logical role for red ocher body color in early human societies. As brain size grew and infants became harder to rear, women would have reduced their number of pregnancies and competition among men to be chosen as a father could well have heated up. In many societies worldwide men paint and adorn themselves for days and weeks in order to attract a mate—someone who will agree to do the hardest part of passing their genes on. Red ocher is far more likely to be a male cosmetic than female menstruation decoy.

Makeup could have given some men a crucial advantage. To put it in very stark terms, imagine two men competing with each other to be chosen by a mate. One has a naturally healthy complexion. The other is actually terminally ill but has recourse to bright ochers. He uses some belladonna to dilate his pupils and dabs oil of muskrat behind his ear. Through this clever sexual culture, it is possible that the ill man can outdo the healthy one in the display-and-attraction stakes and be chosen as the woman's mate. Of course, this may turn out to be bad news for the woman, as she may have to raise the child alone, but her consolation is that the child will have clever, culture-using genes on board. This rather caricatured example shows how culture complicates the business of sexual and natural selection, giving rise to all sorts of complex and sometimes unexpected results. The development of near-total hairlessness in many human communities may reflect the evolutionary victory of svelte body-decorators over hairy types.

Although humans probably had the capability for making art from at least 233,000 years ago, it is not until around 30,000 B.P. that they made much art that was solid enough to survive in the archaeological record. That which has survived is spectacular—a fully formed and mature sculptural style of miniature depictions of women, the Venus figurines of Ice Age Europe. Before considering these sculptures in detail, it is necessary to say something about the cultural development of *Homo sapiens* and Neanderthals from 100,000 B.P. onward. Especially in the Near East, anatomically modern humans seem to have lived side by side with Neanderthals. Whether they actually had anything to do with each other is disputed. It may be that their population densities were so low that they never came into contact. But skulls with both Neanderthal-like and modern-type features, such as those from Cro-Magnon (number 19 in Figure 1.3) suggest that some intermixing of the two populations may have occurred in Europe.

The last distinct Neanderthals lived in Spain around 28,000 years ago. Because the Ice Age Venus figurines date to the period during and following the final Neanderthal disappearance, some scientists have argued that only anatomically modern humans had the capacity for art. This thesis is obviously undermined by the Berekhat Ram figure, even as rough as it is. Moreover, the formality and elaboration of Neanderthal burials leave us in no doubt that Neanderthals had developed aesthetic sensibilities. The most famous site is the Shanidar cave in the Zagros foothills of northeastern Iraq, where a series of Neanderthal skeletons were excavated in the 1950s by Ralph Solecki. The remains of seven adults and two children are dated to somewhere between 60,000 and 44,000 B.P.; four of them were deliberately buried, one apparently with a garland of flowers as an offering.

There is some indirect evidence in Shanidar for a network of social support and for some sort of medical knowledge. The skeleton known as Shanidar I, a 30-to-45-year-old male with a brain capacity of 1,600 cc (compare the modern European male average of 1,415 cc) and around five feet seven inches tall, had suffered crippling injuries, yet he lived on for many years after sustaining them. His left eye socket had been crushed and his right arm had atrophied, along with his right shoulder and collarbone. The forearm and hand were missing, perhaps because they had dropped off, or perhaps because they were surgically amputated. Both his legs were damaged. Such a suite of injuries could easily cause death today and must have left him effectively unable to fend for himself.

That knowledge of medicinal plants definitely existed by this time is shown by new discoveries at the Doura cave site in Syria, dated to 100,000–40,000 B.P. Many hearths have been found that have charred plum stones in them (presumably roasted to get rid of harmful glucosides). Close by the hearths is a vast two-meter-thick deposit of husks from *Boraginacea* — borage or star flower — widely used today as a dietary supplement to alleviate premenstrual syndrome (PMS). The processing of borage seed is very labor intensive, so the reasons for this large deposit are not explicable in terms of calorific returns. It seems likely that the inhabitants of the Doura cave were processing borage for its active ingredients.

The two main active ingredients of borage are gamma linolenic acid (GLA) and alpha linolenic acid (ALA). The first is the one effective in treating PMS; the second, in treating Alzheimer's. It is hard to know to what extent PMS is a modern Western phenomenon; the compensating factor GLA is naturally found in breast milk, and it may be that the intensive and long-term breast-feeding characteristic of premodern and traditional societies provided girl babies with enough GLA in childhood to ameliorate the syndrome in adult life. It seems unlikely that the Doura cave people would process such a large amount of borage unless they had a special need for it. Interestingly, borage has another quality that they may have valued—it is an aphrodisiac.

The evidence from the Doura cave indicates that people were definitely aware of the specific effective properties, rather than simply the basic nutritional values, of the plants around them. It accords with the suggestion (made in Chapter 3) that people could well have been using plants for birth control from an extremely early period. Determining the extent of herbal use is an archaeological problem, since it is rare that the remains of wild-plant gathering survive. Only when there is a major deposit of processing residue, as at Doura, is there any hope of recognizing the traces for what they are.

Rites of Passage

The earliest firm evidence for formal burial of the dead comes from Skhūl Cave in Israel, where nearly 100,000 years ago an archaic *Homo sapiens* was laid out next to a boar's jaw. But no systematic associations between what was buried with a body and its inferred biological sex are known before the relatively recent period, from 10,000 B.P. onward. (The reasons are discussed in Chapters 7 and 8.)

Still, the simple fact of formal burial may tell us something. Formal burial is a "rite of passage"—a term coined by the anthropologist

Arnold van Gennep to describe the way that communities in the modern world mark transitions between different stages of life. As defined by van Gennep, a rite of passage has three phases: the prior state (in this case, the basic state of being alive), the end state (being dead), and the liminal or transitional state. The existence of the liminal state does not mean that death is not sudden, in straightforward biological terms. Rather, it means that what follows after physical death is social death. The interval between the two is marked by ritual. Immediately after physical death the body becomes "liminal"— dangerously in-between; the person no longer breathes, but their physical form exists. For their body and belongings to move on, funeral rites must be held, at the conclusion of which the person becomes socially dead and, to a greater or lesser degree, no longer perceived as active in the community.

Other main rites of passage that van Gennep identified were for birth and for the transitions between childhood and adulthood (notably first menstruation), adulthood and parenthood, and unmarried and married states. Birth, like death, had not only a physical aspect but a social one, usually marked by a naming ceremony. This ceremony was conducted some weeks after the birth, once the infant's life had become established. Children who died before naming had not become social individuals and experienced no social death, hence no funeral. (Archaeologically speaking, neonatal burials rarely occur within formal cemeteries, unless they are accompanying a mother who died in childbirth.) The other, perhaps less fundamental transitions include loss of virginity, a change in residence (moving out to live with a partner), and the act of giving birth. In many societies worldwide, a man's transition to fatherhood is marked by the couvade—a rite of passage in which the man is secluded and acts out labor pains. Among some North American Indian groups, the husband went up into the roof space, from where strings tied to his testicles hung down, to be periodically pulled on as the baby was born.

The archaeological evidence for the beginnings of formal burial implies, van Gennep's insights suggest, a social world in which rites of passage occurred. If death was marked, then so, one imagines, was birth. If birth and death were marked, so might other life-cycle transitions have been. Tantalizing evidence for some of these rites of passage comes from the Upper Paleolithic period in Eurasia, from 40,000 to around 10,000 years ago—a period that witnessed an extraordinary explosion of creativity. Although from around 40,000 B.P. onward the human population of Europe was physically very similar to modern humans, the change from preceding periods was not that sharp. "Modern" humans were in existence before 100,000 and perhaps as early as 150,000 years ago; the Berekhat Ram sculpture suggests an even earlier origin for art. However, the Upper Paleolithic art of Europe starting 30,000 years ago marks the first surviving art on a grand scale and was accompanied by a number of other dramatic changes in culture.

Upper Paleolithic societies inhabited northern Eurasia during the last ice age. The glaciers reached their maximum extent around 20,000 years ago, covering most of the Alps, northern Britain, Scandinavia, and northern Poland. Because the sea level was low, what is now Britain and Ireland was part of a continuous continental tundra, over which herds of mammoths, woolly rhinos, reindeer, shaggy wild horses, and steppe bison roamed. These animals are beautifully shown in cave paintings in southern France and the Pyrenees. Contrary to popular beliefs about "cave men," Paleolithic people did not live in caves. Usually they made tents or huts, although cave mouth areas sometimes show traces of brief occupation. They depended on large game animals not just for meat but for building materials. The remains of many mammoth-bone houses, constructed from piled vertebrae with upward-arching tusks, presumably to keep a covering of cured skin in place, have been excavated in southern Russia. At Dolní Věstonice in the Czech Republic, people kept warm in tents that had coal-fired hearths in the middle. Tallow was burned for light, and bones and ivory were worked into a variety of striking artistic objects of a portable nature.

Evidence for rites of death—as well, perhaps, as representations of complex relationships between living individuals—comes from a small number of Upper Paleolithic burials. Burial was the exception rather than the rule during the ice age. Like many of today's societies, ice age people might have exposed bodies to the elements, scattered ashes, or floated funerary biers off down the river. The normal form of funeral, whatever it was, may have been elaborate, but it does not show up in the archaeological record.

The Red Threesome

One of the most interesting of those few burials that are known was recently excavated by Bohuslav Klima at the important open-air settlement site of Dolní Věstonice in the Pavlov Hills, near Brno in the Czech Republic. It is a triple burial; the three bodies were found lying in a shallow pit, two probable males flanking an individual of indefinite sex, either a light-boned male or—marginally more likely—a female. All were around twenty years old when they died, but the cause of death is unknown. They were carefully positioned in the grave, their relaxed forms indicating that rigor mortis had worn off, and then were covered with branches that were set afire (shown in black in Figure 4.2) before the whole burial was covered with a thin layer of earth. Elements of clothing or body decoration survive in the form of pierced seashells, wolf and Arctic fox teeth. The male to the left had a string of drilled human teeth next to him, possibly part of a necklace. The most striking aspects of the grave are the presence of red ocher (a form of iron oxide) and the positioning of the bodies. All three heads seem to have been sprinkled with red ocher. The central figure has a large patch of red ocher between her/his thighs; the left-hand figure not only gazes at the patch region but extends his hands into it as well. This left-hand figure has had a stake driven through his pubic region, into the coccyx. The middle figure is turned away from him, looking toward the right-hand figure. The latter is turned away, although he has been buried in an unusual facedown position, partially overlying the central figure.

The precise significance of the Dolní Věstonice triple burial may never be known for certain. In the future, DNA testing may be used to determine the genetic sexes of the individuals, which would be important for interpreting the obvious sexual elements in the burial.

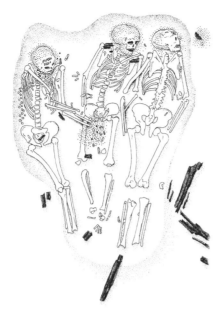

(Fig. 4.2) Ice Age triple burial: Dolní Věstonice in Slovakia. Drawing by George Taylor after Klíma 1988.

(The technique is not yet widely applied in archaeology, partly due to expense, partly because of problems of shipping human remains to labs that are often in other countries.) The youth of the three and the absence of any obvious cause of death suggests that they died together, perhaps from an acute disease, poisoning, or drowning. The possibility that they were put to death in one of these ways, either as sacrificial victims or as a punishment for some indiscretion, should not be ruled out. The positioning of the bodies itself seems to tell a story. If the central figure is female, then we could see her and the right-hand male as a young heterosexual couple. His partially overlapping position and unmet gaze symbolizes some disruption in their relationship. The figure to the left could be the third player in the drama. Was he her illicit lover? What behavior warranted staking his penis in death? Why are his hands between her legs, in an area marked with symbolic blood? Here I undoubtedly overstep the mark in terms of firmly based interpretation, yet it can be said with some certainty that the remains reflect quite complex social and sexual relationships. These relationships may, too, have been projected onto them as unwilling or unwitting victims.

A Venus figurine carved from a solid piece of ocher—

hematite—also comes from the site of Dolní Věstonice. The red ocher that covers the heads of the three buried figures could have symbolized the power of blood in life—a charged material necessary for the transition into death, and some rebirth beyond. The red ocher between the central figure's legs suggests the association of this region—in women, at least—with blood, and it may strengthen the idea that the skeleton is female. Was ocher simply sprinkled onto this region? Or is it the scattered remains, after burning, of some sculpture or object that was carved in ocher and held by the left-hand figure against, or partially inserted into, the central figure's vagina?

Klima himself has suggested that the grave may represent some tragedy surrounding a childbirth gone wrong. He sees the male figures, rather implausibly, as midwives. But he may be right in some respects. The central figure has been examined by physical anthropologist David Frayer, who found it to have suffered from a congenital hip condition, *coxa vara*. (This condition is just discernible in Figure 4.2, where the central figure's left thigh—to the reader's right—is linked to the pelvis by a ball joint that juts from the head of the femur at right angles, as opposed to the normal, slightly less acute angle, as seen in the right-hand male.) Such a deformity would have caused the individual to have a slightly odd walk in life and might have caused problems in childbirth. It remains possible that the central figure was male or some type of intersex individual who warranted a special kind of burial. The aggression displayed in driving a stake through the left-hand male's genital region does not immediately suggest a peaceful "Age of the Goddess," although it could be taken to support a particularly aggressive form of matriarchy.

Whatever the precise meaning of the Dolní Věstonice triple burial, it displays a complex symbolism. Its "narrative" aspect is discernible in the careful posing of the three bodies. The story has clear sexual connotations, and the suggestion is strong that some kind of social judgment has been passed. The burial seems to indicate a society in which sexual transgression could occur and thus a society governed by rules for normal and appropriate sexual conduct. To see how such behavior could have been encouraged and regulated, it is necessary to look in greater detail at Ice Age art.

Chapter 5

Venus in Furs

*"The myth of matriarchy is but a tool
used to keep woman bound to her place.
To free her, we need to destroy the myth."*

JOAN BAMBERGER,
"THE MYTH OF MATRIARCHY"

A great deal of art from Ice Age Europe is known: cave paintings, sculptures, etchings, statuettes, and engraved artifacts. Although this art is high in potential sexual content, let alone functioning, surprisingly little has been made of it, beyond some abstract and rarefied suggestions about the symbolic division of male and female principles. In this chapter I interpret the art objects as part of a complicated sexual culture that, through sexual objectification and censorship, created and maintained power imbalances between men and women.

The Venus Figurines

Perhaps the best-known piece of Paleolithic art, and one of the most pervasive of all prehistoric art images, is the Venus of Willendorf

(Fig. 5.1)   The Venus of Willendorf,
Austria. Limestone, with traces of red ocher
pigment. Photograph: Naturhistorisches
Museum, Vienna.

(Figure 5.1). In 1908 this five-inch-high sculpture of a large-buttocked,
large-breasted woman was found beside the Danube in Lower Austria.
The discovery occurred at an archaeological site known as Willendorf
II. A place where traces of human occupation dating to the Upper
Paleolithic or final ice age period (which lasted from around 40,000 to
12,000 years ago) had been found. The form of the figure is "plastic,"
being carved fully in the round from limestone. Traces of red coloring,
probably red ocher, are discernible, surviving in the deeper folds of the
body. It is thought to have been red all over at one time.

Around 200 Ice Age statuettes of women have been discovered
so far. Despite a fair degree of variation in their appearance, they
have been collectively—and perhaps misleadingly—termed "Venus"
figurines, after the Roman goddess of love. The purpose and function of Venus figurines have been the focus of intense debate. Were
they made by men as the prehistoric equivalent of *Playboy* center-
folds, an ice age "plastic pornography?" Or did they depict priestesses, or ancestral leaders, or images of a "Great Mother Goddess?"
Were they part of a communicative code that linked individuals in
widely dispersed communities? Were they used for sorcery, as a link
between everyday and supernatural powers? Or were they the
product of women's self-affirmation, small-scale self-portraits to
treasure?

At the very least, the Venus figurines are durable *images*. They are the first positive evidence we have for human nakedness, despite the fact (discussed in Chapter 1) that nakedness likely developed far earlier. By carving them, ice age societies were making an important statement about what it took to be human or a particular type of human. Whether or not the figurines reflect the way real Upper Paleolithic women looked, they must have constrained the way that real women were looked at — both by women themselves and by men. They must also have changed the way women, and perhaps men, thought about their physicality. Whereas real Upper Paleolithic women were mortal, with bodies that changed throughout life — and month by month, season by season, pregnancy by pregnancy, according to natural rhythms and the rigors of a demanding ice age environment — the figurines' bodies are fixed in stone, or bone, or ivory so durably that they have survived intact for tens of thousands of years.

The Venus figurines are various in appearance. Some are very fleshy and naked, or almost naked, while others are thinner and have more substantial clothing, such as a parka-clad figure from Bouret in Siberia. The earliest, which comes from the Galgenberg in Lower Austria, is a flat, apparently dancing figure made in greenstone, dating to just before 30,000 B.P. But the majority of the figurines date to around 26,000 B.P. The spatial distribution of the figures runs from the steppes of southern Russia, where they are found within mammoth-bone houses at Kostienki and Molodova, to the Pyrenees in the west, where they are found on cave shelter sites. Many interpretations of the Venuses have been made, which have helped to create ideas about the overall organization of Upper Paleolithic society and the relations between the sexes therein. At present it is not known who made the figurines — women, men, or both — or why they made them.

The best-known theory is that they are images of a "Great Goddess" and that they relate to a period of matriarchy, when women called the shots. This view has been popularized by Jean Auel in her racy best-sellers set in Ice Age Europe, *The Clan of the Cave Bear* and *The Mammoth Hunters*. Among archaeologists this theory has very little support, but nor is there any consensus among

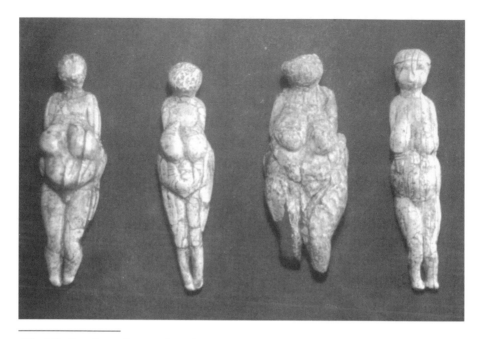

(Fig. 5.2) Four Venus figurines from the Ice Age site of Avdeevo, near Kursk in European Russia. Photograph: Paul Bahn.

them about what the figurines do signify. Over the years many researchers have come up with a whole range of fairly sexist interpretations, which to some extent explains the popularity of the matriarchy theory as an alternative. The prime impetus for the matriarchy theory came from the late Marija Gimbutas of UCLA who, in the last years of her life, produced some splendid volumes — *The Language of the Goddess* and *The Civilization of the Goddess*. These books ostensibly document the religious and political dominion of women both in the ice age and in the succeeding early farming societies of Europe. Her theory was mainly developed in respect to farming cultures (and is discussed in detail in Chapter 6), but she considered that the "Goddess Creatrix" had many aspects, one of which was expressed by the Ice Age figurines.

While Gimbutas's own research was scholarly, that of many of her followers and of those inspired by her work has been less carefully argued. Works such as *The Ancient Religion of the Great Cosmic Mother of All* and *The Great Cosmic Mother*, both by Monica Sjöö and

Barbara Mor, make very broad generalizations about prehistory that have been taken as gospel by the large number of people who are, understandably, unfamiliar with the difficulties of archaeological interpretation. Thus, for example, Nickie Roberts, at the beginning of her otherwise excellent book on the history of prostitution (which I use as an authority for parts of Chapter 6), tells us that

> Sjöö and Mor show that the power of the Stone Age goddess went far beyond the simplistic notion of fertility . . . she was all-encompassing, and thus expressed the original power which animated the universe and the whole of nature . . . the Great Goddess was creator, preserver and destroyer of all life . . . culture, religion and sexuality were intertwined, springing as they did from the same source in the goddess. Sex was sacred by definition, and the shamanic priestesses led group sex rituals in which the whole community participated, sharing in ecstatic union with the life force.

Roberts captions a picture of the Venus of Willendorf with the statement, "In the beginning was matriarchy."

If this were true, we should expect the Goddess to be doing something, as the vigorous goddesses of India do—slaying, giving birth, making love, and so on. However, the Ice Age Venuses are almost completely passive. The only active figures in Ice Age art are men—usually depicted in semi-animal form on the walls of caves and rarely objectified in small-scale sculpture. Some of the figurines may be intended to depict pregnancy, but in none of them is the Goddess giving birth or nursing an infant. Some are shown wearing string aprons, but they are not shown making them; they are not shown hunting or killing or doing anything much at all. Even if they were active, the figurines would not be able to see what they were doing as, although their sexual attributes are shown in considerable detail, the vast majority of them have no faces.

Today's revamping of the Victorian matriarchy theory is broadly related to the feminist movement. Gimbutas's work can be seen as a necessary move to promote new social interpretations of prehistory, alternatives to the deep male sexism of orthodox views. Prior to her work, for example, it was simply assumed that all the Venus figurines were made by men. Of course, they could have been, but any statement in this regard needs to be based on evidence rather than bias.

Plastic Pornography

Karel Absolon, who excavated a number of figurines at Dolní Věstonice, wrote that "sex and hunger were the two motives which influenced the entire mental life of the mammoth hunters and their productive art." A rodlike figurine from the site (Figure 5.3) has two lobes that are considered to be breasts; Absolon (using the quaint chronological term *diluvial*, meaning in this case coming from strata old enough to have been scrambled by the biblical flood) wrote, "This statuette shows us that the artist has neglected all that did not interest him, stressing his sexual libido only where the breasts are concerned—a diluvial plastic pornography." However, the "breasts" could just as easily be seen as testicles, making the piece as potentially phallic as female. Absolon believed that the piece was made by a man, but he did not investigate the idea of gay pornography. It could, of course, have just as well been made by a woman. What is clear is that like a number of similar objects, this figurine is visually ambiguous. We should not rule out the possibility that it had a functional use, "ritual" or otherwise. Modern dildoes display a similar kind of ambiguity, being necessarily phallic, but some have a tip shaped in the image of a woman's face with tressed hair, while others are shaped like dolphins. (Although the Dolní Věstonice phallus is only finger-sized, others measure six or eight inches: Figures 5.5, 5.6, 5.7, and 5.8.)

The idea that the Venus figurines represent ideal sexually attractive women has always run into a certain amount of difficulty. Some

researchers feel that it is a sexist interpretation. Others feel that the Venus figurines
are neither attractive nor erotic. One of
the principal French ice age art researchers, André Leroi-Gourhan, has said,
"Taken at face value, the palaeolithic
woman was an uncomplicated creature,
naked and with curly hair, who kept her
hands folded over her chest, holding her
minute head serenely above the dreadfully
sagging shape of her breast and hips." The
doyen of early ice age art research, the
Abbé Breuil, thought that the figures
showed steatopygia—a pronounced development of fatty deposits on the buttocks—
and wondered whether the women were
from Africa, racially akin to Bushman
women, whose steatopygia was renowned.

(Fig. 5.3) Phallic baton from
Dolní Věstonice, Slovakia.
Drawing by George Taylor
after Marshack 1972.

　　More recently a French gynecologist, Duhard, has proposed that
the Venuses represent various states of clinical obesity. Both Gobert
and Jude argue that they are too stocky to be fertility symbols and
thus represent postmenopausal women. Piette, taking into account the
wide range of variability in size and shape, proposes that they represent two basic types of ice age woman, "adipose" and "svelte," but that
both are equally fertility images. Patricia Rice has argued that they
represent women across the entire age range. She breaks them down
by percentages into what she judges to be young women up to 15 years
old (23 percent), mature pregnant women between 15 and 35 (17 percent), mature nonpregnant women (38 percent), and women older
than 35 (22 percent). It is not clear, however, what value can be placed
on her analysis, since the figures do not represent the population of
one site but are spread over a wide region and display stylistic variations that make any attempt at comparison difficult.

　　Some researchers believe that the statuettes could not have been
involved with enhancing fertility because of the problem of finding

food in Ice Age Europe. Communities would have had to keep tight control over their populations if they were to survive. Henri Delporte, in the fullest survey of female imagery in the Upper Paleolithic, castigates this view, saying, "Having attributed the hunter with bourgeois motivations and having equipped him with Palaeolithic tools, we then declare his situation desperate." Indeed, food on the hoof may have been relatively plentiful, and many of the figurines themselves appear well-nourished. As Delporte's statement intimates, however, the main food supplies were probably procured by men. In the tundra environment the calorific contribution of women from gathering activities may have been reduced, which suggests that the Venus figurines appeared at a time of growing economic inequality between men and women.

Absolon's "pornography" theory has been followed by others who see the figurines as potentially erotic. It is perhaps a truism that old erotica no longer has the power to arouse and may therefore be difficult to recognize. For most of us today, Greek orgy scenes, for all their sexual explicitness, are no more than quaint curiosities, yet in the Victorian period—when even piano legs were considered dangerously erotic and had to be put in skirts—such images were far more sexually charged. Live physical nudity was not a common sight in Victorian Britain, making nudity in art all the more piquant. Nudity during the ice age may have been equally uncommon, packing a similar erotic punch. People had to stay well wrapped in the glacial environment, which for a time was an average of 10 degrees Celsius colder than modern Europe—comparable to southern Alaska today. But the Venus figurines are images without their furs. They may reflect the nakedness of women as they huddled around glowing coals within a well-insulated hut, but such nudity may equally have been a great rarity. Guthrie has suggested that the Venus figurines are the world's first erotica, and he draws direct comparisons with *Playboy*. Their typical form, with small heads and feet, and large breasts and buttocks, stresses—he feels—the most attractive parts, and the legs-apart position of one figure from the cave of La Madeleine, he thinks, suggests "submission and timidity" (though he does not explain why these qualities should be erotic).

According to Devendra Singh, a psychologist at the University of Texas at Austin, the results of a recent survey of the erotic preferences of 195 men support the idea that there is a universally recognized canon of female beauty, with a marked preference for average weight and a low waist-to-hip size ratio—exactly the same ratio, around 0.70, that *Playboy* centerfold pinups have maintained over the last thirty years. But all this conclusion shows is that *Playboy*—with its almost globally pervasive imagery—influences some modern men's idea of the erotic. (It tells us nothing about what sort of women modern *women* may find erotic.) The average weight of Rubens's voluptuous women, with their rippling cellulite and rolls of waist fat, looks much higher. The Venus figurines in their day may have similarly influenced taste; their average weight looks higher than Singh's norm, and their waist-to-hip ratios do not all conform to 0.70.

The Bodies Beyond

It is difficult to know which aspects of the Venus figurines represent real women and which—like the striking lack of faces—reflect stylistic conventions. Fatness, far from being a clinical condition, may have rendered a woman physiologically and reproductively fit to live within a glacial environment. Perhaps a greater survival rate for larger women affected the gene pool. In the Donner Party disaster of 1846–47, where a group of settlers were caught out in the mountain winter on their way to California, the well-nourished women survived best. When it comes to feats requiring great stamina and energy reserves, such as swimming across Lake Ontario, large women do best—and they may be the only people who can do it at all. In Ice Age Europe women of proportions like the larger Venus figurines would have had great endurance potential, which would have been critical for bringing a child to full term when food was uncertain. These figurines are, therefore, not established mothers but potential mothers—those with the reserves and stamina to be successful. It is possible that women did indeed look quite like these representations, for part of the year at least. But who made the sculptures and why?

Leroy McDermott has argued that the figurines' features are best explained if they are understood as women's "self-representations." The fact that women had to look down their bodies, over their breasts, would have emphasized the breasts, McDermott argues, while letting the legs taper away to nothing. This view could also explain why virtually all the figurines are faceless, as you cannot see your own face. But I do not think the Venus figurines are women's self-representations. First, the theory is internally inconsistent: areas like the back of the buttocks and the hair at the back of the head are represented, though women could not see them. Second, if the theory is true, then the women must have deliberately chosen to represent themselves naked; having done so they then went into some gynecological detail (Figure 5.1) yet studiously omitted at any point to sculpt a clitoris. So these would be self-representations in which the focus of personality, the face, and one of the most important physiological foci of sexuality, the clitoris, are absent. In view of these considerations, McDermott's case does not seem strong. But some aspects of the figures lead in another direction.

Sarah Nelson believes that the Venus figurines are too varied to be considered as just one thing, claiming that they "only have gender in common" (by which she means the outward attributes of female sex). Yet while figurines that span several centuries and occur over a wide area could undoubtedly have had different local or contextual meanings, they do in fact share other attributes beyond sex. The essential feature of the Venus figurines is that they are durable. The smooth-worn surfaces of many of them suggest that they were handled often and were perhaps passed around or given. They were portable and exchangeable. The significance of this exchangeability grows when one considers that—with one possible exception—no male figurines are known. Ice Age European society either censored the sculpting of men (although not of phalluses) or made images of men out of perishable materials of which we currently know nothing. The underlying implication is that women, at least symbolically, could be given, while men could not. The type of woman who could be given was typically faceless (her identity did not count) and reproductively fit.

The social implications of "giving women" fit well with other features of Upper Paleolithic society, which was made up of small scattered communities among which communication would have been very important. That the figurines are found over such a wide area suggests that they were a commonly understood symbol. We have no way of being absolutely sure what these figures were used for, and their meaning may not have been constant. Perhaps they were something like marriage tokens, given to a bride's mother as a keepsake when her daughter transferred to a far-off group to bear children for a strange man. They may have been carved by the bridegroom, who had not seen his bride prior to the exchange and so left the face blank, to be given to the bereft parents, who would be better able to envisage the features of their loved one on the smooth surface.

This fanciful suggestion assumes that Upper Paleolithic society practiced marriage—an institution that, however imprecisely defined, is present in all known communities. The idea that marriage began in the ice age is plausible, since burial evidence from the Upper Paleolithic demonstrates the existence of at least one elaborate rite of passage. If one, why not another? Economic and reproductive conditions might have been such that the assertion of individual property rights in another person—which is what marriage, in part, boils down to—became an important issue.

The transferability of women but not men in Ice Age society is supported by evidence from other artistic endeavors during the period, notably cave art. The sexual content of cave art has long been recognized and discussed. Leroi-Gourhan tried to discern a precise gendered "key" to the multitude of representations in the larger caves, dividing all of them into "male" and "female." As with the Venus figurines, we do not know who executed the cave representations. There has been a general feeling, often poorly presented, that men created the art. I believe that men did make most of it, not because women were not involved in "art," but because the cave art that we know about depicts passive "objectified" females and active males.

British prehistoric art specialist Paul Bahn believes that Leroi-Gourhan is mistaken to consider such a great range of abstract symbols to be vulvas, believing that in his case a modern sexual obsession

(Fig. 5.4)   Three rock-cut vulvas;
Angles. Drawing by George Taylor.

has run riot over the actual evidence. "There is little sense in our lumping together signs with different shapes when Palaeolithic artists took pains to differentiate them," he notes. Nevertheless, different artists render the same things in different ways, and there are good ethnographic parallels in Polynesian societies for covering rock surfaces and portable pebbles with vulva motifs. On Easter Island, for example, two-lobed vulva forms with abstractly rendered clitorises (on the whole looking like cartoon cockroaches to the untrained eye) are engraved on a rock at the site of Orongo. The engraved stone was used in the girls' clitoris-stretching ceremony; during the *te manu mo ta poki* or "bird child" ceremony (still part of living memory in 1919), girls stood on a rock where their enlarged clitorises were examined by five priests, who then carved the images on the rocks. As with the Venus figurines, we do not know who made the vulva representations in Upper Paleolithic art. The incised and partly sculpted vulvas found on the walls of Upper Paleolithic caves (Figure 5.4) could have been intended as either erotic or ritual; they could have been designed by men or by women. (Anyone in doubt as to whether women might draw vulvas for erotic purposes is referred to the *Cunt Coloring Book*, a modern lesbian publication.)

In Polynesia, men also had vulva designs tattooed as a sign of virility. Tattooing may very likely have been part and parcel of Pale-

(Fig. 5.5)   Rod from La Madeleine, France. Drawing by George Taylor after Marshack 1972.

olithic art as well. The coloring materials, such as soot, were readily available, as was a technology that could make suitable points; bone awls, probably used for leather sewing, are commonplace. It seems to me almost essential that artists working in the recesses of caves, painting animals on rough protuberances and angles of rock walls by guttering torchlight, had a great deal of prior practice. Tattooing, with its requirement to get it right the first time on a rounded and sometimes moving three-dimensional surface, would seem to provide an excellent training ground.

Although many of the abstract forms in cave art could be vulvas, Bahn is right to counsel caution. What one sees in these more abstract forms is indeed an open question. An engraved bone rod from the cave of La Madeleine is one of several that bear what appear to be phallic representations — in this case, what seems to me to be a lioness is licking the opening of a gigantic human penis, which is hanging down from between the legs of a rather confusingly engraved man (Figure 5.5). Others have seen a vulva somewhere in this picture; Denis Peyrony claims that it is half open, with the hair depicted, while Luquet thought it was an anus and buttocks instead of a vulva. Whatever the truth may be, neither the explicit sexual imagery nor the connection of male human and animal sexuality is in doubt.

Symbols in Action

Many phallic batons carved in the round are found in Upper Paleolithic art. An interesting double "baton" from the Gorge d'Enfer has two explicitly rendered penises set at an angle to each other (exactly as in a modern "double" dildo; Figure 5.9). Unfortunately, many of these batons have not been published with their dimensions given in full, so it is difficult to gauge their potential utility, as opposed to interpreting their symbolism. Generally speaking, the batons do fall within the size range of modern dildoes.

Looking at the size, shape, and—in many cases—explicit symbolism of the ice age batons, it seems disingenuous to avoid the most obvious and straightforward interpretation. But it has been avoided. These phallic objects are variously considered ritual objects, *batons de commandement,* arrow- or spear-straighteners (those with a hole at the base or, in the case of the Gorge d'Enfer double "baton," at the junction of the two penises). Undoubtedly the majority of these phallic objects could have been used for vaginal, anal, or oral insertion. The "baton" from Dolní Věstonice, which Absolon saw as an abstracted woman, could clearly serve as a dildo with a handle; the Gorge d'Enfer double "baton" could easily have been used for vaginal insertion by two women, although other permutations are conceivable; the hole could have been used for some sort of strap. A selection of other phallic batons are shown in Figures 5.6–5.8.

I am not suggesting that these artifacts were necessarily sex toys in the modern recreational sense (although I do not see why that should be ruled out). If the word *ritual* restores credibility, then ritual defloration is one possibility; it is known in a number of societies worldwide. Even if the various batons had other primary or ostensible uses, their dimensions and symbolism do not preclude their sexual use. The presence or absence of dildoes in various human cultures has not, to my knowledge, been systematically documented, but they have probably been a widespread phenomenon for much of human history. The vaginal insertion of objects for sexual pleasure has been observed among primates in the wild. It is something that is likely to have been a part of our own evolutionary and early cultural background, despite the fact that the earliest graphic depictions of the use of dildoes are generally thought to be those found on ancient Greek pottery of the fifth and fourth centuries B.C. However, there may be an ice age example of one in use.

(Fig. 5.6) Phallic baton; Bruniquel.
Drawing by George Taylor after
Marshack 1972.

(Fig. 5.7) Phallic baton; Le Placard.
Drawing by George Taylor after
Marshack 1972.

(Fig. 5.8) Phallic baton; Predmost.
Drawing by George Taylor after
Marshack 1972.

(Fig. 5.9) Double phallic baton; Gorge
d'Enfer. Drawing by George Taylor after
Marshack 1972.

The Grimaldi Figure:
Masturbator or Hermaphrodite?

A phallic artifact may actually be depicted in use in the case of one of
the most enigmatic of the Venus figurines, the Grimaldi "hermaphrodite." This strange sculpture, made of translucent green steatite, is
one of several that are thought to come from the Grimaldi cave but
that were not excavated properly by archaeologists. The figure is relatively conventional in the upper half, with breasts and a bulging
belly. The arms, however, are puzzling. Ice Age sculptors never
found a neat solution for rendering arms on Venus figurines. The essentially objectified and passive subject matter and the sculptor's
striving for a rounded form meant that they were often left off altogether or look curiously sticklike, as in the case of the Venus of Willendorf. The Grimaldi figure appears to have arms that fall straight
from the shoulder, disappear (or are broken off), and reappear at the
top of the thighs, then come around so that the hands can cup what
appears to be a scrotal sac. Leading up from this low-slung lump, a
ridge runs up between the arms and ends beneath the belly. This configuration of forms has been interpreted by Henri Delporte and others to depict hermaphroditism—a figure with breasts and erect penis.
In the light of what has been said in Chapter 2 about the incidence of
intersex individuals in human communities, it would not be particularly surprising to find one represented.

But there are problems with the interpretation of the Grimaldi
figure as a hermaphrodite. The arms do not seem to belong to the upper torso at all. Further, the head of the penis is extremely unclear. In
short, it is equally possible to see the sculpture as showing someone
else's hands coming around from behind, to insert a dildo into the
vagina of the main body. Both interpretations have problems, but the
latter interpretation may be more plausible in the light of the fact that
suitable objects existed. Moreover, in the Dolní Věstonice triple burial, we have direct evidence for a male placing both hands into the
pubic area of a probable female, where he may have held some artifact made of red ocher.

There are other possible explanations for the Grimaldi "her-

(Fig. 5.10) The Grimaldi "hermaphrodite." Drawing by George Taylor after Delporte 1993: fig. 93.

maphrodite." It could, for example, represent a rather contorted copulation scene. Such a scene, differently managed, is known from a cave wall at Laussel. The Laussel scene seems to represent two figures in genital union; they are depicted in mirror image, joined at the groin, lending the picture an emblematic, almost hieroglyphic feeling. Heinz Hunger notes that researchers have been reluctant to interpret the scene as a copulation. Leroi-Gourhan, in his own tracing of it, "felt tempted to tamper with the glyph and 'redraw' the outlines of the copulating pair until he succeeded in converting the composition into an apparently less obnoxious breech delivery," Hunger observes. He argues that the depiction of human copulation presents particular artistic problems, and that the Laussel solution is fairly much identical to that arrived at in many other art styles.

Trances with Bulls

Cave art is concentrated in the Dordogne region of France and the French and Spanish Pyrenees. It has two basic features: caves, and paintings. The paintings were done with red and yellow ochers and charcoal. Traces of wooden scaffolding exist inside some of the caves, erected to position the painters close to the cave roof. Sooty marks show that burning brands or tallow candles were used to light areas

(Fig. 5.11) The Lascaux shaft scene. Photograph: SPADEM.

that were being worked on. If the key quality of the Venuses is their durability and portability, then an important feature of cave art may well be that much of it was created in caves that were deep and sometimes peculiarly difficult to access. So remote and inaccessible were some of the pictures that they could remain secret as millennia passed; indeed, after around 10,000 years ago, it seems they were completely forgotten and passed out of all knowledge until people with scientific interests began to go caving in the nineteenth century.

The best-known images are of large game animals: woolly rhinos, mammoths, horses, bison, and deer. But the greatest number of images are "abstract" motifs (which Leroi-Gourhan divided into two basic types: "full" or female signs and "thin" or male signs). Many people have tried to interpret the art in mythological terms. The revered mythographer Joseph Campbell has described the "crypt" area of the cave at Lascaux in the following terms:

Down there a large bison bull, eviscerated by a spear that has transfixed its anus and emerged through its sexual organ, stands before a prostrate man. The latter . . . is rapt in a shamanistic trance. He wears a bird mask; his phallus, erect, is pointing at the pierced bull; a throwing stick lies on the ground at his feet and beside him stands a wand or staff, bearing on its tip the image of a bird. And then, behind this prostrate shaman, is a large rhinoceros, apparently defecating as it walks away.

Campbell connects this scenario, rather unclearly, to the Australian phallic rite of "pointing the bone." In this lethal magical rite a shaman holds a pointed bone out of sight beneath his perineum, while strewing his own semen or excrement, in an attempt to put the victim to sleep. He then points the bone from under his penis directly at the victim. In the Lascaux depiction, Campbell thinks that the rhino "may well be the shaman's animal familiar. The position of the lance . . . spills the bowels from the area between [the bison's anus and penis]—which is precisely the region affected by the 'pointing bone' of the Australians." It is difficult to know what to make of this interpretation. The detail and the oddity ring true and convince us that the Paleolithic painting did indeed concern something complex and strange. But it is difficult to know how precise our interpretations can be, given the lack of more tangible evidence.

A different sort of approach is to look at gross generalities, like my observation about the remoteness and inaccessibility of the caves. In contrast to the Venus figurines, the cave paintings were hidden from the community most of the time. It is logical to suppose that only certain people were allowed to see them or to know of their existence. It may well be that the caves themselves bore a vulvar/vaginal/womb symbolism. In the cave of Niaux, in the Ariège region of France, is a long, slightly curving vertical fissure in the rock wall. Its latent sexual symbolism was drawn out by the addition of large smudges of red to either side of its lower end, where the rock wall curves under. The smudges conjure an image of open labia, an image enhanced by a liberal dotting of marks suggestive of pubic hair. Populated as they are with (painted) animals, the caves might have represented some symbolic womb out of which the herds would suddenly

(Fig. 5.12) The "sorcerer" of the Trois
Frères cave, Ariège, France. Painted
and engraved figure. Drawing from
Marshack 1972.

(Fig. 5.13) Semi-human bison figure,
the Trois Frères cave, Ariège, France.
Engraved figure. Drawing from
Marshack 1972.

flow, as they appeared to do in reality when they suddenly came in sight around the head of the valley, on the annual migration that the hunters relied on intercepting.

Several male human figures are depicted in the caves; they are often described as shaman figures. Several of them have animal characteristics. Apart from the "bird mask" figure described by Campbell, others are half bison and half stag (Figures 5.12–5.14). Both bison and deer are animals whose sexual organization is of a polygynous, harem-holding nature. Is it too much to imagine that Upper Paleolithic societies took some of their sociosexual cues from the patently successful animals around them? A famous engraved fragment of reindeer bone from Laugerie-Basse in the Dordogne (Figure 5.15) shows traces of a scene in which a stag with erect penis stands over a supine doe-*cum*-woman. Her necklaces and braceleted arm are just discernible to the right, while her rounded, apparently pregnant belly is shown covered with fur, and her legs are those of a deer. A polygynous marriage system would fit well with the interpretation of the Venus figurines given above, although it implies a very different position for women from the Great Goddess theory.

The Secret Art of Initiation

As with the Venus figurines, it is dangerous to attempt an all-embracing interpretation of cave art. It began before 25,000 B.P. and ceased around 10,000 years ago, a period during which there were marked changes in other aspects of life. Various schemes have attempted to fit particular artistic styles to particular periods, but as Paul Bahn says in the best recent survey of Ice Age art as a whole, "One must never forget that art is produced by individual artists, and the sporadic appearance of genius during this time span cannot be really fitted into any general scheme." On the other hand, it is certainly inappropriate to project a modern Western pace of change to the Upper Paleolithic. As Clive Gamble has pointed out, the Ice Age environment was tough: "There would have been no room for individual iconoclasts then. Lack of cooperation meant death." Contrary to popular belief, nonliterate societies are much more likely to do things in the same way, generation after generation, than literate societies. The reason is that the nonliterate must commit detailed cultural knowledge to memory rather than relying on a written record. It is entirely possible that some basic elements of meaning stayed fairly constant for over 15,000 years—because there was no reason to change them.

A source of light was crucial for viewing the cave art in the deeper caves. But instead of seeing these animals in the light of day, it was the animals' own deaths that allowed them to be seen, by providing tallow for lamps. In this interactive symbolism of life and rebirth, the pasty white tallow may have stood for semen (as it was to do in the form of phallic candles, dripped into the font in early Christian baptism, thousands of years later). The tallow/semen would have been carried down into the cave/womb where

(Fig. 5.14) Bison figure with humanoid hindquarters and long erect penis. Drawing from Marshack 1972.

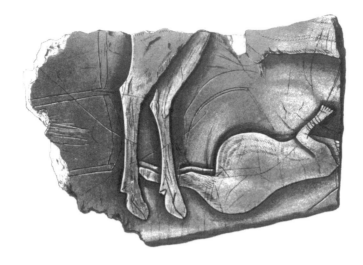

(Fig. 5.15)   Deer-woman, Laugerie-Basse. An engraved fragment of reindeer antler or, more probably, bison shoulder blade. Drawing courtesy of Alexander Marshack.

it would bring a new generation of animals to life. Such a symbolism could have extended beyond the caves to the idea of light itself, and therefore the sun as a male principle or deity and the earth as a female one. (This possibility is discussed in Chapter 6 in relation to farming societies.)

Although such general symbolism seems possible, the precise mythological and social details of the trips Ice Age people made to paint and see such images is probably beyond our ability to decipher. My guess is that the paintings were made by men (as I said, due to the absence of active female depictions in the caves) and were meant to be seen by boys during their rite of passage to manhood. This interpretation is not new, but it has a lot to commend it. It explains the pains taken to create the art, in that to serve as a men's initiation, it had to be concealed from women. This point has been well made by Joan Bamberger, whose fascinating observations on the "myth of matriarchy" helped bring many of the strands of thought in this chapter together.

Bamberger claims that myths of matriarchy—stories of prior rule by women—are relatively widespread in patriarchal societies, and that they function as social charters justifying male power. She cites two myths from Amazonia, both recorded in the early part of this century. The first, a myth of the Yamana-Yaghan people recorded by the Austrian anthropologist Father Martin Gusinde, concerns initiation in the *kina* or men's hut and holds that women were the first to perform *kina* rituals:

> At that time women had sole power; they gave orders to the men who were obedient, just as today the women obey the men. . . . All the work of the hut was performed by the men, with the women giving orders. They took care of the children, tended the fire, and cleaned the skins. That is the way it was always to be.

The women then invented the *kina* hut "and everything that goes on in it." While inside, they dressed themselves up as spirits, then came out to terrify the men, thereby keeping them in "fear and submission." This intimidation continued until Sun-man, who provided game for the *kina* hut spirits, saw two of the young girls bathing with their spirit makeup off. He realized that they were not spirits after all; Sun-man forced them to confess their deception and then exposed them to the men as frauds. The men stormed the *kina* hut, killing the women or transforming them into animals. "From that time on the men perform in the Kina hut; they do this in the same manner as the women before them."

The second myth that Bamberger relates comes from Gusinde's contemporary in Amazonia, E. Lucas Bridges, the son of an English missionary, who worked among the Selk'nam people. Selk'nam men had a hut, the *hain*, from which women were excluded. According to their myth of matriarchy, the women were knowledgeable in witchcraft:

They kept their own particular Lodge, which no man dared approach. The girls, as they neared womanhood, were instructed in the magic arts, learning how to bring sickness and even death on those who displeased them.

The men lived in abject fear and subjection. Certainly they had bows and arrows with which to supply the camp with meat, yet, they asked, what use were such weapons against witchcraft and sickness?

Eventually the "tyranny of the women" became unbearable, and the men massacred the adult initiated women. They had a respite while the younger generation of girl children were growing up; but the men's great worry was that the girls might get together as adults and things might repeat themselves:

> To forestall this, the men inaugurated a secret society of their own and banished forever the women's Lodge in which so many wicked plots had been hatched against them. No woman was allowed to come near the Hain on penalty of death.

The common thread in these myths, Bamberger notes, is that a claim of past misdemeanors is used against women as a justification for denying them initiation: "The utility of a myth that accounts for the origin of the men's lodge, separating men from women in action and in space, is easily demonstrated. As part of a cultural code distinguishing men from women in moral terms, the myth incorporated values that permit males a higher authority in social and political life." At puberty boys are physically separated from their mothers, so as to be taught esoteric lore. At the end of their liminal initiation period, they are introduced ceremonially into the society of adult men. The girls, on the other hand, are inculcated with lifelong prohibitions and restrictions on their behavior. They are threatened with punishments for transgressing, punishments that are actually translated into action among the Kayapo of central Brazil, where the men's house is the scene of the ritualized gang rape of young girls.

On the face of it, these Amazonian myths of matriarchy are very different from the Victorian ones that still have currency in the West today. But Bamberger concludes:

> The elevation of woman to deity on the one hand, and the downgrading of her to child or chattel on the other, produce the same result. Such visions will not bring her any closer to attaining male socioeconomic and political status . . . the myth of matriarchy is but a tool used to keep woman bound to her place. To free her, we need to destroy the myth.

The myths she discusses may have relevance for our understanding of both Venus figurines and cave art. The Venus figurines seem unconvincing as male erotica, yet the society that produced them does not look particularly matriarchal. Perhaps, like the Yamana-Yaghan and Selk'nam, Upper Paleolithic communities had their own "myth of matriarchy," symbolized by the ancestral forms of previously initiated women. The caves would have provided the perfect setting for the initiation of young boys into adult male society—their remoteness allowing them the potential of completely excluding a major section of the community.

S&M on the Steppe

We still have no firm idea how gender was constituted (or "performed," to use Judith Butler's term) in Ice Age Europe. Burials are rare exceptions, and it is impossible to deduce gendered clothing codes from them, beyond the fact that both sexes seem to have been

(Fig. 5.16) Woman with breast straps.
Figurine No. 83-2 from Kostienki.
Drawing by George Taylor after
Delporte 1993.

(Fig. 5.17)   Bound woman. Kostienki,
broken figurine No. 87. Photograph:
Paul Bahn.

adorned with beads, pendants, and other decorations. Only on occasion do the Venus figurines show traces of clothing. The parka worn by the Bouret figure from Siberia is of potentially unisex design, but there is evidence for more sex-specific clothing in the Venus figurines from the southern Russia site of Kostienki.

One of the Kostienki statuettes seems to be wearing some strapping that falls in a *V* from her neck to converge at the top of the cleavage between her full breasts. From this point, two further straps run over the tops of her breasts, then disappear under her arms. Since I have not seen a published rear view of this figurine, I do not know where the straps go around at the back, but the arms are being firmly held down behind, with shoulders back, so that the breasts are pushed forward. That this strapping was in some sense gendered clothing can be deduced from the way the bands accentuate the breasts, an effect that would probably be lost on a male torso.

A second, broken Kostienki figurine represents a vulva, upper thighs, and part of a rounded abdomen, with hands tied together at the wrists resting on it. In both figurines the strapwork or belts have a sort of feathering incision, a convention typically reserved to depict hair (as in the first figurine) or fur (as in many examples, like the doe-woman). It would thus seem most likely that these are bands of fur.

Given the tundra climate at this time, these clothing items can hardly be considered functional in any insulating sense. Nor are they decorous—in our terms, at least—as both breasts and vulva are exposed. Indeed, in common with a standard convention of erotic or sexual dressing, the fur strapping, which fails to be either functional or demure, draws attention to the sexual aspects of the body. The physical poses, and the tied wrists of the second figure, indicate a submissiveness and an inability to resist. Is some form of sexual bondage being played out? Are these representations of women about to be initiated? Are they captives from a raiding expedition?

My necessarily subjective interpretation of these sculptures is that they are explicitly sexual, sharing themes of objectification and possession that I feel are inherent in all the so-called Venus figurines. I also think that these objects were not fantasies without reality. Despite the "unreal" facelessness of the first figurine, the strapwork gives the sense of being modeled after a familiar reality. Similarly, with the second figure, I would submit that a sculptor who can depict hands tied together has a pretty good notion of how hands actually are tied together.

Although much of the Ice Age Eurasian material remains ambiguous, the existence of a vigorous sexual culture is not in any doubt. The overall trend of my interpretation has been to suggest that there were gender differences in both space and activity, with the caves in particular constituting a reserved space for one section of society to the exclusion of another (probably the exclusion of women by men). Such an interpretation begs the complex question, which I first broached in relation to the Hua, of what constitutes a "man" or a "woman" in any particular society. Around 10,000 years ago, the ice age cultural system—its cave art, figurines, and so on—was suddenly abandoned as the ice sheets receded and the climate, within the space of a few centuries, became dramatically warmer.

Chapter 6

The Milk of
the Vulture Goddess

*"There is no finer investment for any community
than putting milk into babies."*

WINSTON CHURCHILL

The colonization of the globe by modern humans was not just a migration, it was a multiplication. As people adapted environments to themselves and crossed continents, they met some dangers, but they mostly found animals that were fatally untutored in the ways of the culture-using, weapon-making, meat-eating, upright-walking ape. The biggest animals vanished from three continents: mammoths from Europe, giant marsupials from Australia, and mastodons from America. Human population rose, and in at least five separate regions of the world, farming was invented, involving the domestication of plants and animals and the creation of the cultivated in opposition to the wild. The effects of settling down to invest in the land were revolutionary, both from a social and an ecological point of view. I argue that while hunter-gatherer sex had been modeled on an idea of shar-

ing and complementarity, early agriculturalist sex was voyeuristic, repressive, homophobic, and focused on reproduction. Afraid of the
wild, farmers set out to destroy it.

Dances with Trees

As the temperature rose and the Ice Age came to an end, tundra
metamorphosed into woodland. In Britain the climate reached a
peak temperature higher than today's, and for a short time lime
trees grew in southern Scotland. Landscapes sprang into abundant
life. The communities of postglacial Europe are collectively known
as Mesolithic, literally "Middle Stone Age." Their stone technology—small, elegant points that were used to tip arrows—indicates
that their economic life had a broad basis. The unfolding wood-
lands provided rich hunting grounds. Human population rose
along with these enriched resources. People often returned to earlier dwelling places in the seasonal round, places that had different
functions.

Star Carr in Yorkshire, on the North Sea coast of England, is
one of the most famous Mesolithic camps and was probably a summer hunting camp. On the basis of a very careful analysis of the animal materials preserved at various places in the area, Pete Rowley-
Conwy has reconstructed the people's seasonal movements. Star Carr
was probably just one location among several. Rowley-Conwy postulates that an entire community moved from Barry's Island, the winter
base camp, to a summer base camp by the sea, from which hunting
parties would take off at times back inland to Star Carr. These
Mesolithic people also used a number of smaller sites in the hills, but
how and when is not fully clear.

The reconstruction (Figure 6.1) shows what a Mesolithic winter
base camp, built on an insulating brushwood platform, could have
looked like. The inspiration for this painting comes from the excavations at Star Carr, which, before the work by Rowley-Conwy and
others, had been thought a winter rather than a summer camp. The
picture is also based on practices of modern hunter-gatherers in simi-

(Fig. 6.1) A Mesolithic hunting camp. Reconstruction painting: the author.

lar environments: the shape of the fish-drying racks is copied from
the North American Copper Indians. Indeed, much of Mesolithic archaeology has grown out of careful observations of living hunter-
gatherer peoples.

Studying indigenous lifeways can help archaeologists working
on the Mesolithic, as well as other periods, know what to look for in
the archaeological record. One study of the Inuit of Alaska has
shown that they have highly complex seasonal movements and specialized sites. In addition to their base camps, hunting camps, and
kill-and-butcher sites, they also have what archaeologist Lewis Binford has recognized as "lovers' camps"—places where new couples
can get away from it all to cement the bonds of their relationship in
peace and quiet. So far, lovers' camps have not been recognized for
the European Mesolithic. But other parallels with present-day indigenous lifeways can be seen.

For the hunters, Mesolithic Europe was a time of plenty. This
abundance is reflected in their art, in the symbolism of intertwining
male and female. In a burial at Skateholm in Sweden, a male and

(Fig. 6.2) The Addaura scene. Rock engraving, Sicily. Drawing by George Taylor after Sandars 1968: plate 84.

female skeleton are apparently cuddling up together in death. In a rock engraving from Addaura, Sicily, two young men are rolling over each other, their erections perhaps indicating some homosexual interest, while around them men and women dance. At Lepenski Vir, in the Iron Gates Gorge of the Lower Danube, the sculptural art associates fish and humans in a series of complex androgynous representations (Figure 6.3) that are impossible to identify as male or female. Although many researchers regard the upright phallic shape at the base of some of the torsos as penises, they are longitudinally grooved, so that they also look vulvar. This ambiguity seems deliberate, playing on the underlying anatomical similarities between women and men.

The sculptures' fishlike faces support such an interpretation. Lepenski Vir was a semipermanent camp on the banks of what was then one of the richest fishing rivers in Europe. The Lepenski Vir people depended for their livelihood on the seasonal breeding movements of fish, and surviving fishbones leave no doubt as to the importance of fish like salmon in their diet. They must have been struck by the salmon's sexual anatomy: salmon heads are clearly male and female, but their genital openings are identical. The androgynous sculptures play on this ambiguity, suggesting a corresponding similarity in humans. Perhaps the Lepenski Vir people mythologized humans as having once been salmon.

(Fig. 6.3) Fish-woman-man sculpture: Lepenski Vir.
Photograph courtesy of John Chapman.

Mesolithic communities differ dramatically from those of the preceding Ice Age in social structure. Obvious signs of gender inequality are fewer, and few durable elements of sexual culture survive. During the glacial period, when survival depended on big-game hunting, the nutritional contribution from gathering may have been relatively small. Women could not hunt big game while they were pregnant, and they may have had to be relatively fat to bring a child to term under the extreme conditions. Men would have been able to take advantage of this vulnerability, as they have been on many occasions throughout prehistory and history.

When the ice melted, however, women gained the potential to be increasingly autonomous at a basic nutritional level. In principle, they could simply walk away. Although men could use violence or the threat of violence as coercion against them, they had lost their basic economic lever—which may be reflected in the relative egalitarianism of the Mesolithic period. Such egalitarianism, if it existed, did not last. The growing population of the Near East introduced yet another economic factor into the equation that was eventually to reforge women's economic inequality in bonds so durable that they persist into the present day: farming, and its concomitant rules of production and property.

Logging the Wildwood

Human beings, far from being cast out of the garden, turned themselves out of Eden. In the space of only a few thousand years, the hunter-gatherer way of life, based on an intimate knowledge of the bounty of nature, has almost vanished from the earth. Although it is often said that "a thousand years ago, a squirrel could cross England from the Severn through the Midlands to the Wash without setting foot on the ground," that forest represented a regrowth. The original great greenwood that spread over Europe at the end of the last ice age had long ago been cut down. Indeed, there have been many cycles of forest clearance and regeneration since the glaciers receded— but mainly of clearance.

New evidence from ancient pollen preserved in peat bogs and waterlogged tree stumps shows that the earliest systematic clearance of the forests took place in Britain between 4000 and 3500 B.C., shortly after the start of what is termed the Neolithic period. While some have spoken of an "Amazon-style felling of ancient oaks," others believe the process of clearing the forests was more gradual and patchy. A second bout of clearance, between 2000 B.C. and A.D. 300, using newly developed metal tools, is estimated to have removed half the entire woodland cover in southern Britain. In mainland Europe the clearances began much earlier—around 6000 B.C. in the Balkans. Why would people who had lived so long among trees — the Mesolithic communities, whose detailed knowledge of the natural world provided them with such a good living—suddenly start removing the pivotal element in their ecosystem, the trees? Why would they turn to the plow and the ox team?

Farming involves the reproductive control of plants and animals by humans for their own purposes. It requires that stud animals and seed corn be managed and that distribution of the food produced be controlled. Communities that farmed had to settle down in villages in order to protect the fields that they had cleared and fenced. Shifting to a sedentary life changes the rules of human reproduction by reducing birth spacing, as we will see. Moreover, with farming, the human relationship with the environment shifts from one of trust to one of exploitation. At the same time, the earth itself is made symbolically female. "Mother Earth" becomes the focus of plowing, crop sowing, and the burial of the dead—a creature who can be made to bear fruit and receive, at the proper time, her human children back into her womb.

The Old Testament, which was written by farmers, describes a world in which men are in control of society, where violence is commonplace, where God is male, and where the earth is female. Adam and Eve were expelled from the garden where they had lived upon the fruit of the trees. In punishment they were to cultivate ground that had been cursed by God. Their sons, Cain and Abel, personify the two principal elements of farming, animal husbandry and the cultivation of crops: "Abel was a keeper of sheep, but Cain was a tiller of the ground." Cain, having murdered Abel, is told in turn by God that he is "cursed from the earth, which hath opened her mouth to receive thy brother's blood from thy hand."

The Great Goddess

A strange modern belief, built up particularly around the work of Marija Gimbutas, holds that the first farmers lived in an idyllic, goddess-worshipping *pastorale*. (For Gimbutas's theories on the Upper Paleolithic, see Chapter 5.) Female figurines have been found in great numbers during excavations of early Neolithic farming villages, though formed of clay rather than carved out of stone or ivory. "In art and mythical imagery," Gimbutas wrote, "it is not possible to draw a line between the two eras, Paleolithic and Neolithic." People in both periods worshipped a supreme female deity, the "Goddess Creatrix." But Gimbutas considered the farming communities to be more civilized than their hunter-gatherer forebears'. They were settled and, she argued, they were settled around women. Men married into households where descent and inheritance passed through the female line—a culture that was "matrifocal and probably matrilinear, agricultural and sedentary, egalitarian and peaceful."

One of Gimbutas's followers, meteorologist-turned-ancient-mysteries-researcher George Terence Meaden (whose work she endorsed) has claimed that the farming cultures of Britain—like those who built Stonehenge—were a "classless, balanced society" that enjoyed "the serenity of the Age of Goddess." This notion has a wide appeal and has found a place as "fact" in the writings of feminist sociologists and New Age mystics alike. This chapter shows why they are misguided. I believe that the first farmers in Europe had a fundamentally exploitative attitude toward everything, including sex—being violent, unbalanced people, whose idea of a good time was felling trees, erecting great stone phalluses, and sanctifying them with sacrificial victims, often women and children.

The Genesis story was probably first written down around 900 B.C., almost 3,000 years ago, but farming originated much earlier, at the end of the last ice age. Its emergence may have been connected to the changes in environment that were then taking place. Around 12,000 years ago the glaciers were making their final retreat. While meltwater raised sea levels and caused coastal flooding in some areas, in other places the removal of the great weight of ice caused the land to spring back up, so that new coasts appeared. The Bering land bridge was created, forming a corridor between ice and sea over which people could move out of eastern Siberia and into North America. These hunters subsequently ate their way south through herds of mastodon.

In the meantime the sea level rose in the Levant, at the eastern edge of the Mediterranean Sea. The hunter-gatherer communities of this region had knowledge of at least 250 useful species of wild plant, which they gathered as they carefully moved around the landscape according to the season. They hunted gazelle and fished and lived well. In fact, at the time when the sea level rose, their population was increasing. Suddenly their rich maritime resources were gone, lost to the rising waters. Communities were hard pressed, and it is therefore not surprising that they turned to an alternative mode of food production: cultivating the land.

One of the earliest farming villages was Jericho, which was

built in the earthquake zone of the Jordan valley. Jericho was occupied from around 8500 B.C. to 73 B.C., when Herod relocated what was by then a city. So frequently renewed were Jericho's defensive walls over the millennia that they became the subject of biblical legend. The Jericho people came to depend on about a dozen plants, cultivating wheat and barley in the adjacent floodplain. Wild wheat and barley had never grown naturally on the plain, since the seasonal flooding rotted any seed. But humans could manage the fertile margin, planting and harvesting it and holding back grain for the next season's planting. The implications of this system were profound.

The transition to farming was a one-way street for humans and plants alike. Humans quickly lost the detailed knowledge of wild plant foods that had been cumulatively built up over the preceding tens if not hundreds of thousands of years. In turn, the few plants they harvested rapidly became dependent on humans for their propagation. When an ear of wild barley is ripe, a shake of the stem will dislodge the grains, which fall to the ground to germinate the following year. On a lake edge the grains that fall when the plant is cut rot. Only those with a slightly tougher "rachis" connecting them to the stem remained for the people of Jericho to gather in and thresh, keeping some back as seed corn. Grown from this reserve, the next season's crop stayed on the ear better, and the same process of selection was again made at harvest time. At every stage of human processing some grain was lost, and on average, it was the smaller grains that were lost. Soon barley and wheat became domesticated. Their grains had grown larger and did not fall easily unless threshed.

Just as the reproduction of plants became dependent on human society, so society came to depend on the plants. By investing time and effort in cultivating the land, and by protecting their investment from wild animals and other human groups, people at Jericho and other locations in the Near East became tied to one place and developed new ideas about ownership. People began to erect fences and claim the land within as their own. (The idea of property began, according to nineteenth-century political thinker Pierre-Joseph Proudhon, when they found someone stupid enough to believe them.)

Although prehistoric hunter-gatherers had often stored food and invested effort in managing the natural returns of the environment, agriculture put these activities on a qualitatively new plane. The seed grain was crucial to individual survival, and it had to be stored and protected. Whoever controlled it had political power of a sort not seen before in human history.

The Domestic Round

Australian archaeologist and prehistorian V. Gordon Childe thought that there had been three great revolutions in human affairs: the Farming or "Neolithic" Revolution, the Urban Revolution, and the Industrial Revolution. Each was accompanied by population increase, political centralization, and an extension of human control over the environment. The term *Neolithic* means "New Stone Age" and was adopted because the stone-tool technology of the new farming cultures was different from what had gone before. Instead of being simply chipped, tools were now also ground, so as to produce a smooth, rounded surface. Other kinds of grinding became essential in early farming communities too, as grain had to be ground into flour. Theya Molleson of the Natural History Museum in London has conducted studies of 162 Neolithic skeletons dating to between 11,500 and 7,500 years ago from the farming village of Abu Hureyra in modern Syria. She believes that women had ground the grain, on their knees, leaning forward over a "saddle quern"—a flat slab that was slowly worn into a concave shape as a flat grindstone was moved back and forth across it. Her conclusion is based on the marked repetitive strain injuries that damaged the vertebrae in female skeletons and caused severe osteoarthritis of the toes, curvature of the thigh, and "housemaid's knee"—the growth of bony extensions on the kneecaps.

Any economic upheaval has the potential to alter gender relations, but it is hard to predict how. When the prehistoric Caddoan Mound Builders of Texas switched from hunting and gathering to farming, the sexual dimorphism in height between men and women was markedly reduced. Women's size increased dramatically, while men's increased only slightly. Farming may have brought nutritional improvements from which women benefited disproportionately. When farming was adopted in the Mississippi valley, the reverse happened: everyone got smaller, but the women much more so; sexual dimorphism thus became more marked.

Molleson's studies were enabled by the Neolithic fashion for burying the dead. Their treatment of the dead suggests that human societies underwent a marked shift in religious ideas. In political terms, burying the dead in the ground can reflect not only a concern with lineage—the sequence of human generations and the associated property inheritance—but a general territorial claim by the entire society. One's ancestors invested their labor in tilling the earth, and when they died, they were physically incorporated back into it. The position of the dead in Neolithic graves is often contracted, with the knees up and arms tucked in, in the fetal position. Arranging the corpse in this way required special treatment, usually involving binding the limbs into position. It is impossible not to reach the general conclusion that the earth itself was now considered as a sort of womb, with the buried body awaiting rebirth.

The farming cycle itself involved a cycle of rebirth through the opening of the earth, the planting of seed, and its seasonal germination; after harvesting the corn in its prime, the residue—the seed—is kept aside for the next year. At Jericho new faces were plastered onto skulls using the fertile floodplain mud, and cowrie shells to represent the eyes. Cowries are a near-universal "natural symbol" for female genitalia and suggest the female power of birth required for rebirth. But at Jericho the skulls also remind us of the creation of Adam in the Book of Genesis, sculpted from mud by a patriarchal God.

Women became ever more involved in birth in the Neolithic. The simple fact of staying in one place reduces the spacings between births. The problem of accumulating sufficient body fat was essentially eliminated with the advent of a generally reliable, cultivated food supply. Other factors probably contributed to more frequent childbirths too. The loss of detailed hunter-gatherer plant knowledge may have meant that the contraceptive uses of many plants were forgotten. More significantly, the routines of corn grinding, hoeing, and harvesting are less compatible with continuous breast-feeding than are hunter-gatherer lifeways. Among hunter-gatherers, breast-feeding on demand and late weaning are the norm, with all their contraceptive benefits. (See Chapter 3.) The most important element in such contraception is not the amount of milk the child takes but the frequency of feeding. A three-year-old may drink as much or more milk as a three-month-old, but a woman's chances of conceiving while nursing a three-year-old are much higher because the frequency of the nursing sessions is reduced to a point where prolactin levels in her body are too low to inhibit ovulation.

The backbreaking work of grain processing, and the sharply defined and intensive work periods demanded by the agricultural year, particularly at harvest time, must have encouraged Neolithic women to schedule breast-feeding at intervals rather than do it nearly continuously. They thus would have run the risk of their prolactin levels dropping while their infant was still young. Although we have no direct evidence for this precise mechanism, population did rise, and by 5500 B.C. there is clear evidence of deliberate weaning. It was for this purpose that fired pottery seems to have been invented. According to Theya Molleson's analyses of tooth wear in Neolithic infants, fired pottery allowed grain to be boiled into porridge gruel that could be used as a weaning food.

It is hard not to conclude that the position of women deteriorated in the Neolithic period. Yet from burials in the earliest periods there is no particular evidence that men were conspicuously wealthier. Further, many of the key innovations, such as the domestication of plants and the making of pottery, were most closely associated with women. The broad gender division of labor of the old hunter-gatherer days seems to have been retained, as it continues into the present. Margaret Ehrenberg cites a study of 104 modern horticultural societies—those that raise crops on small plots without using plows or heavy machinery—that found that women were solely responsible for cultivation in 50 percent of cases, as opposed to only 17 percent where men were solely responsible. Ehrenberg notes that this gender division of labor continues in such societies despite "decades or even centuries of contact with societies whose ideology would encourage men to take on greater roles in production." Men tend to get involved in farming at the point where animals become important, initially for meat, but later and more significantly, for pulling loads — enabling heavy plowing and bulk transport.

There are many different ways of farming. The "package" of techniques and technologies varies from place to place, as do the environment and the people who live in it. Around 8500 B.C., two thousand years after the first systematic cultivation of plants, men who had previously hunted gazelles began to pen animals, notably sheep, close to their villages. In this way sheep, and later goats and cows, became domesticated. The fattest and best of the wild population were selected, and those with unpleasant tempers were sorted out. The animals that remained became larger and more docile and provided a year-round source of meat for the villagers, as well as manure that could be put back on the land to help retain its fertility.

There is much debate among archaeologists about how "revolutionary" Neolithic farming actually was. My view is that the significance of the change can hardly be overestimated. At different times within the last 10,000 to 12,000 years, the switch to farming seems to have occurred independently, in five or six different parts of the world, including China, India, and the Americas. In the Americas the hunters who helped wipe out the mastodons eventually settled down in places such as coastal Peru and began to cultivate maize by around 5,000 years ago. In each region farming led to a second revolution: the development of cities, dense populations, craft specialization, political hierarchy, and complex recording and accounting systems, including calendrics, mathematics, and writing. The reason for the switch to farming, however, was not necessarily the same in each region. That is to say, people may have chosen or been forced into deliberate cultivation for a number of reasons. Still, in every case it was necessarily a one-way process, characterized by loss of hunter-gatherer knowledge and a rising population to support. Nevertheless, a preceding steady increase in global population probably played some part. By 10,000 years ago, humans had reached most of the places in the world where they live today. Under pressure, they could no longer easily move to a better area, since the next place was already occupied. Once people made the switch to farming and their populations rose above the carrying capacity of their cultivated territory, there was a pressure to expand by displacing others.

It was by such overspill colonization that farming was brought to Europe, where its impact on existing societies was dramatic, fundamentally altering cultural attitudes toward sex and reproduction. The retreat of the ice from Europe had prompted many changes in human life, but the switch to farming had not been one of them. The Mesolithic communities that used sites like Star Carr and Lepenski Vir did experience a general rise in population, consistent with the fact that the congenially warm post–ice age environment was created very rapidly and had originally been very thinly populated. Although it is hard to get good estimates, Mesolithic population growth may have been beginning to level out just when farming was introduced. By the time farming became fully established, the population of the Continent had probably increased fivefold.

The initial movement of farming people into Europe, around 6000 B.C., was from modern Turkey into the Balkans. Farming then spread around the coasts and islands of the Mediterranean. Sometimes migrants introduced it, but in other places local Mesolithic populations adopted elements of the agricultural repertoire—pottery, or domesticated animals, or cultivatable plants, or some mixture of these—that were already available. This mixture of colonization and adoption was reprised in central and western Europe more than a thousand years later, beginning around 4500 B.C., and reached Britain around 3800 B.C. The earliest Neolithic societies in the Balkans—and in the Mediterranean—produced large numbers of clay figurines in the shape of human females. These figurines are Gimbutas's principal evidence for the existence of a goddess-centered farming religion, built on old roots but refreshed by contact with Anatolia. Much of her theory of a matrifocal, goddess-worshipping, agricultural society rests on the interpretation of these figures and on evidence from one of the most famous of the Anatolian farming villages—Çatal Hüyük, on the Konya Plain of modern Turkey.

Çatal Hüyük

During the 1960s archaeologist James Mellaart excavated fourteen buildings in a settlement of almost urban proportions at Çatal Hüyük, dating to between 6200 and 5500 B.C. The houses were originally entered from above, by ladders. Their internal layout, sculptures, and wall paintings are well preserved, and the burials were under the floors. Mellaart's publication of the primary evidence has been erratic; current work by Ian Hodder of Cambridge University may shed light on some of the mysteries. Gimbutas reads the symbolism in the houses as relating to worship of the Great Mother Goddess, personified for her by a clay idol depicting a "majestic enthroned Goddess, flanked by felines . . . giving birth to the child who emerges from between her legs." But it is hard to make the child out clearly—it may be there, but then again it may not; the position of the woman's knees suggests that she is sitting rather than squatting. It is clearly not a familiar depiction of childbirth. It may well be, as Gimbutas claims, an image of a deity giving birth, but that does not make it the principal or supreme deity for the whole of Old Europe.

Some of the Çatal Hüyük houses have great sculpted horned bull's heads sticking out from their inner walls. Although they are rather virile-looking, Gimbutas claims that they too are symbolic of the goddess. She compares the curved configuration of the paired horns on either side of the muzzle with the layout of the uterus, fallopian tubes, and ovaries in the human female. This comparison is hard to take seriously. It is of course possible that the Çatal Hüyük people had a fair conception of internal anatomy. Human viscera were probably well known, as indicated by the evidence for violence in the Neolithic (which, incidentally, runs counter to Gimbutas's claims for a peace-loving matriarchal society). The phenomenon of *Mittelschmerz* (ovulation pain; see Chapter 4, on menstrual synchrony) might have led Neolithic people to understand the reproductive significance of the ovaries. But a formal comparison between a highly schematic modern medical diagram of the female reproductive tract and the equally stylized prehistoric depiction of a bull's head

(Fig. 6.4) The "Great
Goddess." Drawing by
George Taylor after
Gimbutas 1989.

and horns is unconvincing. Nevertheless, Mellaart too has claimed—
without proper photographic documentation—that mural paintings
within the houses depict women giving birth to both human children
and horned bulls. We know that cattle were of major importance in
the settlement's farming economy.

The most difficult evidence from Çatal Hüyük for the Gimbutas
theory is the so-called breasts—paired mounds of clay that are stuck to
the inner walls of the houses. Female figurines from Çatal Hüyük have
breasts with the nipples prodded in—little dents rather than protru-
sions—which is probably of little significance beyond the fact that
dented nipples were easier to make in miniature than raised nipples.
But the mounds on the wall have nipples made of vulture beaks.
Griffon vultures—the species in question—also seem to appear in wall
paintings from the site (although again, these are not yet convincingly
published). In the light of what has been said already about weaning,
perhaps these sculptures represent the moment of independence from
the mother, when the child must turn away and, like the vulture, pick
at meat. Perhaps they symbolize a connection between the baby, nega-
tively envisaged as parasitic on its mother's flesh, and the vulture,
thought of as a parasite of corpses. Certainly in some societies weaning
is accomplished through negative conditioning, sometimes by coating
the nipples with lemon juice or another bitter substance. The attach-

(Fig. 6.5)   Temple of the Vulture Goddess, Çatal Hüyük. A molded breast form juts from
the left-hand wall above the bull's head; the far wall carries images of the "Vulture Goddess."
Reconstruction painting by Alan Sorrell, reproduced courtesy of *Illustrated London News*.

ment of vulture beaks to the nipple is not known, however. But then
the mounded bumps on the wall may not have been meant as breasts at
all. Not all of them are paired, and some occur one above the other.
Not all have vulture beaks—some have foxes' teeth, some have wild-
boar tusks, and one has a weasel skull.

Women of Clay

Ian Hodder has been particularly interested in the symbolism at
Çatal Hüyük. He does not necessarily believe that it supports the
"Great Mother Goddess" theories, but he does see evidence of a general tension between the wild and the domestic, ideas that only really
took form when humans stopped living with nature and began,
through farming, to oppose themselves to it. For my part, I do not see
much in Çatal Hüyük that strongly supports the existence of a peaceful matriarchal religion. The things on the walls are creepy and sug-

gest a community ill at ease with the world. I would rather have one of British artist Damien Hirst's sheep pickled in formaldehyde in my living room than protruding vulture-beaked breasts; it would be less disturbing. The Çatal Hüyük evidence hints at a society whose attitudes toward children were far more complex and perhaps more systematically exploitative than those of the preceding Paleolithic and Mesolithic periods. This is borne out to some degree by other evidence from Neolithic Europe.

The central problem with Gimbutas's Mother Goddess theory for the European Neolithic is that, just as with the ice age Venuses, very few of the clay figurines are distinctively *mothers*. Generally speaking, the depiction of motherhood has presented no great problem in art. From the Virgin Mary to the Indian goddess Hariti, the standard imagery is of a child suckling (see Figure 8.8). Alternatively, an artist may show a child sitting on its mother's knee, being born, or dangling on the end of the umbilical cord—a popular depiction in prehistoric rock paintings, from Aboriginal Australia to South Africa. Strangely, among the several hundred known Neolithic figurines, there is only one image of a mother breast-feeding—the so-called Madonna from Gradac, from a 5000 B.C. site in the valley of the Morava River in former Yugoslavia. Sculptures of childbirth are also extremely rare.

Possibly sensing this difficulty, Gimbutas relied on a wide variety of other, possibly supporting indications for motherhood, such as symbolization of the length of pregnancy. A small female figurine from the temple site of Hağar Qim in Malta, dating to the fourth millennium B.C., has nine deep-incised lines across her back. Gimbutas describes the figurine in the following terms: "With upraised legs and hand at swollen vulva, this figurine appears ready to give birth. Do the nine lines across her back represent the nine months of gestation?" This speculation rests on the assumption that the woman is depicted as pregnant, which seems arguable, and on the symbolism of nine. But in fact no natural symbolism of nine attaches to pregnancy. The length of pregnancy may be nine months on our modern twelve-month calendar, but it is ten months by the lunar calendar, which was almost certainly the one used in the Neolithic period.

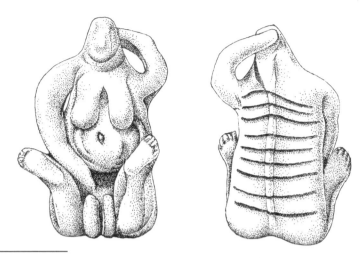

(Fig. 6.6)   Masturbating female, Hağar Qim, Malta, showing back and front. Drawing by George Taylor after Gimbutas 1989.

At the time of Hippocrates, the reckoning of full term was calculated as ten naturally observable lunar months from the last menstrual period. The lunar month is 29 days, 12 hours, 44 minutes, and 3 seconds long, but it is observed simply as 29 days: on this basis, 10 months are equal to 290 days or 41 weeks and 3 days. Modern calculations of gestation time vary and are based on variations of Naegele's rule that reckons the estimated date of delivery as nine calendar months plus seven days after the first day of the last menstrual period—that is, between 280 and 283 days, according to the length of the months included. Actual lengths of pregnancy vary: one study showed the average length of first pregnancy to be 288 days, and 283 days for subsequent ones. Different societies opt for different estimates: the French calculate the due date as 41 weeks from the time of last menstruation, while the British and Americans reckon 40 weeks.

In any case, the nine stripes on the back of the Hağar Qim woman are unlikely to symbolize full-term pregnancy. Judging from the figure's recumbent position, with one hand languidly reaching behind the head and the other reaching down to the top of the labia, she is more likely to be masturbating than giving birth. A recumbent position is a very bad one in which to give birth and was virtually unknown before the modern period, when it came to be imposed by male obstetricians who wanted to wrest active control of the process away from women.

But what was the purpose of the Hağar Qim figure? Was it educative, symbolic, or erotic? If the Neolithic figurines in general are not Mother Goddesses, then what are they? One clue may lie in the clay itself, the basic material of agricultural fertility. These figurines personify the earth as female. They do not have children because the earth does not bring forth children—it produces crops. Furthermore, the seed only germinates in the ground with water and sunlight. The clay for the figurines must be wetted to be worked, and then subjected to the heat of the kiln, the terrestrial version of the solar flame. Perhaps the figurines each contain a seed, sown in the clay.

Watchful Matriarchs

Female figurines are much less common outside the East European–Balkan and Aegean–Mediterranean areas, even though it was from eastern Europe that farming was first brought into northern and western Europe. The community that introduced farming is known to archaeologists as the LBK culture—the *Linearbandkeramik,* a German term that refers to their pottery, which is incised with curved and geometric lines reminiscent of field boundaries and row upon row of crops. The LBK people spread swiftly from the Hungarian plain and western Ukraine into what is now Germany, the Netherlands, and northeastern France between 5500 B.C. and 5000 B.C. Traces of LBK villages are found exclusively on light, sandy loess soils—the easiest to clear and cultivate but also the most rapidly exhausted. There is good evidence that clearings were used for a number of years, abandoned, and then returned to when some of their fertility had come back. The evidence includes overlapping patterns of postholes relating to successive villages, each comprising several distinctive longhouses.

The longhouses are among the most distinctive features of the LBK. Measuring around 20 feet wide and 50 to 100 feet long (with some shorter, and some at 150 feet), the longhouses were designed as permanent dwelling structures and were probably single-storied. Their ground plans show a consistent yet enigmatic division into three parts. The size of an LBK longhouse was probably related to the sort of family that lived in it, although parts of the house could have been used for stalling animals. A comparison of one-family housing in different societies today shows that matrilocal extended families tend to construct bigger houses than patrilocal families. One reason is that in societies where men marry into a community from the outside so that sisters stay together in a community with their various husbands, the women are more likely to share tasks under one roof. In societies where women marry into a new community, brothers tend to maintain their own separate households within the village. As Ehrenberg has pointed out, the LBK longhouses fall within the defined parameters of a typical matrilocal residence pattern. Some researchers have suggested, on the basis of a very limited modern survey, a correlation between monogamous marriage and rectangular houses and polygamous marriage and round houses, on which basis the LBK communities would have been monogamous. LBK monogamy is highly speculative, however, as no convincing connection has been established between marriage type and house shape.

The archaeological traces of the LBK culture reflect a frontier mentality. Like white settlers moving in wagon trains across the Old West, through the traditional hunting grounds of the Indian tribes, the lives of LBK settlers must have been hazardous. They moved much more slowly than did those on the Oregon Trail, taking around five hundred years to reach the Atlantic seaboard. We do not know whether they were aiming for the coast, or whether their advance was simply the result of a growing population that gradually spread farther west. But whatever the case, rising population was an essential component in their advance. Some archaeologists argue that the switch to farming in northern and western Europe was the result of the adoption of available techniques, domesticated animals, and crops by indigenous Mesolithic communities, but this can be only a part of the story—a part that occurred on the fringes of the main spread of intrusive colonizers.

That the LBK people were settlers in a strange land is clear from the uniform appearance of the LBK culture as it spread. The longhouses, the pottery, the mode of burial—crouched, fetal-type burials within villages, sometimes beneath the house floors—all speak of a conservative tradition. As with the North American pioneers, a rigidly ordered way of life may have bolstered the Neolithic incomers in their adversity. The preexisting Mesolithic communities were unlikely to have given up their forest environments willingly. Archaeologically speaking, the evidence for violent death in this period is quite extensive. Both "sides" were efficient killers. The Mesolithic development of ever more efficient arrowheads was answered by the Neolithic development of the barbed-and-tanged arrowhead, which had good penetration, caused extensive internal hemorrhaging, and stayed in the body if the shaft was pulled out. It may have been specifically designed for killing people and was certainly used to great effect to do just that, as two male skeletons from a Neolithic site in Spain show. One of the men seems to have been shot from below, as if he were hiding in a tree or standing on a fortification. The shot penetrated his abdomen and lodged in the inner face of one of the lumbar vertebrae; it was accurate and skillful and would have caused almost instantaneous death.

French obstetrician Michel Odent associates aggression principally with the way babies are born and how they are treated in the very first weeks of life. The most aggressive societies, he notes, tend to separate mother and baby at the moment of birth and withhold colostrum, the yellowish protein-rich, antibody-packed nutrient that the breasts produce for the first few days after birth. This separation not only contributes to higher mortality rates among the constitutionally less robust, it provides the ground conditions for a kind of primal anger in the infant. Withholding colostrum disrupts the subsequent flow of normal milk and makes nursing harder to establish. Such societies may place additional limits on the infant's access to the comfort and security of the breast, by "timing" feeds, isolating the infant in a cot at night, and weaning early.

The production of children must have occupied much of women's time, and Neolithic women probably had more of them than Paleolithic women. Although we do not have direct evidence for Neolithic birth spacing, comparisons between modern hunter-gatherer and sedentary communities suggest a birth spacing of around five years for the former and one to two years for the latter. One reason agricultural women had children more often, as previously mentioned, was the erosion of demand breast-feeding among many sedentary agricultural societies. The ready availability of weaning foods—like porridges, which could be cooked in the distinctive round-bottomed LBK pots—could have contributed to early weaning among the LBK. So could the demands of a heavier work schedule—modern hunter-gatherers, even those who have been pushed into marginal environments (as most of them have been) appear to work much less in order to stay alive and well than do farmers. It is also unlikely, at first, that the Neolithic settlers would have known much about the contraceptive effects of the plant species they encountered in their push north and west. They may even have deliberately encouraged population growth: in frontier situations it is often the side that physically expands fastest that succeeds. Finally, farmers may also value children for their labor in a more direct way than hunter-gatherers do: farming involves many simple and repetitive tasks, such as weeding, that can be delegated to the young. The Mesolithic economy of postglacial Europe was a thriving one, yet it gave way, mile by mile, ineluctably, to a farming economy.

The Roots of Homophobia

The idea that longhouses were the focus of extended matrilocal families is supported by evidence that the inner, domestic sphere was at the cultural heart of the earliest farming communities. It has been argued that the advent of permanent houses meant that sex became more private, allowing an intimacy between two people that had been denied in the open mobile communities of the hunter-gatherers. It seems to me, however, that the reverse is likely to have been the case. Among pastoral steppe dwellers today, a couple merely places a marker on the ground and retreats into the lush grass beyond it to ensure perfect privacy. But the big-family atmosphere of the longhouse, with a hostile forest beyond, must have provided the perfect structure for elders to monitor the reproductive lives of their sons and daughters.

The voyeuristic side of sex was probably encouraged by the close proximity of animals. Children's first ideas about sex must have come from observing stud animals, the behavior of bulls with their harems. Both at Çatal Hüyük and in the LBK villages, it seems most implausible that the culture regarded the bull as an embodiment of the "Great Mother Goddess," with fallopian-tube-shaped horns. More likely, the bull was considered an embodiment of quick and functional male sexuality with a succession of relatively passive females. This sort of sex education, coupled with the abject lack of privacy in the closely confined rooms of the Anatolian village and in the peep-through wattles that partitioned rooms in the European longhouses, must have done little to encourage the finer aspects of heterosexual lovemaking.

Longhouse society might even have been polygynous. The evidence for violent death among men may indicate that there was a skewed female-to-male ratio among the living, allowing wealthy stockbreeders to behave like their own stud animals.

Speculating further, conditions for homosexual liaisons were probably still more abject, while the lives of intersex individuals may have been brief. I believe that the Neolithic period saw the true birth of homophobia; the Old Testament, which is in part the manifesto of a rural farming society, is stiff with it. Domestic animals display homosexual behavior relatively often, but it is not "functional" in the eyes of the stockman; if the whole herd did it, the system would collapse. Therefore, as eagerly as the fertilizing activities of the stud bull are encouraged, alternative, "dysfunctional" behavior is not. There is evidence that the birthrate of intersex animals goes up under domestication; such animals were probably not allowed to live long and may have been taboo as food, due to worries about contagion. Human children born with similar ambiguities might well have been treated the same way.

The new permanence of houses and villages heralded the establishment of a number of binary oppositions, between wild and domestic, inside and outside, male and female, that took meaning from each other. These binaries were conceived of as necessary opposites. The products of nature were domesticated and brought inside, while the products of culture were spread outward, into the wild. The boundary was always clearly marked, by a door or a fence. Ownership was stressed to a far greater degree than in previous societies. The very decoration of the pottery betrays an obsession with demarcation. The definition of the sexes and of sexual activity was no exception to this pattern and was soon symbolized in an explosion of massive anthropomorphic landscape monuments.

Chapter 7

The Grave of
the Golden Penis

The childhood shows the man,
As morning shows the day.

JOHN MILTON,
PARADISE REGAINED

I do not believe that women built Stonehenge. Perhaps they had a hand in it, and a woman was certainly sacrificed in one of its foundation ditches, but like guns and rockets, it is essentially a male monument. I believe that the making of Stonehenge was ordered by a man and that he was unhappy. When the midsummer sun rises over the heel stone and penetrates the center of the circle with a shaft of light, it is a sign that the sun is at the height of its powers. It can be seen as a sexual symbol—the sun god firing his semen into the hollow space. But it can also be seen as the fulfillment of a prediction, a massive overstatement of the power of human calculation and, by extension, power over the forces of nature.

In this chapter I argue that the familiar landscape of prehistoric

Britain, the great standing stones and earth mounds, was not only created as a stage for a cosmic sexual symbolism but is a huge exercise in psychological compensation for the loss of control, and attendant rage at the world, that Stone Age boys were made to feel when they were first weaned. I believe that males, in particular, were singled out for a harsh initiation into life by an increasingly populous and belligerent society that required warriors.

Children of War

A grim insight into the realities of early farming life comes from the excavation of a mass grave on the edge of an LBK village near Talheim in southwestern Germany. Thirty-four contorted skeletons were found, thrown into a single pit. The bone traumas of most are consistent with killing by stone axes and cudgels. But two of the individuals were shot dead with arrows. The lack of any characteristic "parrying fractures" — injuries sustained while defending oneself — suggests, with the rest of the evidence, a surprise attack followed by summary executions. The corpses were stripped of their belongings, then dumped. Some believe that the Talheim pit contains virtually the entire population of the LBK village. The dead comprised seven children in the one-to-six-year age range, nine juveniles, and eighteen adults. As far as sex and age can be determined, there were nine adult men, three of whom were over fifty years old, and one who was between sixty and seventy, and seven women, six of them of childbearing age. There are two interesting omissions in the group: babies less than a year old (completely absent) and older women (only one).

The absence of young infants in the Talheim mass grave suggests to Konrad Spindler (the archaeologist who heads the Iceman team) that the reason for the massacre was "child abduction, practised by some primitive people to add new blood to their own population." That is, the village was exterminated to capture the children. "Certain age limits were set in order to facilitate the linguistic and cultural integration of these young children into their new community." Moreover, "there was no cannibalism," Spindler notes, "as has

(Fig. 7.1) Goat suckling human infant. After Brüning 1908, Fig. 13; reproduced courtesy of the Wellcome Institute Library, London.

not infrequently been observed at other Neolithic sites. The Talheim bodies lack the tell-tale cutting and slaughtering marks on their bones." The fact that the bodies were in fact buried—hygienically disposed of—suggests that the attackers wished to take possession of the entire village, "complete with houses, livestock, fields and stores." If the massacred group was indeed the entire population of the village, then the impression is that it was a patrilocal extended family, with a group of senior men and their younger wives but no women "elders." Further analysis, such as genetic testing of the bones, may throw more light on this.

Spindler's hypothesis suggests a grisly scenario in which these orphaned children grew up as the helpmates of their parents' murderers, unwittingly toiling close to the unmarked mass grave. In Spindler's scenario, some of the young infant survivors from the Talheim massacre might have been too young for full weaning. Several solutions for keeping young infants alive after the death of their mother suggest themselves. First, the infants could have been raised on cereal gruels alone; their mortality on such a diet at such an age would have been high, however, as it would have been nutritionally inadequate and would have given them no antibody protection. Second, the infants could have been wet-nursed; this diet would have provided good nutrition and some antibody protection, but it would have depended on the availability of women to do the job—women whose own babies had died. The third option would have been to suckle the infants directly onto a domestic animal, such as a goat. This third option, bizarre as it at first seems, was standard practice in foundling hospitals in Renaissance and early modern Europe. Animal nursing provides some level of nutrition, although there appears to be no antibody benefit; in fact, the child is exposed to the animal's diseases. We will never actually know if the Talheim massacre was in part a baby raid or if it was, if the infants were nursed by animals. But we do know that the use of nonhuman milk became widespread in the later Neolithic period.

Baby Booming

By around 3500 B.C., fifteen hundred years after the peak of the LBK culture, some Late Neolithic communities in Europe were definitely using animals to produce milk for human consumption. We know this from the range of pottery vessels used for manipulating liquids and semiliquids—jugs and cups, strainers and boilers. Archaeologist Andrew Sherratt has termed this development, which also involved the use of oxen for draft and sheep for wool, the "secondary products revolution," to distinguish it from the use of animals for their primary products alone—meat, leather, and bone. Evidence of these uses can be found in the Near East during the same period: they are clearly depicted in art. The use of animals for plowing was certainly a later Neolithic development—only then did human settlement move away from the loess soils to the potentially richer but harder to work clay soils. But animal milk may have been utilized much earlier than Sherratt initially suggested. Archaeologist Peter Bogucki has argued that the age and sex structure of LBK cattle herds suggests that they were kept as dairy animals; he has also identified some strainers among LBK pottery.

Direct infant nursing by animals seems the most likely path for the development of dairy farming. Perhaps the original venue was within the longhouse itself, where infants could be left in the care of older relatives, with the odd goat on tap, while the parents toiled in the forest clearings. It must have seemed like a natural progression—

(Fig. 7.2) A breast-shaped weaning vessel:
Barton-upon-Humber, Anglo-Saxon period.
Photograph: Kevin Harvey.

human babies and young animals alike drink milk, and both women
and female animals produce it. But despite our modern Western fa-
miliarity with the idea, for *adult* humans to regularly drink the food of
calves and lambs without ill effect is, on the face of it, rather bizarre
and would have taken some time to become established. Only then
could it become culturally elaborated, involving specific types of vessels — strainers and weaning cups. Weaning cups are known from
early farming cultures in France, Italy, and the Carpathian basin, as
well as from the grave of twin babies at Jebel Moya in the Sudan,
dating to the early introduction of pastoralism to Africa in the first
millennium B.C. Such vessels, initially used solely for children, were
later joined by jugs, cups, and bowls for grown-ups. These vessels
were used not only for raw milk (which may not have been drunk
much at all) but for foods never before seen — cheese, yogurt, and alcoholic koumiss. (Such close contact with animals was not without
risk. Skeletal studies demonstrate that tuberculosis was first spread
from cows to humans in this period; its first transmission could have
been during direct infant suckling.)

Although weaning regimes typically result in higher infant mortality, in purely demographic terms they are outweighed by the greater number of conceptions that can be sustained to full term. The increase in population during the European Neolithic is similar to that which took place in other parts of the world during the transition to farming. It may have been at some level deliberately manipulated, certainly by the time animal management began to figure largely in the economy. One of Marija Gimbutas's main contentions was that the later Neolithic and early Bronze Age periods were characterized by obvious gender inequalities. She thought that these inequalities arose rapidly and were the result of the immigration of pastorally based communities, the Kurgan cultures, from the steppelands of eastern Europe. But it is possible to accept immigration to explain increased gender inequality while not subscribing to the view that the earlier Neolithic was characterized by peaceful equality between the sexes. The management of herds, developing as it did out of the hunting in hunter-gatherer economies, tends to be principally associated with men, as indicated by male burials with paired oxen.

Men and Animals

Pecked rock art stretches from upland Britain and Ireland, Scandinavia, and the Alps in the northwest, eastward into Uzbekistan, Siberia, Mongolia, and beyond. In many places it suggests a continuous tradition of territorial marking by shepherds and cowherds that began in the Neolithic and has lasted into the present day. Individual images can be dated more or less accurately using various stylistic criteria; in the Val Camonica in northern Italy, for example, some men carry long halberds of a type known from the adjacent lowland Bronze Age cemeteries.

One scene from the Val Camonica (Figure 7.3) shows four human figures. The one on the left is holding a goat and leading two oxen, one of which is definitely male. The oxen are harnessed to a plow that is being driven by a second figure. The bulge beneath the legs of this second figure could suggest biological maleness, but it is not certain. Behind the plow team appears a stooping figure who is

(Fig. 7.3)   Plowing, hoeing, and infant-carrying: Val Camonica. Drawing by
George Taylor after Anati 1965.

hoeing and carrying a baby in a papoose on her/his back. Whatever
its mythographic significance, the basic elements of the drawing show
a sexual division of labor—that babies are not carried by those who
plow. The conventional interpretation would be that the plow team
figures are male and the hoeing, baby-carrying figure female.

The association between men and animals is also made clear in
a number of scenes of bestiality. In one from the Val Camonica, a
man is penetrating what appears to be a donkey. Those from Siberia
are particularly interesting, showing copulation among moose, as
well as men copulating—or attempting to copulate—with moose, the
man in one case being on skis (Figure 7.5). These animals are not
domesticated but, as social anthropologist Tim Ingold has observed
among modern herders in Lapland, managed herds of wild animals.
Bestiality scenes seem to stress the power of the penis. In several
rock engravings from southern Scandinavia, the penis is to the fore,
where it links figures together, making it difficult to see who the
penis belongs to or what sex each person in a group is. A "marriage"
scene from the Bohuslan site may have homosexual content, some
have suggested. Homosexual imagery seems fairly clear in a group
of three figures from Mongolia, published by the Russian rock art
researcher Nora Novgorodova; but the touching penises may be
nothing more than a symbolic juxtaposition, merely indicating the
essential maleness of two combatants. Other images, as yet unpublished by Novgorodova, show clear sex scenes, with a central
woman fellating one man while having vaginal (or possibly anal)
intercourse with another. Novgorodova believes that these scenes

(Fig. 7.4) Man having sex with donkey: Val Camonica. (Part of the novelty of this scene is that donkeys were a recent introduction to Alpine Europe at the time the image was created, around 3000 B.C.) Tracing of rock surface: Christopher Chippindale.

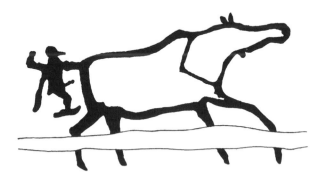

(Fig. 7.5) Skier attempting intercourse with moose: Angara River. Tracing from Martynov 1991; fig. 25.2.

are of purely ritual or symbolic significance. But what can be drawn can be done, and it would be surprising if a community that was this explicit in its art did not actually engage in the activities depicted. Still, I suppose a question mark must hang over the plausibility of the ski scene with the moose.

The fertilizing power of the penis and the reproductive value of semen must have been well known to those who managed animals. The essence of keeping a meat or dairy herd is not just in the patterns of slaughter but in controlling the ratios of the sexes and their mating patterns. Minimally, only one stud bull is needed to ensure the continuity of a dairy herd, but oftentimes he must be kept separate from the cows. The control of animal sexuality by men may have had its analogue in control of the sexuality of human females. The rise of the idea of property, in land, in herds, and in women, would have placed new emphasis on exclusive rights of sexual access, as promised by certain forms of marriage. In an exploitative economy, virginity may have been valued in both land and women. Early farming societies were probably the first to formulate rape laws, not so much to protect women as to defend property and lines of inheritance. The penis as an image, so obvious in ice age art but virtually absent from the surviving archaeological record of the Mesolithic period, again comes to the fore in the Neolithic.

Varna: Grave 43

In 1968 a cemetery of more than 250 graves was discovered at Varna, on the Bulgarian Black Sea coast. They date to a little before 4000 B.C.—after the main LBK spread and only about seven hundred years before the Iceman lived, at a time when copper and gold were being used on a grand scale for the first time in eastern Europe. (The copper ax that Ötzi carried with him may well have been traded from somewhere in this metal-rich Balkan region.) Some of the graves were too poorly preserved to tell much about, and some were devoid of bones; the remaining 150 or so have been classified as either men's or women's graves. Grave 43 is one of the richest burials, containing

many wonderful metal objects. The skeleton held a ceremonial copper ax in its right hand. The wooden haft survives only as a series of
beautifully finished gold bands or cylinders. There are gold arm rings
and gold disks with holes that show that they were once sewn onto
an elaborate garment.

The most unusual object in Grave 43 is a sheet-gold artifact that
in shape and size resembles the end of a penis. It was found between
the legs of the skeleton. It is usually referred to as a "penis sheath,"
but because it is both unique and incomplete, and because I do not
want to prejudice any other conclusions that might be drawn about
its function, I call it a "penis piece." It is made of a single piece of
hammered sheet gold and is about two inches long and almost an
inch and a half in diameter. Small perforations dot the "rim," suggesting that it was once sewn to some organic material, such as calfskin.
(The people buried at Varna kept cattle, as we know from the animal
bones found in settlements of this period, as well as from gold cow-
shaped clothing appliqués found in other graves in the Varna cemetery.) The thing was clearly an object of beauty, made to be seen. But
the question is: Did it have a particular function?

It seems unlikely that the gold-tipped penis piece from Varna
was a particularly fancy condom, as the tip has a hole in it. But this
hole in itself suggests that the piece could have been actually worn on
the penis, as it would have allowed both urination and ejaculation. It
could, of course, have functioned as a condom in the sense of providing some protection against sexual disease transmission. It is, after
all, made of a hypoallergenic material, suitable for contact with delicate body tissue. The piece might have been sewn to some condom-
like animal membrane, although it could have been sewn directly
onto the skin of the penis itself. (Anyone with any doubts about the
feasibility of such a thing need only glance at one of the specialist
magazines devoted to the increasingly popular art of decorative genital piercing.) Could somebody have ejaculated out of the Varna penis
piece in a bizarre fertility ritual, either copulatory or masturbatory?
Its diameter would certainly have made it a snug fit for an erect penis, but then people are various, and we do not know what the average size was for Varna males at that time. Its "erect" dimensions

(Fig. 7.6) The Grave of the Golden Penis: Varna cemetery, Grave No. 43; 4000 B.C.
Photograph: Vitaly Vitanov Agency.

would seem to fall at the lower end of the normal modern range. The penis piece would cover the glans area and part of the shaft, leaving the rest of the shaft of the penis, membrane-covered or not, open to sensory contact.

Similar to the Varna penis piece are the penis sheaths that are worn quite widely among tribal peoples of the world's tropical belts. Despite their name, such sheaths are not for contraception, although they typically have no hole in the end. A comparative survey by anthropologists suggests that they have usually been worn as a mark of modesty or decorum. The men who wear them wear little clothing elsewhere on the body. Although such sheaths are necessarily phallic in form, they are never lewd and reflect none of the anatomical detail of a penis. Their purpose is to symbolize manly status in an abstract way. They are rigid and opaque, and they keep the real state of the penis private. In essence they are fig leaves, but effective ones. As such sheaths have no hole, they are removed when the man wishes to urinate.

The Varna penis piece does not look like a device of this sort because of the hole in the end and because the climate in which it was worn was not tropical. (Gilding one's penis is hardly modest in any context.) Although the summers may be hot along the coast of the Black Sea, the winters are fairly bitter, and from the clothing evidence from this period, we can infer that people were well covered. Indeed, the positioning of the gold fashion objects and appliqués in Grave 43 suggest that the body had bare arms that were adorned with arm rings, but a covered torso and legs. The torso had a fair density of small sewn-on gold buttons or sequins, while each knee had its own golden disk decoration, originally sewn onto trousers or, more probably, leggings like the Iceman's. There was also an elaborate headdress, with rows of large gold disks.

In this context the gold-tipped penis piece seems more akin to a Renaissance codpiece—emphasizing the possession of an organ that was actually well covered (and presumably flaccid) beneath. Like the briefly fashionable Renaissance examples that stood out and up, the piece might actually have been padded so as to appear erect rather than dangling, which would certainly have made a dramatic show of the hole, otherwise not easily visible. It is clearly a piece that was made to be seen. But the reconstruction of the clothing of the corpse complicates this reasoning.

If a body is buried "fresh," with clothes on, it will decompose in the ground amid much movement. The viscera will swell and possibly burst, sometimes causing small items, such as necklace beads, to ricochet around the coffin when their threading gives way. Even with a corpse that has been buried without a coffin—that was lowered into the grave pit on a bier, for example—and directly covered over with earth, small jewelry items may subsequently be found some distance from their original places. It is possible to restrict such movement by placing the body in a tight winding cloth, or by trussing the legs and arms into a fetal position for a "contracted" burial, lying on one side. There are three basic grave types at Varna: ones where the body is laid out long on its back (extended inhumation), ones where the body lies on one side, with knees up (contracted inhumation), and ones with no body (possibly representing those lost at sea).

The grave with the penis piece is an extended inhumation, with little sign that clothing and jewelry items have been much displaced. This probably means that the body was displayed for some time following biological death and before the social death marked by the funeral rites. During this time the body would probably have been secluded in a death hut, from which a terrible stench would have emanated, signaling the swelling of the viscera and their subsequent relaxation as the stomach gases were vented and the initial putrefaction processes ran their swift course. The body would then have been in a floppy and fairly stable condition, at which stage it could have been dressed. The indications of clothing excavated at Varna are, therefore, traces of grave clothes. It is possible that the penis piece was worn only in death, a symbolic penis for use in the afterlife.

The Golden Penis: Male Ornament or Female Substitute?

In only one grave in the Varna cemetery does a penis piece survive. (There may have once been others, made entirely of perishable mate-

rials, of which no trace has been found.) Could it have been the grave
of some unfortunate who—unlike Ötzi—had been emasculated? The
answer is unknowable, but then, no such scenario is really necessary
to explain the penis piece, as Grave 43 is probably the "richest" in the
entire cemetery in terms of the number and wealth of the status objects and clothing elements within. Whoever was buried in it was a
person of considerable importance to the community, in death at
least. The Renaissance codpiece comparison again seems to fit best.
This was an individual of high status—the "Man with the Golden Penis." . . . But was he really a man at all?

If the penis piece was primarily a symbolic status symbol, it
need not have been worn over a real penis. The erect codpieces of the
Renaissance were self-standing fashion items, strapped on over un-
dergarments. The penis piece *could* have been worn by a biological
woman, either in life or in death. Obviously, before speculating further we should ascertain the sex of the skeleton, which we have simply assumed until now to be male.

At this point certainty begins to slip away. Although the excavation report for the Varna cemetery records the skeleton as male,
the criteria by which this determination was made are open to question. (The skeleton on which the grave goods are displayed in photographs is not the original skeleton; it is in fact a plastic model.)
Grave 43 may have contained the body of someone who was in all
respects male, who had a masculine skeleton and a standard XY sex
genotype. Or it may be the skeleton of a person who was genetically
female—a priestess perhaps, who ritually played out some myth.
(The Hazda of Ethiopia have a myth about a woman who ties a
zebra's penis to herself and uses it to satisfy her beautiful wives.) Or
the skeleton might easily be of "uncertain" sex. Out of a cemetery of
more than 150 surviving skeletons, one or two might represent the
remains of intersex individuals of one kind or another. Grave 43
could thus contain the remains of a genetic woman who, for example, had AGS—a condition that caused her gender orientation to be
"male" in life and that left various malelike features on her skeleton,
so that the physical anthropologist—perhaps already influenced by
the grave goods—pronounced the bones male. This would be one

way to explain why only one skeleton in the entire cemetery had a gold penis piece.

The person buried in Grave 43 was clearly singled out in death to wear a striking and extraordinary appendage — a gold-tipped phallus. Since, unlike the erect codpieces of the Renaissance, this object had a hole in the end, we must consider it a strong possibility that it was designed to ejaculate — most probably by being worn over an erect penis but possibly artificially, by having something pumped up through it. A comparable modern object would be the strap-on ejaculating dildo (mass produced and widely available on a global level, but not often discussed). Such plastic or rubber penises have a hole in the end with a tube running down to a fake scrotum, which can be filled with something such as cream; squeezing the scrotum causes the cream to ejaculate. The gold-tipped penis piece was certainly part of something more complex. It *could* originally have been fitted up with some natural membrane and tubing from the cattle and sheep kept by the Varna people, and the small — and thus rare and valuable — amount of milk and cream that these early domesticates produced could have been used as the fake or symbolic semen.

I am not saying that the Varna object *is* the surviving part of a strap-on ejaculating dildo. For one thing, its context is clearly alien. The modern dildo is used during private sexual activity or in sexual performances of one kind or another; it is not usually associated with funerary rites. Nevertheless, the Varna piece does look as if it were made to function — the hole in the end would have been a bit of a letdown if nothing had come out of it. And if something did come out of it, then it seems likely that it was as part of a public "ritual" display.

I realize that I could easily be accused of anachronism, of back-projecting the weird and wonderful sexual activities of the modern world onto the clean-living, simple, and wholesome peoples of the prehistoric past. Many people believe that in the past, closer to our "cave man" and "cave woman" roots, we can observe the "natural," free from the confusions and decadence of modern civilization. But people of the same biological type as us — our species — have been

(Fig. 7.7) Masturbating
male; Larisa. Drawing by
George Taylor after
Gimbutas 1989; fig. 281.47.

around for 100,000 years, with the same underlying curiosities and
fascinations about life and death. As soon as there are written
records, from around 5,000 years ago in the Near East, we find references to many of the sexual practices—homosexuality, male and
female transsexualism and transvestism, masturbation—familiar to
us today.

The Masturbating Godhead

That a religious ritual, whether performed by a man or a woman,
could have focused on the male ejaculatory function is clear from
ancient Egyptian and Sumerian texts. In surviving Egyptian religious documents, male masturbation is the basic act in the most popular creation myth. Pyramid Utterance 527, dating to around 2600
B.C., says that "Atum [the sun god] was creative in that he proceed-
ed to masturbate with himself in Heliopolis; he put his penis in his
hand that he might obtain the pleasure of emission thereby and
there were born brother and sister—that is Shu and Tefnut." This
creative masturbation was most often thought of as taking place in
water, sometimes with the help of the hand goddess, Iusas; the cul-

minating ejaculation formed the Nile flood, upon which the whole civilization depended. Temple priestesses at Karnak were known as "hands of god" as they facilitated the divine annual spasm. Similarly, in Mesopotamian literature, Enki "stood up full of lust like an attacking bull, lifted his penis, ejaculated, filled the Tigris with flowing water."

A small clay figurine in the form of a masturbating male figure, from the Greek Neolithic Dimini culture, dates to the same time as the Varna cemetery (5000–4500 B.C.). Found near Larisa, it has parallels with the masturbating woman from Hağar Qim. The idea of semen as a natural "fertilizer" was not confined to agricultural society. The Zuñi of North America used to take one of their "men-women"—anatomically male cross-gender people—and lead him/her out over the mesa in the "spring riding" ritual, during which he/she would be masturbated in order to ensure the return of wildlife.

The Invention of Mother Earth

The emphasis on the generative power of the male organ, the engendering of the earth as female, and the distinctive psychological outlook induced by early weaning and a harsh attitude toward infants may perhaps constitute a series of intertwined influences on the British Neolithic. Together they may throw new light on the underlying motives for constructing monuments like Stonehenge and the elaborate long barrows into which the dead were placed.

The switch to farming in Britain is in many respects enigmatic. The earliest phases of forest clearance, dated according to the pollen record, are not associated with many traces of permanent settlement, and nothing like the longhouse villages of the LBK is known. Instead, there are field monuments. It seems likely that these monuments were erected in a preexisting practical and symbolic landscape—a network of routes and special places that had developed during the preceding Mesolithic. Apart from these monuments, the main observable change that came with farming was in the treatment of the dead. For the Mesolithic we have little idea about standard modes of disposing of corpses, except that they were not buried in the ground. Bodies were returned to the cycle of life in some way, quite possibly by being exposed to the elements and carrion birds. Exposure platforms and mortuary enclosures seem to have a continuing significance, but at sites such as Fussell's Lodge they are associated with long mounds, within which are stone-built chambers—charnel houses or "keeping places" for the dead—in which bones were arranged and rearranged many times.

The basic symbolism of grave mounds derives from the practical fact of displaced soil. If you dig a hole and place a body in it, then shovel the earth back, some soil is left over. The amount is in direct proportion to the size of the interred body. By enlarging the mound with extra soil, the symbolic importance—the imagined "size" of the person interred—can be increased. In farming cultures, the cycle of death and rebirth in the agricultural year suggests an analogy with human life and death and seems to cast light on the mystery of what happens next. In the long barrows, bones are placed like seeds in a womb of earth, as if waiting for the moment of rebirth. Often, the ground beneath the barrows has been plowed. British archaeologists have usually considered this plowing fortuitous—the construction of a ritual monument sealing evidence of basic economic life. Yet some of the plow marks have a strange vigorousness, as for example those under South Street Long Barrow. The plow marks are probably not coincidental. Patzold believes that similar plowing under German round barrows was deliberate, serving to prepare the ground for the "planting" of the dead.

The shape of many of the long barrows suggests genitals. Most notably, the long form has often been considered phallic. Indeed, the long form of the earthen mound is appropriate for symbolizing the propagation of a male patrilineage, the documentation of a land claim, and the inheritance of property from father to son. The way into the long barrow, however, has a female anatomical aspect. It is often described as an opening between two "arms"—an unfortunate coyness that obscures the obvious fact that arms do not converge on an opening, legs do. The feeling of entering into one of these places has been appropriately evoked by the archaeological photographer Mick Sharp, here talking of an English Neolithic burial mound:

> Dark, damp, and smelling of the earth pressing in from all sides; Hetty Peglar's Tump in Gloucestershire retains well the atmosphere of the earth mother's womb. The place from which we were born again, through the constricted entrance, the souls of the dead, and where the bones rested securely in the belly of their creation.

Across the English Channel in Brittany, and in the chalk-cut tombs of the Marne region, the female associations of Neolithic tomb shapes are enhanced by stylized but unambiguous female representations on the walls of the inner chamber, depicting face, breasts, and neck ornamentation, or simply paired breasts on their own. At Carnac, Brittany, a remarkable virtuosic representation, worthy of Picasso, succeeds in being both a large vulva, viewed in close-up, with breasts above and beyond, and at the same time a face—the breasts also serve as eyes.

How were the dead thought to rise? A particularly dramatic scenario is suggested in the orientation of many of the tomb entrances, perhaps best illustrated by the passage grave of Newgrange in the Bend in the Boyne, Ireland. Newgrange is a great, pregnant-looking round or slightly kidney-shaped mound, edged around its base with curbstones that are decorated with swirling designs (to which Gimbutas and others attribute vulvar and "Great Goddess" significance). A stone-lined passage that leads into the mound terminates in a burial chamber with a stunning vaulted roof, formed of dry-laid, corbeled courses of stone. The outer entrance to the passage is curious, in that it has a main doorway, above whose lintel is a narrow slit, as if for letters. The whole monument is oriented so that on one day of the year—the winter solstice of December 21—a shaft of sun-

(Fig. 7.8)　Midwinter sunrise at Newgrange. Co. Meath, Ireland. Photograph: Con Brogan.

light can enter the narrow opening and strike the back wall of the burial chamber. The effect lasts for some seventeen minutes.

The idea conveyed by the whole is of the sun as a male fertilizing power, whose shafts of light have analogies with the fertilizing penises of men and stud animals, as well as connections with the earth-penetrating power of the plow and the fork. (*Fork* is an Indo-European word that was originally at one with *fuck*.) The idea of the female sex as a field into which grain is sown is common among farming cultures and can be found in Talmudic, Egyptian, and Vedic writings. The idea of the female earth mound being entered by the male force is startlingly embodied at Newgrange. The resurrection of the bodies of the dead is symbolically connected to the resurrection of the year itself—the point of exact midwinter, after which the sun must begin to come back or there will be no spring. Such symbolic orientations are known from other Neolithic sites, such as the vaulted tomb of Maes Howe in the Orkneys. The relative positions of sun and earth at different times of year have altered somewhat since the monuments were first built, but it can be calculated that, if one had stood by the phallic stone of Kintraw in Scotland in 1800 B.C. (Figure 7.9), one would have witnessed a spectacular sight. As Mick Sharp writes, "Looking over the site from what may be an artificial platform on the hillslope to the north-east, the midwinter sun, after setting behind a mountain peak on Jura, would have briefly flashed into life again at the bottom of a V-shaped cleft." At Stonehenge it is the midsummer sun that rises over the heel stone, as seen from the central sanctuary area. Many of these effects could have been directly observed only by a small group of select people, even though the monuments themselves often embody the labor of many hundreds.

Erecting Stones

It is hard to say whether all the Neolithic megaliths have one over-arching meaning. These great architectural stones, found on both sides of the Channel, in Britain and in Brittany, were erected singly, in lines, or in circles. At Stonehenge they were slotted together at

(Fig. 7.9)   Standing stone; Kintraw. Loch Craignish, Mid Argyll, Scotland.
Photograph: Mick Sharp.

their most complex. In one sense they are a replacement for the trees
that were felled to create the vistas in which they can be seen. But
they also have an undeniably phallic aspect. Among the impressive
monuments around Carnac in Brittany is the Grand Menhir Brisé,
which lies broken in three fragments, possibly after toppling at the
moment of its unsuccessful erection (around 4000 B.C.), but which
would have stood over sixty feet high.

From around 2500 B.C. onward, as the long barrows were going
out of use, communities in Britain began to put up stone circles. The
detailed geometry and astronomical alignments of these circles have
often been overstated—particularly in the 1960s and 1970s, when a
variety of nonarchaeologists claimed that the circles were prehistoric
computers and celestial observatories. Even if the weather in
Neolithic Britain was slightly better than it is today, the rarely observable star sets would have made getting any detailed alignments
subject to cloudy disappointment. The monuments could only function if there was a degree of leeway in their erection, and they were

oriented toward major events—midwinter and midsummer sunrises and sunsets, and various moonsets—that would be seriously disrupted only by a whole week of completely overcast weather.

To investigate the basic motives for megalithic architecture, it is necessary to examine the social organization of early farming cultures and in particular the enculturation of children. I have argued that during the Neolithic period as a whole, children were increasingly seen as a potential labor force whose numbers could be increased by early weaning. Attitudes toward them were not sentimental, as witness the Talheim massacre and a number of archaeological discoveries in Britain. At the site of Woodhenge—a wood-built counterpart to nearby Stonehenge, which survived only as concentric circles of large filled-in postholes and a shallow-ditch-and-bank perimeter—the body of a three-year-old girl was found, her skull split by an ax blow. John Barber, who has excavated many sites in Scotland, suggests that several infant burials around passage graves—ten at Quanterness, twenty-four at Isbister—represent systematic infanticide of neonates. At Stonehenge a woman and child were buried in the great ditch close to the entrance to the monument. Attitudes toward (at least some) women seem to have been no better than those toward some unfortunate children. There are many potentially sacrificial burials of women at Neolithic sites, such as one from the Curragh Henge in Ireland, where a woman appears to have been buried alive. Ian Kinnes of the British Museum remarks that "while there are not many bodies, where there are they tend to be women, and people are thinking in terms of special sacrificial dedications."

It may be time to risk a psychological profile of Neolithic society. Such a thing has been attempted from time to time, most recently by Peter Ellis, who sees the megalithic monuments as evidence of a "collectively held obsession" creating "a landscape of detached sexual objects." This idea is suggestive, and when it is brought together with theories of developmental psychologists and of obstetrician Michel Odent, the combination may indicate what lay at the root of Neolithic culture.

In many hunter-gatherer societies, children continue to nurse to the age of five or six, and they derive great comfort from the unconditional love that breast-feeding represents, embodying the principles of trust, reliance, and sharing. On the basis of this early experience, far from becoming dependent individuals, they display remarkable autonomy based on a strong inner sense of their own value. Early weaning practices are generally associated with the opposite psychological tendencies. Warrior societies, for example, often withhold colostrum from a newborn infant and give him or her water instead. The infant is understandably angry about the fact, except that it lacks the cognitive abilities to understand anger, so the event becomes an unconscious primal focus for aggression in later life. Deliberate weaning comes in two forms or stages. First, nursing is limited, and finally the mother ends all breast-feeding. Early weaning, as we have seen, is common in farming societies, where birth spacing is reduced.

The specific results of such conditioning processes vary from community to community. They may manifest themselves as a cultural obsession with breasts, idealizing them to the point where virtually no one feels she possesses or has access to precisely the "right" sort (as in modern America). But there may be more systematic effects as well. In particular, the weaning process typically arouses resistance in the child—it cries. For weaning to succeed, the crying must be ignored, as it also must be if the child is to sleep alone. The modern term for this approach is "controlled crying," where the child is allowed to cry a little more each day before its needs—for food, comfort, or attention—are attended to. The child eventually shuts up. The reason it does so is connected to a basic animal instinct that can be precisely observed in the young of most mammals and birds. The instinct, stated as a rule, is: "If you cry and no one comes, you have been abandoned; because you have been abandoned, you are in grave danger and you will increase your chances of survival by conserving energy; crying is costly in energy terms; therefore stop crying." The human child does precisely this. Before it ceases crying, however, it must adopt the psychological state equivalent to knowledge of abandonment.

The conditioning brought about by "controlled crying" connects closely with one of the most influential theories of depression, Martin Seligman's theory of "learned helplessness." Seligman argued that if a particular response to a situation—such as crying when one is hungry—is met with no relief, or if it is not possible to correlate the relief that comes with the experience of any internal physical or psychological state, the person begins to feel detached from reality and powerless to affect it. The depressive effects of this early experience of powerlessness can, however, be mitigated by arranging one's life around predictable events. By having a rigid routine and being able to predict what will follow, the person is able to compensate for their primal distrust of the world.

With this in mind, we can look again at the megalithic monuments, of which Alison Sheridan, an archaeologist at the National Museum of Scotland, has said, "The message may have been 'We can control time and the seasons. We can compel the sun to appear in the same place.'" Sheridan sees this control as important for a farming society, dependent on the procession of the seasons. But the basic organization of the agrarian calendar does not need the grand architecture of Stonehenge. I believe that British Neolithic society was in some way soothed by the massively overstated predictive power of the monuments. They were therapeutic. As Samuel Johnson so percipiently put it, faced with the Great Pyramid of Cheops, "I consider this mighty structure as a monument of the insufficiency of human enjoyments."

Never Mind the Quality

All these predictive monuments, be they passage graves, standing stones, stone circles, or long or round mounds, have a form that is at times suggestive of a "landscape of detached sexual objects," yet their size may have been closely related to an agricultural ethos of "bigger is better." In contrast to foraging societies, in which people's main concern was the identification and gathering of almost infinitely varied resources, agricultural society depends on the maximization of only a few resources. The basic idea is to generate a surplus. Quantity thus supplants quality—in food, in labor, in children, in sex. The big monuments of the Neolithic seem to project ideas of big penis power and big womb power onto a depleted natural environment.

Of course, these ideas were probably not starkly conscious. The Neolithic communities must have believed in a male force flowing from the sun god and a female one embedded in earth, and the complexity of their myriad local nuances must forever elude us. As historian of religion Jane Harrison wrote in 1921:

> Man has made himself representations of beings stronger and more splendid than himself, he has lost all sense that they are really projections of his own desire and to these beings he hands over his conflict, he no longer needs to banish conflict into the unconscious but gods will see to it and fight on his side.

The basic dyad of a bountiful yet passive Mother Nature, and a virile, potentially vengeful, bearded man ruling the heavens, is an idea that took firm root in Eurasia during the Neolithic. Incorporated into grand systems of religious thought, its influence can still at times be strong. Christian belief and symbolism incorporate much of it. The film *2001: A Space Odyssey* projected "god" as an inscrutable but clearly phallic megalith that makes its appearance on various planets and moons—where the passive, spherical female ova awaited its creative touch. Most profoundly, the idea of a basic dichotomy in the world, of a struggle between man (in the deliberately sex-specific sense) and nature, is what lies behind our continuing lunatic progress toward ever deeper ecological disaster.

Chapter 8

Shamans
and Amazons

"You're born naked and the rest is drag."

RuPaul André Charles

Dismissed by its critics as fanciful nonsense, Herodotus's *History*, the lifework of a fifth-century B.C. Greek from a polyglot town in Asia Minor, is the earliest and still one of the most remarkable accounts of human diversity. Ostensibly the story of how the small yet democratic Greek states beat the might of authoritarian Persia, it is in reality a vehicle for talking about the history of all of the peoples of the world, as far as Herodotus had been able to know them through his extensive travels. His brand of history was not narrowly political. Amazons and eunuchs, transvestite shamans and cannibals, werewolves and griffins—all are included in his mélange of firsthand observation, merchants' tales, and carefully recorded myths. All are astutely assessed for their value in understanding different social customs, religious beliefs, and sexual mores. Today archaeology is in a position to corroborate much of what Herodotus believed.

One of the best known of the ancient myths concerns the Amazons. According to Herodotus's account, the Amazons were a race of warrior women, enemies of the Greeks, who lived in the steppelands of what is now Ukraine and southern Russia—lands known in Herodotus' time as Scythia (to the west of the Don River) and Sauromatia (later called *Sarmatia,* to the east of the Don). This myth has exerted a powerful hold over the male psyche. In the nineteenth century it influenced Johann Jacob Bachofen when he formulated his idea of the politics of *Mütterrecht* or matriarchy. Equally, the myth has been dismissed as nonsense, notably by Bachofen's detractors.

In this chapter I argue that social gender increased in importance from the end of the Neolithic onward, with the growth of political complexity in Europe. The development of more intensive plow agriculture, the increasing use of metals, and the growth of trade in the Bronze and Iron Ages allowed individuals to become rich. Their insignia of rank, stressed in elaborate and ostentatious personal burial monuments, used an insignia of sex—the elaboration of codes of dress for men and women—for credibility. If people accepted that men and women naturally dressed differently, then the naturalness of other divisions, such as between rich and poor, that are actually supported by no biological reality, was more believable.

But the insignia of sex was actually an insignia of gender. From the earliest establishment of a system of "men's" and "women's" burials, a significant minority of biological women and men were buried with opposite grave furnishings—women cross-dressed as men, and men cross-dressed as women. Culture began to co-opt biology in the Iron Age with the creation of new physical categories, such as eunuchs, and the use of the earliest known hormone treatments to feminize biological men. Sexual diversity and sexual knowledge blossomed when the Celts adopted techniques derived from oriental Tantric yoga. But for the spread of Christianity, at precisely this time, the sexual culture of Europe might have developed along very different lines.

Buried Gender

In the Neolithic long barrows, differentiation by sex was not particularly clear or consistent. Occasionally we find spatial separations between male and female skeletons, as in the Cotswold-Severn-type tomb at Lanhill, where females predominate in the south chamber and males in the north. Gender categories for the dead became more marked in the succeeding Beaker period (2600–1800 B.C.), when metal was coming into use in northern and western Europe for the first time. The so-called Beaker people were usually buried singly, accompanied by a bell-shaped pottery beaker; the female skeletons were buried facing south or southwest, the males facing north or northeast. The most likely reason for this distinction is that the dead in Beaker society were considered to rise and move off in different directions according to sex, implying a sex-segregated heaven.

In Britain and on the Continent, male graves typically include a little copper dagger, which—along with "spacer plates" that may have functioned as archery wrist-guards—expressed some notion of manhood. Men got the richest grave goods and were buried alone, under round barrows. Such barrows dot the environs of the earlier megalithic monuments and seem to have supplanted them, at the same time drawing on their physical authority as statements in the landscape. The association of men with daggers, however, is not consistent. In cemeteries near Brno in Moravia, some biologically female graves have also been found with copper daggers, suggesting that as soon as a standardized sex-gender burial practice was established, it was subverted by those who did not fit into it easily.

The advent of metal provided a new focus for sexual divisions of labor and the creation of ideas of gender. Metal was associated with the male principle at this time, an association that correlates with the disappearance of megalithic monuments and remains fairly constant thereafter. The new phallic symbols were daggers and swords. Again, the distinction between sex and gender must be fully appreciated. As Andrew Reid and Rachel MacLean note in a recent anthropological study of iron production in Igurwa, in the old Karagwe kingdom in present-day Uganda:

Frequently, the presence of women, and more importantly
the presence of female fertility, is regarded as threatening
to the act of smelting and is therefore prohibited . . . [but]
it is not "women *qua* women" who pose the danger, as children and postmenopausal women may not be excluded; it is
rather the dangerous, ambiguous, and therefore uncontrol-
lable, power of a woman's fertility. This power could damage the embryonic iron and therefore, to prevent failure,
not only are women excluded from the smelt itself, but
smelters are frequently prohibited from engaging in sexual
intercourse before and during the smelt.

As more and more of Eurasia was brought under the plow, the
new metal technology developed further, with soft copper alloys giving way to tin-bronze, and then iron. Mining became widespread. In
the southern regions urban centers sprang up, and networks of trade
and exchange spread out, dealing in amber, colored glass, and eventually slaves. As Eurasia became more densely populated, society became more ethnically mixed. Functionally specialized groups
emerged that could survive only within the framework of the broader
economy. The elite horse-riding Scythians of the steppelands, for example, were at the apex of an economic system that extended across
the whole of the Old World, linking Europe to China and India.
Within this system were local patterns of subsistence—sedentary
agriculture, seasonal pastoralism, and fully nomadic pastoralism;
there were traders and professional soldiers, engineers and pirates,
nobility and slaves.

Previously—in the longhouses of the Neolithic, for example—
people's place in society had been governed by birth, which fundamentally established their identity in the eyes of their family and
tribe. But the specialization and nonautonomy of many Bronze and
Iron Age groups meant that they had to enhance their images in order to be recognizable in the crowd. They accomplished this by using
marks of allegiance—tokens of ethnicity. One of the freeze-preserved
Scythian-culture bodies at Pazyryk in the Siberian Altai is heavily

tattooed in the "animal style" art so typical of the steppes. The tattoos served to identify him anywhere in the world, in life or in death. Along with the Celts, Thracians, Persians, Greeks, and others, the Scythians also adorned themselves with fine decorated metalwork. In the preceding tribal-agricultural period, a village could express its personality through the nuances of its pottery designs, but the elite arts of the Bronze and Iron Ages were portable and unbreakable; the objects were to be worn on the body, and to move with it.

Buried Wives

Particular Bronze and Iron Age communities at times displayed relative equality between the sexes, and women could even become leaders within some—as did Boudicca (or Boadicea), queen of the East Anglian Iceni tribe, who in A.D. 60 led a revolt against the Roman occupation. But men and women more often had unequal access to wealth. As a rule, women were economically disadvantaged, which is often reflected by their position in burial. Herodotus says that when a Thracian chief died, his wives would vie with one another to be adjudged the favorite; whoever was chosen had the honor of being put to death by the graveside and passing into the other world with him. The wives who were not chosen were publicly shamed. Archaeological evidence that is at least congruent with this story comes from a grave at Vratsa in Bulgaria, excavated by Bogdan Nikolov in 1965. Around 350 B.C. a mature male was buried, and next to him a female with a dagger in her ribs. Whether she was a willing participant is beyond archaeological method to determine.

Single female skeletons often occur next to those of wealthy men in the richer barrows of Thrace and Scythia. This seems to contradict Herodotus's very clear statement that Scythian nobles might make a number of diplomatic marriages. It may be that although polygyny was practiced, a man's wives were ranked. Behind the polygynous facade might lie complexity, with concubines, diplomatic-exchange wives, and a lineage wife—the principal lady and mother of the legitimate heirs. Scythian kings certainly seem to have kept their options

open, as inheritance passed through the male line—but by the unusual practice of ultimogeniture, or everything going to the last-born.
Ultimogeniture may have been a mechanism that attempted to ensure
the allegiance of one's older and more experienced sons, who could
not hope to inherit, while keeping everybody guessing as to the identity of the true heir (the king could continue to have children as long
as he lived).

The jewelry and ornamentation that people wore or carried with
them often bore portrayals of activities—parts of stories, perhaps—
from the lives of gods or heroes. A set of beautiful fourth-century-B.C.
silver-gilt horse harness decorations, found at Letnitsa in north-
central Bulgaria, seem to show various scenes from a narrative. Both
men and women are depicted, as well as what appears to be an ambiguous or intersex figure. Perhaps the most striking of the Letnitsa
plaques displays a scene that is most usually described as a *hierogamy*
or sacred marriage (Figure 8.1). The explicit sexuality of this scene
seems to have blinded scholars to what is really going on, as it is not a
sexual marriage between equals, whether humans or gods, at all.
Rather, it seems clear that the man is being seduced, even raped.

The biological sexes of the figures are indicated clearly enough.
The male is seated, wearing a mail coat and trousers, his head tied in
a topknot; his erect penis projects from his clothing, and his testicles
are also clearly on view. He is being straddled from above by a female, whose clearly drawn vulva, surrounded by pubic hair, envelops
his penis. One of her feet appears to the bottom right, beneath and
behind the man. (It could easily be mistaken for a little cushion.) Although she is also clothed, her femininity is emphasized by the circular depiction of breasts on the front of her dress—possibly the
depiction is intended to be realistic, with her breasts actually poking
through holes in the garment, but more likely it is an artistic convention. My interpretation of this scene as a male seduction or rape is
not based on the female-superior position depicted here; it was, after
all, one of the most commonly used positions in the Hindu, Chinese,
and Egyptian civilizations, as well as among communities worldwide
up until the arrival of English and American missionaries with their
own peculiar ideas of sexual propriety.

(Fig. 8.1) The Letnitsa
"seduction." Bridle
decoration, Letnitsa,
Bulgaria. Photograph:
National Historical
Museum, Sofia.

Rather, my interpretation is based on the presence of the second woman, who stands to the left of the couple. This "attendant" holds two objects. In her right hand she carries a vessel, presumably containing some beverage, alcoholic or otherwise; in her left she holds a leafy branch, which arches over the couple and obscures the man's vision. The artist has positioned this branch very carefully, to show that the man cannot see who is having sex with him. His semi-clothed, seated position, coupled with the mysterious drink, suggest that he was drugged. We may never know precisely what story lies behind this picture. It could just be a metaphorical depiction of the blindness of love, but it seems much more physical and conspiratorial than that. If its central motif is in fact forced sex, the piece would be virtually unique, in that the seducer and her helper are female. Whether this plaque depicts a myth, a real event, or something imagined by the silversmith we do not know. It seems either to embody a male fear of being overpowered by women, or a female fantasy of control and domination.

Amazon Power

Other fears about the power of women surface in the legend of the ferocious Amazons. Its resonances have gone wide and deep, so that when sixteenth-century Portuguese explorers found fighting women in a region of the Brazilian rainforest, they named the region and its principal river accordingly—the Amazon. The precise meaning of the word *Amazon* is unclear, but one possibility is that it means "without a breast"—*a-mazos* in ancient Greek. According to the legend, Amazons only had one breast. Hippocrates discussed the Amazons at some length, saying that mothers cauterized their daughters' left breast region before puberty so that it would not later develop. The purpose was to facilitate shooting from the bow, during which the breast might get in the way. Although this idea seems far-fetched, women archers today do use a leather restraint to keep their breast clear of the bowstring—but in this case the right breast. If Amazon women once existed, why would they have wished to remove the left breast? One answer is that it would have been difficult to wear a chest restraint while riding. The steppe nomads rode small, agile, fast horses, and they had to combine strength with suppleness to control them. In modern archery the reason the right breast is restrained is that the longbow draw goes back to the right-hand side of the body. With a short, composite reflex bow fired from horseback, however, the draw is short and across the body. The left nipple is in the firing line, and the firing line would not have been a good place to be, when one considers the power of these bows: they could fire armor-piercing arrows with a speed approaching that of a crossbow bolt.

Another possible explanation of the one-breasted story is that it is symbolic, representing women who were half men. Some of the hermaphroditic deities of India are depicted with one side of the body female, with a voluptuous breast, and the other side male and flat. It is also possible that both things are true: that it was a real practice with symbolic overtones. According to Hippocrates, Amazon women fought until they had killed and scalped three of the enemy, at which point they were free to marry and have children (for whom they would need their remaining breast). Subsequently they had no need to ride "unless compelled to do so by a general expedition." Herodotus says something similar and gives us the indigenous name for these women: *Oiorpata,* which meant "slayers of men."

Herodotus records a tale about the Amazons that purports to

explain the origin of the strange half-Scythian language spoken to the east of the Don River in Sauromatia. A band of young male Scythians skirmished with an alien band, the story goes. When they stripped the dead of their armor, they discovered that they were in fact women—the Amazons. They decided not to fight the Amazons anymore but instead to court them, figuring that the offspring of their matings would be noble and ferocious warriors. The Scythian lads pitched their camp opposite the Amazon camp and waited until about noon, when the women would come out in pairs to urinate. Two of the Scythians crept up on a pair of Amazon women and, being received by them, had sex with them. Although neither could speak the other's language, they resolve to return the next day, each bringing another friend. So it went, until the two camps were lustily amalgamated. The Scythians could not learn the Amazons' language, but the Amazons showed rather greater ability in learning, albeit imperfectly, the Scythian tongue. The Scythians then suggested that the Amazons return home with them to their parents' dominions to be their wives. But the Amazons retorted, "We cannot live with your women. For we and they have not the same customs. We shoot the bow and the javelin and ride horses but, for 'women's tasks' we know them not." The Scythians settled with the Amazons in what was Sauromatia, and because the Amazons never quite mastered the Scythian language, Sarmatian arose as a dialect variant. Herodotus's mythical account indicates that the area to the east of the Don River, known in classical times as Sauromatia, would be the place for archaeologists to look for traces of these warrior women.

Burials of warrior women first came to notice in the mid-nineteenth century, when some graves in the Caucasus Mountains on the Terek River were opened. One grave contained a skeleton of strongly female type, buried with armor, a sheaf of arrows, a slate discus, and an iron knife. A series of graves from a nearby site at Aul Stepan Zminda contained many female warriors and their mounts, although they were dated later than the Scythian period. Modern excavations around the royal barrow of Chertomlyk in Ukraine found that four out of fifty warrior graves were of this "Amazon" type: one of them was buried with an arrowhead embedded in her back, an-

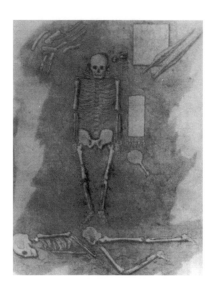

(Fig. 8.2) Burial of an "Amazon." Mound No. 20
at Cholodnyi Yar, Ukraine. The principal burial
appears biologically female, with a young male at her
feet. Source: Bobrinskoi 1887–1901 in Rolle 1989.

other had a massive iron shield, and a third had a small child. This
last burial suggests a slight variation on the accounts given by
Herodotus and Hippocrates.

Around forty female warrior burials are currently known in the
Scythian region, while in Sauromatia around 20 percent of all the
Iron Age warrior burials are said to be female. Striking though this
percentage is, it is likely to be an underestimate. The skeletons have
been sexed through comparison with modern populations, yet they
are likely to display a higher frequency of traits designated "masculine." That the Amazons were, according to Hippocrates, able to regulate their reproductive lives may indicate that they used oral fertility
controls (such as *Artemisia* and *Ferula,* effective agents that grew in
the region). But it is also possible that they were amenorrheic due to
the extremely physical nature of their training. Like some female athletes today, they may have traded their body fat for muscle to the
point where they were not fertile. Whether or not this was so, the
Amazons likely retained narrow malelike pelvises later into life than
would normally be the case. Not only is this hormonal factor likely to
hinder the archaeological identification of their skeletons, but short-
term sexual selection pressures may have endowed such women with
physiques that were genetically more "masculine."

The Amazon rule that only women who had killed three of the enemy could start a family would mean, if strictly adhered to, that only those women with the greatest military prowess would pass on their genes. Under such conditions any woman with a masculinizing hormone imbalance, such as adreno-genital syndrome, would actually be at a reproductive advantage. Rather than being ostracized for excessive masculinity, she could take her pick from among the best suitors. This notion is of course hypothetical, but the underlying point is that a radically different set of physical qualities were valued in Scythian women as opposed to ice age women. The Amazon burials occur alongside more "feminine" female burials in Scythia, demonstrating that it was not obligatory to serve as a warrior woman.

The story of the Amazons is deep in the popular psyche. For many women today, the myth conjures up images of greater empowerment. Yet from a sociological point of view, the existence of such women in the Iron Age steppelands is thought to be anomalous. Engels argued that pastoral nomadism marked a new stage in the oppression of women by men, and many Marxist-inspired sociologists followed in this approach. Maria Mies writes, for example, "It is most probably correct to say that the martial pastoral nomads were the fathers of all dominance relations, particularly that of men over women." Could the Amazons have emerged because of this dominance?

More modern ethnography provides many examples of females cross-dressing and adopting male roles. Walter Williams has recently surveyed them in *The Spirit and the Flesh: Sexual Diversity in American Indian Culture*. The Amazonian Amazons were described thus by Pedro de Magalhães de Gandovo in 1576: "They wear their hair cut in the same way as the men, and go to war with bows and arrows and pursue game, always in company with men; each has a woman to serve her, to whom she says she is married, and they treat each other and speak with each other as man and wife." These Amazons maintained what Williams calls a *heterogender* relationship, despite their biological homosexuality; wives did not consider themselves lesbian. If the marriage terminated, they could marry a biological man without any trouble. This is a common pattern in North

America, but it differed in Scythia, at least as far as the Greeks understood it.

Among several of the Alaskan peoples, such as the Kaska and the Ingalik, having a son was extremely important, as the family's survival depended on big game, the hunting of which was a male gender pursuit. Thus a family that had only daughters would select one of them—usually around the age of five—to "be like a man"; such women-men often became outstanding hunters. Among the Ingalik they would participate in the men-only sweat baths, where their biological sex would apparently be ignored.

Economic factors may have been important in Scythia too, especially economic factors introduced by outsiders that caused deep changes in Scythian society. Such a phenomenon, too, has a historical analogy. In sixteenth-century Canada the arrival of European fur traders sharply tilted the existing power balance between native men and women. Before European contact, a fairly sex-egalitarian society had existed, like that proposed in Chapter 6 for Mesolithic Europe. To be sure, there was a gender division of labor, where most women did food-gathering, weaving, and so on, while most men hunted. Some men and women did each other's work, often cross-dressing in the process, but only on an individual, personality-trait basis. Either sphere could provide a path to wealth and a position as a revered elder. When the Europeans arrived, they were interested only in furs, for which they traded guns and blankets. In the process they made the native hunters—the vast majority of whom were men—much richer than the women. In the face of marked gender inequality, biological women increasingly adopted male gender roles as they vied to maintain their personal status—if not that of their gender. The pattern for Scythia may have been somewhat similar.

The reason Herodotus and Hippocrates knew so much about Scythia was that the Greeks had set up trading colonies along the coasts of the Black Sea. Through these colonies flowed grain and slaves for Athens and other city-states. It was against this background that, between 700 and 350 B.C., the nomadic martial elites of the steppes rose to power. Their game was slaving and extortion, and their rewards were some of the finest artworks of gold and silver that Greek craftspeople ever made. Herodotus mentions that the Issedones, one of the tribes that lived farthest from the Black Sea, probably somewhere around the Ural Mountains, had a society where women and men exercised equal political power; closer to the colonies such was not the case, and it is clear archaeologically that here the richest and most elaborate burials of all are those of men.

The real Amazons behind the myth, the heavily armed women of Chertomlyk, may well have been a group of women in the higher echelons of steppe society who took their chances to go on raids and trade slaves with the Greeks for some financial reward. Female participation in lucrative raiding may have hardened into a system of military obligation, as Hippocrates implies. That women might have been drafted during this period is supported by reports from discoveries at the other end of the steppe, in China, where a female army of life-size terra-cotta figures is said to have been excavated.

The rise of farming societies and, subsequently, urban states has always tended to produce an economically disadvantaged position for women. The reasons are complex but have something to do with the fact that child-rearing is hardly ever recognized as a job in market economic terms. If resources are allocated on the basis of market production, and the production of children is omitted from the category of gainful work, then women who have children will not have the same opportunities to earn social credit (money). Under such conditions, as women's perceived economic importance diminishes, female sexuality typically becomes a commodity, with all that this implies for the experience of sexuality in general.

Sex Slavery and Recreation

By the Iron Age, there is increasing evidence in Europe for female sex professionals, as well as sexual slavery. Perhaps the best archaeological guides to the incidence of prostitution are the so-called brothel tokens of ancient Rome. These little coinlike objects have long been improperly understood, and the sexual imagery that appears on them

(Fig. 8.3) Roman brothel tokens. Three examples, showing obverse and reverse. Drawings by George Taylor from images supplied by Aleksander Bursche.

has consigned all too many of them to the locked basements of museums. Each brothel token has a sex scene on one side and a number on the other, an arrangement that puzzled experts until recently, as there appeared to be no obvious relationship between the two sides. But Aleksander Bursche of the University of Warsaw, a coin specialist, has recently been able to order the tokens into a chronological sequence from the early to late Roman periods, on the basis of minor stylistic changes.

The Roman era as a whole was inflationary, a fact that allows Bursche to show two things. First, the later tokens had higher values; and second and more important, the particular positions depicted on the tokens of each period—early, middle, and late—accord with the tokens' relative values. To the untrained eye, it might be difficult to see why fellatio should be cheaper than vaginal intercourse from the rear, but Bursche was able to confirm his hunch that a systematic relationship indeed existed by conducting a blind test on present-day Warsaw prostitutes. He asked them which positions and acts they charge more for. Their scale accorded precisely with the Roman scale. For prostitutes who see a lot of clients, one of the greatest hazards is vaginal soreness; thus deep penetrating positions, such as sex from behind, are more painful and therefore cost more.

The brothel tokens also have broader sociological importance. Found all over Europe, wherever the Roman army went, they represent an institutionalized form of professional sex that crossed all language barriers. A mercenary from Libya or Dacia could decide what he wanted and obtain it from a Caledonian prostitute during his tour of duty on Hadrian's Wall. She, on the other hand, knew precisely what the man had paid for. The tokens imply an established sex industry that did everything from design and manufacture the tokens themselves to maintaining brothel premises. Although the women must have been able to keep a tally of the remunerative value of their work, they did not have control over the finances. The people who ran the brothels received the money. It may be that the women never received any money at all and were slaves. Or they may have done the job in return for protection and a roof over their head in a war-torn and increasingly lawless society.

The prostitutes in a given place were not necessarily of local origin. Herodotus, writing of the Thracians in the fifth century B.C., says that they sold their daughters into slavery in Greece; the most attractive or skilled women may well have been traded elsewhere. Careful analysis of skeletal pitting can now prove that syphilis was present in Roman Europe; it must have been spread in part through the brothel network, although its incidence seems to have stayed fairly low.

The brothel tokens provide unambiguous evidence for the existence of an established repertoire of "sexual positions." How this repertoire emerged, and when, is presently unclear. Unusual depictions of sex occur in earlier Iron Age Europe, notably on the great bronze wine-drinking buckets or *situlae* of Etruscan culture in northern Italy and the southeast Alpine Hallstatt culture. The pictures document many items of everyday use that do not normally survive in the archaeological record. Beds and mattresses, for example, are shown in wonderful undulating movement beneath a pair of explicitly depicted heterosexual lovers. This Iron Age *situla* art provides some of the first direct evidence we have for sex on beds in prehistoric Europe, although beds are likely to have been used since much earlier times. One princely burial from Hochdorf in Germany, dating to the same period as the *situla* (the fifth century B.C.), contained a splendidly ornate bed, presumably supplied for pleasure as well as rest in the afterlife.

Nor was sex confined to the bedroom in the *situla* depictions. Scenes of apparently simple merriment—with people drinking and feasting, while trials of personal strength go on around them—often have a sexual edge as well. One type of scene occurs again and again on the *situlae*. Two men are involved in some form of competition with each other; the prize, a *situla* of wine, usually stands on a jardiniere placed between them. Their competition may be physical—sometimes they strip down and do something that involves holding up dumbbells, their erect penises defiantly facing each other across the tournament floor. Or the competition may be cerebral, as when they sit at either end of a chaise longue, with musical instruments, trying to outdo each other's virtuosity.

The most extraordinary scene of this type involves sex. It occurs on a short piece of beaten-bronze belt plate. Although it is unfortunately fragmentary, the image can nevertheless be recon-

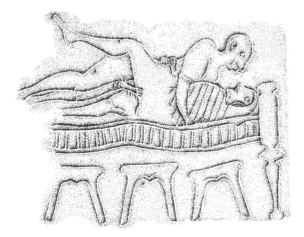

(Fig. 8.4) The missionary position; Sanzeno. Scene from a bronze *situla*, Italy. Drawing by George Taylor after Kastelic 1965.

(Fig. 8.5) A competitive sex game, Brezje. A fragmentary bronze belt plate from Brezje, Slovenia. Decorated in the "*Situla* Style." Author's reconstruction, drawn by George Taylor.

structed with confidence, due to the formulaic nature of such scenes. Given the prudery that has often hidden or destroyed such archaeological evidence, we are perhaps lucky that this piece survives at all; its fragmentary state may well have resulted from an attempt to destroy it at some time. In the fragment, a couple are having intercourse; the woman is perched on a stool with her legs high, to facilitate the man's entry, and she is wearing a heavy head scarf. The man is looking away from her, back over the prize stand, where the amphora of wine is clearly in view. Here the scene ends, but it is virtually certain that it was replicated on the other side of the stand, with the other man looking back over his shoulder too. Clearly a sexual competition of some kind is depicted, apparently primarily between the men. But what were the rules? Are they trying to stare each other out? Or is it a case of seeing who can last longer, or succeed in defloration more quickly, or perhaps simply ejaculate first? Is the woman, along with her lost counterpart, a prostitute, or is she the wife of the man, or does her rather demure headcovering indicate that she was a virgin?

What does seem clear is that this competition did *not* focus on the woman's desire or pleasure. The man is more interested in his sporting rival than in his partner. Her blank expression carries no hint of mounting orgasm but implies that she is an alienated vessel for his temporary use. Certainly the bronzesmith felt no need to hint at pleasure, or indeed any other explicit emotion, when her features were traced.

Transvestite Shamans

Not all Iron Age men were rampaging macho boors. Although the Scythian nomads of the Black Sea steppes were one of the most ferocious military forces of the period, they were also, according to Hippocrates, "the most impotent of men," especially the warrior elite. Not only did they spend "most of their time on their horses, so that they do not handle the parts but, owing to cold and fatigue forget about sexual passion"; they also wore pants, and the "constant jolting of their horses" made them unfit for intercourse. Hippocrates concluded that "the great majority among the Scythians become impotent, do women's work, live like women and converse accordingly . . . they put on women's clothes, holding that they have lost their manhood." That is, they were transvestites. Herodotus says that they suffered from the "female sickness."

Was there any reality behind this description? From what we know about Hippocrates, it seems unlikely that he would make up factual evidence, although his explanation of underlying processes might not be acceptable in modern terms. The idea that the constant jolting of horses can make men unfit for intercourse mirrors a well-known modern complaint. In Australia it is known as "geographer's balls," brought on by the bumping of Land-Rovers across the outback. It is also documented among avid cyclists. Damage to the testes caused in this way can be lasting. First blood appears in the semen, and later the ejaculatory and erectile functions are lost. The appearance of blood may provide a clue to the mysterious "female sickness," but there are other possibilities as well. Spending too long in the saddle is not just bad for the genitalia, it is also affects the anus. The English surgeon John Arderne pioneered operations on knights returning from the Hundred Years' War (1337–1453) to cure them of anal fistulae—holes that appear in the anal and rectal wall as a result of poor blood circulation and partial atrophy in some muscles during many years in the saddle. Scythian military adventures were of similar long duration to the Hundred Years' War campaigns. Herodotus records one campaign that lasted twenty-eight years.

Hippocrates's reference to the problems of pants-wearing also makes sense in the light of modern medical knowledge. In primates the testes are on the outside of the body, so that sperm develop at a lower temperature. Sperm that can survive at a couple of degrees below core body temperature may have a better chance of hanging on for an extended period in the vagina. In any case sperm do not develop properly at core body temperature levels—levels that can be artificially produced by wearing tight-fitting pants. The Scythians' style of life could have caused them to suffer from a variety of ailments around the genital region, some of which could have produced symptoms that were recorded as a "female sickness."

Herodotus, for his part, described the transvestites among the Scythians as "androgynous" and said that they were known as Enarees. Because the Scythians spoke an Iranian language, one of the constituent languages of the Indo-European group, their words can be connected with related words in other Indo-European languages. The Sanskrit word *nara* means "man," so that *a-nara* or *e-nara* could mean "without manhood." Herodotus wrote that the priestess of the temple of Ascalon had smitten the Enarees with the sickness and that they thereafter became diviners or prophets. They carried out divinations for kings and other leaders in some fashion that involved braiding and unbraiding strips of lime bark. Their position was at once elevated and vulnerable: their pronouncements were revered, but if they turned out to be incorrect, they were put to death.

In the light of the general correspondences between Herodotus's other descriptions of Scythia and the archaeological evidence, we should be inclined to trust him on the transvestite soothsayers, the Enarees. There is a great deal of evidence from around the world for people similar to the Enarees as Herodotus describes them. In North America the general term *berdache* is used for males who dress as females. Like the Amazonian Amazons, they may be involved in long-lasting relationships that are culturally heterogender but biologically homosexual. The men who take up with such partners are considered no different from other married men. Among some Plains Indians, berdache were ritually and physically created by making prepubescent boys ride bareback until their testes were destroyed, causing feminizing hormonal changes in their development. Rough equivalents to the berdache occur or occurred in Polynesia *(mahus)*, India *(hijras)*, Europe *(castrati)*, and parts of Asia and Africa, sometimes involving alteration or mutilation of the genital region. Transvestite shamanism is also well known from modern Siberia, a region that the Scythians had great contact with in their time.

According to Hippocrates, the transvestite Scythians constituted a large part of the biologically male elite population—those who rode horses and were subsequently disabled by it. Herodotus, on the other hand, implies that they had a much more specialized role as prophets or soothsayers. Whoever the Enarees were, they cannot be simply identified as effeminate or homosexual men. There was gender-crossing but no gender-blurring in Scythia; one noble male who began to dress in Greek fashion, in long flowing robes rather than trousers, and to frequent taverns with Greek men, among whom homosexual behavior was a relative commonplace, was lynched by his Scythian peers on the ground that he had become effeminate. Clearly there was a crucial difference between effeminacy and "losing one's manhood" to become a soothsayer.

Love Potions and Gender Drugs

Could the Enarees have made themselves look like women? Scythian men are depicted in Greek art as having great bushy beards; any gender-crossers among them would have had to cope with that—unlike the berdache of the Americas, where male beard growth is typically slight or nonexistent. Did they shave? Certainly good bronze razors had been available in Europe since the middle of the preceding Bronze Age, but they are not usually found in Scythia. A solution to this dilemma and a clue to the true identity of the Enarees comes from the first-century-B.C. poet Ovid, who was exiled to Tomis, a Greek Black Sea colony on the edge of the Scythian steppe where he wrote his famous love poems. In *Amores* 1, verse 8, Ovid writes: "She's a witch, mutters magical cantrips, can make rivers run uphill, knows the best aphrodisiacs—when to use herbal brews or the whirring bull-roarer, how to extract that stuff from a mare in heat." This final, puzzling reference to horses is repeated in the poem *On Facial Treatment for Ladies:* "Put no faith in herbals and potions, abjure the deadly stuff distilled by a mare in heat."

An extract of pregnant mares' urine is marketed today under the trade name *Premarin,* by Ayerst Organics, Inc., of Canada, and is used by male-to-female transsexuals as part of their hormone therapy. It is a rich source of complex conjugated estriols that feminize the skin, suppress beard growth, and cause a degree of breast development. Could it be that Ovid learned his witch's potions in Tomis? Scythia had been known since the time of Homer as the land of the mare-milkers, and strange as it may seem, it is not at all unusual for pastoralist people to drink the urine of their animals. Indeed, camels' urine is a national drink of Mongolia today. This practice might have given the warlike Scythians distinct tactical advantages at times: if you are unsure whether the water sources ahead of you have been poisoned or polluted by your enemy, it may be a sensible measure to "filter" it first through your horses. All in all, it seems most unlikely that the Scythians would not have known what effect pregnant mares' urine could have on male physical development.

Ovid also refers to more dramatic physical modifications. In *Amores* 2, verse 3, he writes: "Bad luck that your mistress should have a keeper who is neither male nor female, who can't enjoy true sex! The man who was first to sever boys' genital members should have been castrated himself." The original Greek text seems to imply a castration involving both the penis and testicles. It sounds a little like the creation of *hijras* in modern India—feminized boys with amputated sex organs who earn a living by dancing, divination, and prostitution.

Although Ovid's writings throw important new light on the

possible identity of the Enarees and how they might have managed their female appearance, they have yet to be identified archaeologically. Some burials, such as that of a Sarmatian "priestess" from the Sokolova barrow on the southern Bug River, dating to the time that Ovid was writing, contain such strange grave goods that they arouse speculation that the remains of an Enaree lies within. The skeleton in the Sokolova barrow is described as that of a 40-to-45-year-old woman, but the published metrical data are inconclusive. The grave goods include rare Egyptian imports, as well as various models and symbols—a phallus, a cowrie shell (a traditional vagina symbol), and a sculpture of a woman in childbirth. In addition, there is a unique bronze mirror— usually a female cosmetic aid. Its handle is made in the form of a bearded man sitting in a lotus position, wearing a long dress, and holding a ritual drinking vessel of a type that accompanied the body in death. Although little can be said for certain without a fuller analysis of the bones, the soft-tissue reconstruction of the face is definitely masculine. Any subsequent work conducted in the light of the Greek written evidence would have to take into account the fact that the skeleton of a biological male who had drunk pregnant mares' urine out of a ritual container all his life might well be difficult to recognize as male by today's standards.

(Fig. 8.6) The "priestess" of the Sokolova Mogila, southern Bug region, Ukraine. Reconstruction from Kovpanenko 1991.

Tantric Sex in
Iron Age Denmark

An ambiguous Enaree-like person—beardless, with flowing robes, yet also breastless—is depicted holding a mirror and standing in the company of a three-legged serpent on one of the Letnitsa plaques (see "Buried Wives," earlier in this chapter). Another figure, very like the one on the Sokolova mirror handle, occurs on one of the greatest art objects that the prehistoric world produced—the Gundestrup cauldron—although the Gundestrup figure has no beard and is clearly androgynous. The cauldron itself was made in the second century B.C. in southeastern Europe, probably in what is now the Transylvanian region of Romania, and was lost on waste ground in Jutland, Denmark, some years later. A bog grew up around it, and it was rediscovered by peat cutters in 1891.

The cauldron is made of several silver plaques that fit together around a great hemispherical bowl. They are decorated with fantastic scenes of people and mythical beasts. The outward-facing plaques depict gods and goddesses, and since the gods have beards and the goddesses have breasts, they set up a kind of pictorial grammar for expressing gender. In contrast to them there are a number of androgynous figures. The most striking seems at first to be sitting in a cross-legged pose, eyes in trance, wearing a stag-antlered cap and holding a neck ring in his/her right hand. A rather phallic ram-headed snake is in the left hand, and the figure—often identified as the Celtic god Cernunnos—is surrounded by animals. The figure is of indeterminate sex, with neither breasts nor beard. What is most important is the pose. The legs are not actually on the ground but are raised up. Although it is hard to see it at first, the whole figure is

(Fig. 8.7) Androgynous figure; Letnitsa. Bridle decoration, Letnitsa, Bulgaria. Photograph: National Historical Museum, Sofia.

(Fig. 8.8)   Goddess on the Gundestrup cauldron. One of the outer plates: The small figure resting in the crook of the goddess's arm probably represents a breast-feeding infant. Photograph courtesy of Flemming Kaul.

(Fig. 8.9)   Androgynous horned figure; Gundestrup. Detail from one of the cauldron's inner plates. Photograph: Nationalmuseet, Copenhagen.

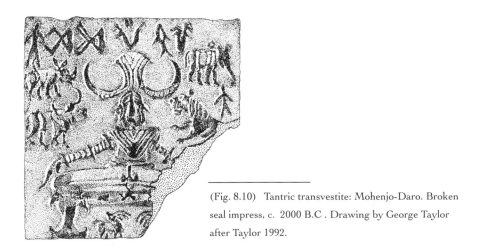

(Fig. 8.10) Tantric transvestite: Mohenjo-Daro. Broken seal impress, c. 2000 B.C. Drawing by George Taylor after Taylor 1992.

levitated on one toe. (The ground line is clearly defined by the adjacent stag's hooves.) The right heel is sandwiched between the left thigh and the crotch, so as to put pressure directly on the perineum—the point between the scrotum and anus. The figure has been depicted in one of the advanced positions *(asanas)* of Tantric Yoga, a type of yoga that varies from the more recent ascetic tradition in that it focuses on animal energies. Those who practice it may use both sex and drugs in order to reach altered states of consciousness.

A closely similar image to the one on the cauldron comes from the great city site of Mohenjo-Daro, in the Indus valley of South Asia. It is dated to an earlier period, around 2000 B.C., and appears on a seal stone rather than a piece of decorative metalwork. Nevertheless the type of person represented is very similar. Through comparisons with other images from the Indus valley civilization, it is possible to say that the figure is dressed as a woman within the canons of the time. Yet the figure also clearly displays testicles and an erect penis. This man-woman wears great horns and is, like the Gundestrup figure, surrounded by animals. Most strikingly, the figure too is in a Tantric *asana,* this time with both heels placed against the perineum. Thomas McEvilly of Rice University has investigated the background to this figure and concluded that it marks the earliest de-

(Fig. 8.11) Androgynous and part-bestial figure (showing bare breasts and hairy shoulders); Gundestrup. Photograph: the author.

piction of Tantric or sexual yoga on the Indian subcontinent. The Tantric yogic and steppe shamanic traditions, McEvilly notes, are closely interwoven.

The figure on the Gundestrup cauldron seems to represent a particular type of individual, someone with intersex or ambiguous sex qualities—a person who brought together the female, male, and animal worlds in one body. He/she seems to have a shamanic nature and to have entered some sort of altered state of consciousness by channeling sexual energy. A second shamanic figure is shown on the base of the cauldron, wielding a sword, with animal hair on the shoulders and distinct breasts (Fig. 8.11). These figures may represent the Enarees Herodotus spoke of.

It is ironic that such a sophisticated form of sexual expression should have reached Europe with Christianity following so closely on its heels. Had historical circumstances been different, the courts of Medieval Europe might have thrilled to the erotic dances of Indian-style courtesans, surrounded by voluptuous sexual imagery, as on the Hindu temples of the Deccan. But things did not turn out that way. The connection between ritual and sex went underground, when it was not incorporated in obscure fashion into the fabric of the Catholic Church.

Bad Sex

In both Pagan and early Christian Europe, in the centuries that followed the fall of the Roman Empire, brutal interdictions on inappropriate sex can be archaeologically traced. Interpretation is hampered, however, by a lack of properly thorough forensic reports on some of the most important human material, such as the large number of bodies preserved in the bogs of Scandinavia and parts of Britain and the Low Countries, many with traces of violent and possibly ritualized death. The historical data is much better and supports various speculations about the archaeological evidence.

In the early medieval period King Harald Bluetooth had his unfaithful wife Queen Gunnhild drowned in a bog. Hers was apparently a standard penalty for adultery and was sometimes also applied to the female victims of rape and incest. Such executions required no judicial process and would follow extremely swiftly on discovery. As semen can remain identifiable in the vagina for about ten days, the bodies would almost certainly have contained semen at the time of death, and owing to its chemical composition, it would stand a fair chance of being preserved along with everything else. The Roman author Tacitus, writing in the early second century A.D. about the German tribes, says that "adultery in that populous nation is rare in the extreme, and punishment is summary and left to the husband. He shaves off his wife's hair, strips her in the presence of kinsmen, thrusts her from his house and flogs her through the whole village." Her ultimate punishment would probably have been like that recorded by Tacitus for other evildoers: "drowned in mire and swamp with a hurdle put over them." Yet when the body of an adolescent German girl of the first century A.D. was found in a peat bog at Windeby in Denmark, naked, shaven-headed, blindfolded, and weighted down with a halter around her neck, the forensic scientists made no attempt to identify traces of semen.

There is also some archaeological evidence for rape that casts light on the attitudes toward it. The skeleton of a sixteen-year-old female—excavated from a sixth- or seventh-century A.D. Anglo-Saxon cemetery at Worthy Park, Kingsworthy, in Hampshire—has lesions on both thigh bones. The lesion on the right thigh is at the top and was caused when two of the main tendons that connect to the pelvis were torn away from the bone. Archaeologist Sonia Hawkes and pathologist Calvin Wells, writing in 1975, concluded that the "tearing of [these] tendons, which is very uncommon in young persons of this age, is almost invariably due to violent separation of the thighs while trying to resist this and bringing them tightly together. . . . In other words, this lesion is typically the result of a brutal rape. . . . The lesion on the back of the left femur, just above the knee, could have been the result of forcing her knees upwards in order to facilitate penetration." Although pathologists today would not draw quite such firm conclusions about the specific causes of bone lesions, important additional evidence supports their case.

The young woman was buried without grave goods of any kind—a very rare circumstance and one that may be considered a mark of some less-than-honorable status. The young woman in Grave 78 was buried not only without grave goods but facedown, and judging by the position of her bones, she may have still been alive when the earth was shoveled in over her. These observations become relevant in the light of contemporary historical evidence for attitudes toward rape victims. Wulfstan's *Sermo Lupi ad Anglos* describes an Anglo-Saxon man being made to stand by while his wife was raped by a dozen Vikings. Wulfstan stressed the man's shame rather than any concern for the woman. From what is more generally known of Anglo-Saxon society at this time, it seems quite likely that a raped woman would be put to death to expunge the dishonor that her rape brought on the man's house.

The tradition of religious transvestism, documented for the later Iron Age communities of the steppes, seems to have continued into Pagan Europe. Tacitus says that among a particular tribe of Germans, the Naharvali, an ancient form of worship is conducted in groves, where "the presiding priest dresses like a woman." The historian Bede, writing some six centuries later about the pagan religion of the Germanic Anglo-Saxon settlers in the British Isles, is notably coy about details, although he does let slip that the chief priest had to ride a mare rather than a gelding (perhaps an on-the-hoof source of conjugated estriols?). It is interesting that in surviving folk tradition, shamanistic or wizard powers are associated with divination using a willow wand, as willow also is a source of conjugated estriols. Archaeologist Christopher Knüsel has recently begun to search for burials of possibly transvestite priests among the records of already excavated Anglo-Saxon graves.

In the end, Christianity may have used the transvestism of the local pagan priesthood for its own purposes. The standard explanation for modern clerical garb is that it derives from the togas of Rome, but one has to ask precisely why this mode of dress—which is not associated with any inherently Christian values—was retained as Christianity spread north. It may be that it neatly fitted local expectations of priests in dresses. Sexual elements in the church service persisted into recent times, particularly in the sacrament of baptism. In the later medieval period baptism was for adults; those who were to be baptized would appear in church naked, to be dunked into the font, the life-giving forces of which would be activated by shaking of hot wax from a large white candle into the water. No clearer reference to the male and female principles could be envisaged. This basic ritual carries us back in time to the grave of the golden penis and perhaps beyond, to the painted caves of Lascaux.

Chivalry had been born as far back as the Iron Age. It had its original inspiration among the horse riders of the steppes who, far from home, pined for their loved ones. In Medieval Europe it was transformed into the ideal of the wandering knight out to win the chaste, slender princess locked in her father's tower. Eventually, as in the epic poem *Sir Gawain and the Green Knight,* love ideally became quite removed from physicality. Sex would spoil it. The complexity of the issues raised by this separation is intimated in Malory's *The Death of Arthur,* where the king's love for Queen Guinevere is necessarily

(Fig. 8.12)   The Men-an-Tol, Cornwall. Photograph: Mick Sharp.

unconsummated because of his "groin" injury. Lancelot cuckolds
Arthur and thereby confirms male fears about the promiscuity that
lies just beneath the chaste exterior of the noblest lady. Guinevere,
for her part, could easily have managed a sexual relationship without
getting pregnant. Knowledge of herbal birth control continued down
to the very end of the medieval period and was a significant factor in
demographic stability.

Of course, all sorts of other sexual activity went on. Homosexuality was widespread in the monasteries, as penitentiary records
make clear, and it was a common service that a young man on his first
campaign rendered to older warriors. The segregation of men and
women within the medieval castle created opportunities for discreet
lesbian liaisons of the sort that, throughout evolutionary time, prehistory, and the early modern world, have left little material evidence.

The sexual imagery of the past was either reinterpreted and
kept alive, or else it was reinterpreted and suppressed. At an
unknown date the ring-cut stone that had served as an entrance to
the Neolithic Men-an-Tol grave, which the shafts of the sun god

(Fig. 8.13) The Cerne Abbas Giant, Dorset.
Photograph: Bob Croxford.

once penetrated, was set up in the open between two stumpy phalluses and used for various folk rituals that healed through symbolic
rebirth. The great prehistoric chalk hill-figure of Cerne Abbas, who
once stood guard on the outer slope of a hill fort, wielding a club, his
penis erect in a show of virility and aggression rather than sexuality,
played host to a midsummer's-eve orgy of village lads and lasses.
Young women who were having difficulty getting pregnant would
walk up the hill to spend the night sleeping on the giant's penis. Less
affirmatively, Cernunnos, the horned god—the Celtic translation of
Indian Tantric practice and a symbol of religious transcendence
through sex—was translated by Christianity into none other than
the Devil.

Sex and the Laws of Sumptuary

As prehistory progressed toward the present, the rather varied natural bases of human sexuality seem to have become ever more stereotyped by culture. Before the Bronze Age, burials can be sexed only
by reference to biological features of the skeleton (with all the attendant uncertainties), but later a firm code of grave goods emerged that

symbolized gender and masked sexual ambiguities. Gender objectified difference but at the same time overrode biology.

It can happen that a dead person is not represented bodily as the
sex that we would classify him or her as being in life. The ancient
Egyptian grave "1770" is an elaborate burial of someone who seems
skeletally to be a young female. She was buried with gold nipple covers (as is usual in female graves) but also with a prosthetic penis
(made of wrapped bandages; these are often provided in male
graves). After careful analysis, Egyptologist Rosalie David concluded
that the person probably drowned in the Nile and was recovered in
such a poor state that the biological sex was no longer clear. The em-
balmers hedged their bets, she believes, by providing both male and
female attributes for the journey to the other world. Another Egyptian mummy was thought until very recently to be female, until X rays
showed that it is in fact a male who was deliberately buried as a
woman—with careful bandaging to pad his/her hips and breasts. It is
important to distinguish here as elsewhere between the biological sex
by which we classify a body today and the original social gender of
the person when alive.

The appearance of gendered clothing is the moment when a
more complex social hierarchy can begin to develop. Baby-carrying
slings, as I argued in Chapter 1, were probably developed by hominid
females to carry their infants, but they could also have been used by
males. The context in which a thing is used gives it the potential to
become gendered—to take on, despite its inanimate nature, a sexual
identity. In reality, the division between people and things is not quite
as clear as we may imagine, when it comes to sex and gender. In most
societies menstrual pads have a clear association with fertile women,
by virtue of actually containing some of their biological matter. To a
lesser extent, clothing absorbs the smells and secretions of the
wearer. It becomes "theirs," and in a society where a sexual division
of labor exists, it also becomes a generically gendered item.

Specific men's and women's clothing probably emerged at the
point when clothing first was made, designed to meet a combination
of functional requirements—allowing access to breast-feeding or different modes of urination—and codes of mutual sexual attraction. In

the archaeological record, however, it took a long time before grave goods took on a consistent association with biological sex. The reason for the delay may be that in many small-scale prehistoric communities, over long time spans, the issue of "who you were" rested on your individuality and your own special contribution to group life. Only after the development of farming, as population rose, did a grosser classification—*first* a woman or man, *then* an individual—come to the forefront.

The emergence of strictly gendered clothing, of uniforms for men and women that it was a crime to subvert (transvestism was a grave Old Testament offense) aided the entrenchment of social inequality. When a king wearing a crown looks down on a shaven-headed slave, his symbolic impact and thus social power are strengthened by the fact that all around him different grades of people—guards, courtiers, ladies-in-waiting, scullery maids—are wearing clothes that convey their different statuses. If they were wearing anything they pleased, the king and slave would appear to be just two more revelers at a fancy dress party.

Court clothing has the power that fancy dress lacks because it is rule-governed. The very existence of gendered clothing lends clothing denoting other kinds of status something of the force of nature. When women wear one type of clothes and men another, the clothing is evidently different just as the biology is different; each sex wears their "natural" clothing. This logic can be extended, by sleight-of-hand, to justify the "natural" clothing of kings and paupers and thus to naturalize the very existence of social hierarchy. Gender rules are extended into sumptuary laws. It is therefore no accident that the societies where gender-crossing is most visible are those that have the most rigorous laws about the "proper" garb of sex and class. Paradoxically, they are the societies least tolerant of sexual ambiguity; the clothing *is* the sex. In Scythia, as we have seen, the Enarees could dress as women and talk as women, but when one of their kings, Scyles, blurred the boundaries by dressing in Greek robes and participating in Dionysiac orgies, he was killed.

Identity can be defined in many ways. Biological sex, gender, and social status all play their parts, as do physical type, temperament, and personal taste. How these and other aspects of a person are projected after death is largely up to those who bury them. How archaeologists sort out the different parameters hundreds or thousands of years later is problematic. A cause célèbre is the burial of the so-called Princess of Vix, a spectacularly richly endowed grave of the early fifth century B.C., discovered in 1953 near the ancient citadel of Mont Lassois in Burgundy. Some people believe that the grave is that of a wealthy woman, others that it belonged to a transvestite male priest. The costume jewelry on the corpse is ambiguous, and so are the bones. Although there were likely more wealthy men than women in Iron Age Europe, some women did possess great wealth.

As the pelvis of the fragmentary Vix skeleton did not survive, the only way, in the absence of DNA testing, to sex the remains is to measure the skull. But then the skeleton's racial type becomes a crucial factor. If the deceased was Nordic European, belonging to the blond, tall, and robust physique commonly found in Denmark, then the skull looks comfortably female. But if the "princess" belonged to the more gracile Mediterranean stock, then "she" could easily have been male.

Whether we like it or not, race is just as important in the definition of self as sex. It arises out of sex—out of the specific mate choices that different people make. Yet its boundaries turn out to be just as ambiguous as sexual boundaries.

Chapter 9

The Return of the Beast
with Two Backs:

Sex and the
Prehistory of Race

"Certainly no normal human being of modern times would willingly copulate with any of the australopithecines."

JOHN BAKER,
RACE

Race is, at first sight, a strange subject to deal with in a book on the prehistory of sex. It is also a sensitive subject, having a history checkered with claims that do not bear scrutiny. Race is where culture meets biology at a political level. Its dynamic is controlled by sexual attraction and reproduction, on the one hand, and the appalling realities of genocide on the other. Are human races ancient in origin, marking distinctly different evolutionary paths? Or are

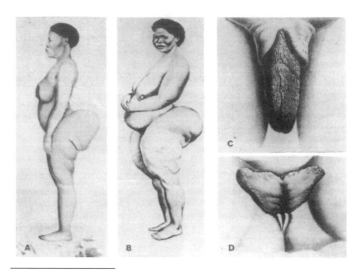

(Fig. 9.1)   Sexual anatomy of two nineteenth-century San women. (A)
The so-called "Hottentot Venus" (Cuvier 1824). (B) A woman of the
Korana tribe (Friedenthal 1910). (C) and (D): external genitalia of a San
woman (Lesueur 1800); (C) shows the long labia minora hanging down
together; (D) shows them separated. From Baker 1974, by kind permission of Oxford University Press.

they relatively recent phenomena, created as a function of the rapid
geographical and numerical expansion of anatomically modern
humans across the globe? Only the study of prehistory can provide
answers.

   Genitalia are among the most wonderfully varied of all human
attributes. Different lengths and shapes of clitoris, labia, penis, and
nipple are common to different peoples around the world. Such differences fascinated Charles Darwin, who noted them down, along
with differences in natural hair growth in men and women, and the
variations in skin hue that were locally judged most beautiful. He
thought that these differences had arisen through sexual selection,
that different societies had different ideas of beauty and framed the
reproductive choices of individuals accordingly. Even less obvious
differences, Darwin believed, arose on the basis of such choices. For
example, when the Sandwich Island maidens transferred lice to the
crews of European whaling boats, the lice failed to live on board, in-

dicating to Darwin some subtle difference in the constitution of the blood of the sailors and the natives. Yet humans were, for Darwin, clearly one species: matings between people of markedly different appearance resulted in the birth of children as certainly as did matings between people who looked alike.

The voyage of the *Beagle* brought different races together, but it was not a unique event. Throughout time people have been on the move, and as certainly as isolation and chance have fostered local peculiarities in their makeup, people have met and merged with others of different peculiarities. Some groups were temporarily isolated, like the Tasmanians, cut off by rising seas. Given enough time alone, the Tasmanians could have become a separate species, unable to interbreed with other humans. But such a process would have required an almost geological timescale; in reality, their isolation was rudely interrupted by Europeans. Indeed, the Tasmanians soon ceased to exist as a distinct group. Those who did not intermarry died of disease or were shot to provide specimens for Victorian museums and collectors. In 1877 the last distinctive Tasmanian died—it was not a species extinction but the genocide of a historically distinct people.

As the fossil record shows, many groups of hominids emerged only to die out. Human evolution has been part of a complex pattern in which species seem to have divided off into various types and lived in close proximity to one another for hundreds of thousands of years before evolving further or becoming extinct. (See Chapter 1 and Figure 1.3.) It is an understatement to say that we do not fully understand the differences between these ancient hominids, whether they could have interbred despite the separate species and genus labels that we have attached to their bones. The claim made by John Baker, an Oxford zoologist, that normal moderns and australopithecines would not have mated is untestable since australopithecines are extinct. But 1.6 million years ago, when our direct ancestors lived cheek by jowl with several other types of hominid, opportunities must have abounded. Did mutual sexual repugnance keep them apart, as Baker implies? Were they genetically incompatible or merely behaviorally unsuited to one another?

I think that racism existed in prehistory. It was one of the forces that powered the diversification of early hominids into separate species and that ultimately forced the extinction of some groups. The last to go were the Neanderthals, whose extinction around 26,000 years ago finally left us as the only species of upright-walking hominid left on earth. But the legacy of our early prehistory lives on. Although our genetic endowment shows us clearly to be one species, we periodically and persistently respond to outwardly different groups *as if* they were separate species—animals to be hunted, and occasionally eaten.

But a different and complementary game was also played. Hybridization—the crossing of distinct types—produces new forms with new qualities more quickly than does the continued evolution of either of those two types alone. One of the most startling features of the hominid fossil record, as archaeologists and paleontologists uncover it, is its variety, which consistently challenges interpretation. Just how many separate species were there at any one time? Such is the variation that almost no two fossils look exactly the same, giving the impression of massive and continuous flux over several million years. Hybrid types clearly have to be clever to stay alive, as their numbers start low. Our emerging intelligence may have been sharpened by the challenge of such physical diversity around us.

Increased population and the relative ease of global travel today bring dramatically different kinds of people into daily contact with one another on a scale that makes the total erosion of racial differences a logical possibility. If people met and reproduced at random, then we would soon become homogenized, in the state of panmixia; but we never actually do reproduce at random. The boundaries of race, however fluid, represent differences in taste, in fashion, and in identity that often become criteria for choosing mates.

Plato's Two-Backed Hermaphrodites

Racial thinking dates back at least 2,500 years. When Shakespeare used the phrase "the beast with two backs" to describe the consummated love of Desdemona and Othello, he may have been subtly twisting an idea of love personified as two-individuals-in-one, first found in Plato. In his dramatic debate on the nature of love, *The Symposium*, Plato has the comic playwright Aristophanes claim that originally, "each human being was a rounded whole, with double back and flanks forming a complete circle; it had four hands and an equal number of legs, and two identically similar faces." Each had two sets of sex organs. There were three different sexes: not only females and males but hermaphrodites, who had a mixed pair of male and female sex organs. Despite these, the original "processes of begetting and birth had been carried out not by the physical union of the sexes, but by emission onto the ground, as is the case with grasshoppers." These primal humans moved with a rapid cartwheeling motion and were proud and strong, so much so that the gods felt threatened by them. Finally Zeus ordered Apollo to humble them by cutting them all in half. Ever since, the individuals created by this division have attempted to find their "other half" and appeared as male homosexuals, lesbians, and heterosexuals accordingly. As Plato concludes Aristophanes's speech, "The way to happiness for our race lies in fulfilling the behests of Love, and each finding for himself the mate who properly belongs to him."

The Greek words translated as *our race* here can be broadly understood to mean humans in general, but Plato's dialogue implies a narrower sense of *race* too. The "true" other half that should complete each of our symmetries must be of the same color—as like as possible to ourselves. Plato's Beast with Two Backs story is to explain not only the force of homosexual and heterosexual love but the maintenance of outward physical differences between Greeks and non-Greeks, black-skinned Libyans, pasty-pale Scythians, and people of different appearances who often worked as slaves in Greek households. As in the American South, much later, the easy sexual access that owners had to those they owned must have produced many children whose physical aspect publicly betrayed the asymmetrical circumstances of their conception.

When he returned from his Black Sea travels, Herodotus described a dual-race society in Scythia, centered on a large wood-fortified city (of a type now well known from archaeological excavation).

The society, he wrote, was made up of two ethnic groups speaking separate languages, the nomad Budini, "the true natives of the country," and the sedentary Geloni, who were "anciently Greeks who moved away from their trading posts and settled among the Budini." Herodotus makes clear that the Budini and Geloni were physically distinct, the Budini "with very blue eyes and red hair," the Geloni like them "neither in shape nor in colouring."

The physical idiosyncrasies of these two groups had been established before they met, but while they lived together in Scythia their distinctiveness was maintained (and possibly enhanced) through their different although symbiotic ways of life. The Budini and Geloni were not in competition with each other, and they had little need for intermarriage as a diplomatic tool to keep the peace. Their individual patterns of property inheritance—one based on agrarian land ownership, the other on mobile flocks and herds—meant that marriages *within* each community were encouraged. Their different physical appearances were probably important social identifiers, incorporated into the sense of identity, the ethnicity, of each group.

The Chosen Ones

From A.D. 1400 onward the European "voyages of discovery" brought markedly different peoples from widely separated parts of the globe into greater proximity with one another. While the ancient Greeks seem to have believed that when the gods made humans, they simply made them various, a Judeo-Christian framework with a single god allowed that one people might be more "chosen" than another. The theory of polygenesis, enthusiastically promoted by the Calvinist thinker Isaac de la Peyrère in 1655, held that only the Jews had descended from Adam, while other human groups had been the result of earlier, less-practiced exercises in divine creation.

Polygenesis gave intellectual support to the exploitation of West African slaves and indigenous Caribs in the plantations and mines of the New World. The modes of life of non-European, nonurban, and nonliterate peoples worldwide were considered primitive and uniform. The stone tools that some communities used suggested an explanation for similar objects that had been found in Europe—prehistoric artifacts that had at first been thought the work of elves or fairies but that now could be explained as the traces of "pre-Adamites."

During the eighteenth century, as opinion weighed in against the institution of slavery, French and Scottish Enlightenment thinkers stressed the "psychic unity" of humanity—the belief that all the peoples of the world share similar emotions and intellectual capacities despite individual differences in aptitude. Their different levels of technological progress, it was thought, had to do with differences in environment, time, and chance; "progress" could be made by all. More radically, Jean-Jacques Rousseau promoted the idea of "the noble savage," the claim that both prehistorically and in so-called primitive society, people had lived in a harmony with the world that Western civilization with all its attendant ills should rightly envy.

But these Enlightenment doctrines were inconvenient for those who benefited from the cheap labor of oppressed peoples. Although polygenesis was no longer spoken of, nineteenth-century European imperialism and romantic nationalism were associated with an emphasis on national "character" or "spirit"—qualities that came to be seen as not simply cultural but deeper, bred in the bone. These ideas were most influentially encapsulated in the writings of the French royalist Count Joseph-Arthur de Gobineau, whose *Essay on the Inequality of the Human Races* (published in separate parts from 1853 to 1855 and never fully translated into English) set out to solve the problem of why civilizations decline and fall. He expected to find a single cause, and after examining economic and ideological factors and rejecting them as too inconsistent to qualify, he resorted to a racial theory.

Gobineau believed that only some peoples were culturally creative and that their ability was borne in their blood. When creative people joined together to form nations, they intermarried and became homogenized, but the cities that they built attracted outsiders—migrant workers, traders, and slaves. This diversity created an international society in which people who had not shown themselves capable of initiating civilization intermixed with those that had. Gobineau singled out ten peoples, racially defined, as specially blessed, capable of producing civilization: the Chinese, Egyptians, Assyrians, Indians, Greeks, Romans, Mexicans, and Peruvians (all of whom produced great urban monuments and systems of record), along with the "Allegheny civilization"—the mound-building Indian tribes of the Appalachian plateau, stretching from Ohio down to Mississippi—and finally "the Germanic races." Also-rans included the Armenians, who had produced civilization despite a rocky, unfavorable homeland, and the Jews, "a people capable in all it undertook, a free people, a strong people, an intelligent people." That the Jews had not managed to build pyramids or create a great empire was because they had—according to Gobineau—"hybridized" to some degree with the Hamites, the descendants of Ham who were thought to have colonized Ethiopia and Abyssinia. (This speculation, as we shall see, was later developed for an overtly political purpose by Heinrich Himmler.) Gobineau was thoroughly derogatory about other, blacker Africans: "The European cannot hope to civilize the Negro."

Darwin's concept of human evolution strengthened beliefs in innate racial inequality. The first edition of Félix-Archimède Pouchet's treatise *On the Multiplicity of Human Races*, which came out in 1858, the year before *Origin of Species*, proposed that the various races had been the result of separate acts of spontaneous generation. But swayed by Darwin's evolutionary biology, Pouchet revised the second edition to suggest that a single apelike prehuman ancestor had given rise to several distinct species of modern human, each of which was more closely related to the ape-ancestor than to each other. Carl Vogt, on the other hand, argued in 1863 that the evidence of racial difference "leads us back not to a common stem, to a single intermediate form between man and apes, but to manifold lines of succession, which were able to develop, more or less within local limits, from various parallel lines of apes." Vogt believed that progressive improvement in these various lines would tend to cause convergent development, bending the branches "so that their tips came closer again to one another." Many Europeans and Americans found it convenient to argue that nonwhite races were quite simply earlier stages in human evolution that had somehow fallen out of the mainstream and stagnated.

In *The Descent of Man, and Selection in Relation to Sex*, Darwin supported the idea of a single common ancestor for modern humans. He held them to be one species, whose regional differences were nevertheless explicable in terms of their more recent evolution. These differences were not brought about primarily by the challenges of the external natural environment but came from within the social environment, where fine-tuned discriminations in mate choice led to the selection not only of different visible features, such as eye and skin color, but of mental differences too. Darwin envisaged a continuous selection-driven moral ascent, from lowly, selfish, animal instincts to elevated Victorian morals. Battle lines were thus drawn not just between races but within them. Male temperance and female chastity were on the rise, he thought, along with fidelity and courage, because the richer social classes were outbreeding the poorer "intemperate, profligate, and criminal classes," whose high fertility was outweighed by heavy infant mortality. In 1878 his protégé, George Romanes, addressed the British Association on the subject of mental evolution, illustrating his theme—in the absence of real prehistoric ancestors—with a living exhibit of what *The Times* described as "savages, young children, idiots, and uneducated deaf-mutes."

Darwin's belief, which he maintained in the absence of any fossil evidence, that modern humans emerged in Africa was not shared by most of his contemporaries. In 1856 a strange skull had been discovered in the valley of the river Neander, near Düsseldorf, Germany. This skull, along with two skeletons discovered in Belgium in 1886, convinced many scholars that the evolution from ape to human had in fact occurred in Europe. The problem, however, was that the "Neanderthals" were not really very apelike; early reconstructions were based on a badly arthritic individual who gave every appearance of stooped apedom to an ill-informed public. In fact, behind the heavy brow ridges and receding chins of Neanderthals were brains that were as large or larger than those of modern people (though they *may* have been less intelligent; see Chapter 1).

In 1912 human ancestor status was claimed for stranger-looking

and ostensibly older bones discovered at Piltdown, in Sussex. "Piltdown Man" was eventually exposed as a fake. A deliberately stained
orangutan jaw with filed-down teeth, plus parts of an old but anatomically "modern" human skull, had been planted together at a site
where genuine extinct woolly rhino bones were being found. That
Piltdown Man was accepted at all was due to the anatomical combination of a large braincase and brutish jaw, which neatly fitted with
the Enlightenment belief that "man" had improved his natural, bestial
condition through the application of a rational intelligence.

Which of the several eminent scientists involved with the
Piltdown site falsified the primary fossil evidence remains a mystery, but their motivation presumably involved nationalism, if not
downright racism. Most Englishmen believed that their greatest-
great-grandparents must have been Englishmen too, or at least
European—certainly not African. If the supporting evidence had not
yet appeared, what harm would there be in preempting it? Such
nationalism still has immense appeal today. When a half-million-
year-old leg bone of archaic *Homo sapiens* was recently discovered at
Boxgrove (not far from Piltdown), the press hailed it as "the first
Englishman," notwithstanding the fact that Britain had no island
existence at that time (and notwithstanding Germaine Greer's caution about sexing leg bones). And in 1995, the "first European" was
promoted on the basis of new fossil finds from Orce in Andalusia,
even though, at this writing, it is not clear whether the limb bones
belong to *Homo erectus*, as some researchers claim, or to an unidentified four-footed carnivore.

While Darwin saw sexual selection as the key to the creation of
human variation, he believed that groups like the Maoris could be reduced by a process of "natural selection." As he dryly observed in his
Beagle notebook, "natural selection is now acting on the inferior races
when put into competition with the New Zealanders." Francis Galton, one of Darwin's cousins, focused on the postulated intellectual
aspects of human breeding, arguing that all moral and mental traits
were hereditary in humans. He called for better, more scientific
breeding, as was already applied to racehorses, so that the "nobler
varieties of mankind" would prevail. These eugenic ideas later in-

spired Marie Stopes to popularize information about contraception, as a way for the English lower classes (and those who wore glasses) to let off sexual steam without swamping subsequent generations with their inferior traits. Since in Galton and Darwin's time, genes remained undiscovered, Galton believed that the secret of heredity lay in the blood, and his house overflowed with rabbits of assorted breeds whom he subjected to regular transfusions of each other's blood, in a vain attempt to get them to change coat color.

Nazis Prefer Blondes

Gobineau thought that blood of special nobility was to be found in "the Germanic races"—northern Europeans of "Nordic" type—tall, blond, and blue-eyed. He considered Nordics a branch of the greater "Aryan race," inventors of the original Indo-European language, who took their name from the Aryas, who appear in Indian epics as northern invaders. The Aryans—allegedly—lay behind every Old World civilization except the Assyrian; they had taken civilization from India to China. A version of this view of history—global cultural progress through the activity of a single, innately brilliant people—was later developed by the English anatomist Grafton Eliot Smith, although his hereditary geniuses of choice were the ancient Egyptians. It has been most recently applied by Thor Heyerdahl in his strange quest to demonstrate that all pyramids and large stone statues, including those of the Americas and of remote Easter Island, must have been the work of the roving priests of Ra.

The most fervent promoter of the superiority of the Nordic race was the German physical anthropologist and prehistorian Hans Günther. Günther surveyed all the local physical types in Europe in his book *The Racial Elements of European History*. "A race shows itself in a human group which is marked off from every other human group through its own proper combination of bodily and mental characteristics, and in turn only produces its like," claimed Günther. He went on to define five races that could be found in both "pure" and "crossed" form in Europe: Nordic, Mediterranean, Dinaric, Alpine, and East Baltic. Günther considered himself Nordic and felt that "Nordic eyes often have something shining, something radiant about them." Mentally, Nordics were claimed to be fit for "statesmanlike achievements," an assertion supported by a careful choice of portraits showing eminent American and European "Nordic" men.

Günther measured other races against the blue-eyed wonder boys: "If the Nordic race inclines to a sharp, bold profile, the Mediterranean inclines to a pleasant, agreeable, as it were more womanly, profile" and "shows but a slight sense of law and order." Dinaric people, with "very prominent nose," brown eyes, and dark hair, found especially in Bavaria, Austro-Hungary, northern Italy, and parts of Poland and Romania, are slightly better: "For mental capacity I would put the Dinaric race second among the races of Europe." The East Baltics, found on the marches of Russia, were "opposed to all individuality, and always cultivating a dead level of thought for all"; they had "little cleanliness, whether personal or in the home." Finally, the Alpine race was "reflective, hard-working, and narrow-minded," but also plagued by "petty criminals, small-time swindlers, sneak-thieves and sexual perverts." Günther's comments on other groups with a history in Europe, notably the "Hither Asiatic strain" (the Jews) and the "Negro strain," were extremely derogatory.

In all his thinking, Günther connected an—to him—unpleasant outward physical appearance with the—to him—weaknesses in the cultural and social lives of people who were not—like him—German. In his view, civilization deteriorated "in the direction of the lessening of the strain of Nordic blood." Yet there is no such thing as Nordic blood; it is not a distinctive strain, like a yeast culture. There are of course blood groups, but these do not form pure and exclusive units, and they are distributed at greater or lesser frequency worldwide. If Günther's own blood had been supplied to a blood-compatible Tierra del Fuegan, the latter's cultural behavior would have been altered not one iota.

Mythical ideas of pure-breeding were a central part of the Nazi-led neopagan revival in Germany—an ideology that was underpinned by archaeology. The foundations had been laid by one of the most influential prehistorians, Gustav Kossinna, who at the end of the nineteenth century developed the important concept of the "archaeological culture"—the material manifestations of a pure people who shared the same religion, appearance, and mentality. Kossinna claimed to be able to trace a distinctively German type of settlement back into prehistory. He believed that villages where German-speaking people had lived could be distinguished from those of the ancient Slavs, Germany's modern neighbors to the east, by virtue of their orderliness, cleanliness, and attention to fine architectural detail.

Kossinna believed that some symbols, such as the *Hakenkreuz* or swastika, and the runic alphabet were essentially German. Since the swastika appears on ancient Greek pots and in Indian decorative motifs (where it is an array of nine points representing principal Hindu deities), Kossinna concluded that Nordic German genius lay behind these civilizations. Using his archaeological technique, he traced German settlements back to the time when Tacitus wrote his *Germania* and beyond, into the Neolithic period. Kossinna was particularly interested in proving that the Ostmark, the eastern region of what is today Poland, was archaically German. After the German defeat in the First World War, he was delegated to prepare a deposition for the Treaty of Versailles, pressing Germany's claim to the region—a claim that was rejected. After the war, Kossinna's students came to fill influential positions in German universities, and after his death in 1921, many were involved in the nascent Nazi party.

According to Günther, cultural progress began with the invention of farming, an achievement that he—wrongly—attributed to the tall, blond-haired, and blue-eyed Nordic race of Denmark (recently annexed by Germany). This cultural benefit, he thought, had been brought south around 1200 B.C., when the Nordics were believed to have swept into Greece from the north and laid the foundations of classical civilization. Thus—for Günther—all the achievements of the Greeks were marked down to Germany. The high point of this racial lunacy was the bizarre claim that the Nordic nature of the best Greeks could be seen in their marble statues. Simply by viewing them, with almost psychic skill, Günther was swiftly able to infer that they had had blue eyes and blond hair. Nordics were thought to have powered the rise of Rome too, but in this case their success supposedly brought disaster. As the peoples of the empire mixed, Günther believed, the precious Nordic blood must have become dangerously diluted.

Günther termed this imagined process "denordization," and he thought that it had triggered a wholesale decline, during which Hither Asiatic moneylenders moved to Rome and began to contaminate the genes of the ruling elite. Apparently desperate when they realized their mistake, the Romans tried to look more Nordic. Günther marshals some wonderfully selective evidence to support this ludicrous theory: the poet Juvenal saying that Messalina used to hide her black hair under a fair wig; "rich upstarts *(homines novi)*" who "made their black-haired wives and daughters buy fair hair from Germany"; and Herodian's description of the emperor Caracalla "of African-Asiatic blood," who often used to "put on a fair wig and walk about in Germanic garb." In reality, it is as easy to find references to the idle classes dressing up as Egyptians, or as donkeys, or as the opposite sex. In the colorful world of ancient Rome, playing at "barbarians" was one among many entertainments. The fact that, according to Günther, Nero possessed congenitally blond hair and blue eyes can do little to inspire confidence in alleged Nordic mental characteristics.

Because of all the mixed blood, Günther argued, the fall of Rome was inevitable. Weakened by miscegenation, the empire crumbled. The first intimation was the battle of the Teutoburger Wald in

Figs. 224a, 224b,-Julius Caesar
E, dark? H, dark; tall, fair-skinned

Figs. 240a, 240b,-Lucius Caccilius Jucundus,
banker in Pompeii.
Predominantly Hither Asiatic

(Fig. 9.2) *The Racial Elements of European History.* Two images from Günther 1927. Reproduced by kind permission of Methuen & Co.

A.D. 9, when the Romans suffered their first major defeat at the hands of the Germanic tribes of the north. Nordic blood—in the form of an influx of Germanic mercenaries—subsequently stayed Rome's fall for a while, Günther believed. Ultimately, however, the invidious influence of "Hither Asiatic, Oriental, Hamitic, and Negro elements" and of Alpine and Dinaric people intruding in the north signaled—in Günther's version of events—"the end of everything, a true racial morass, whose degeneration and decomposition bred those repellent things we learn of from the last days of Rome."

For the Third Reich, the implication of this fanciful and deliberately offensive race history was clear. Only by patrolling the boundaries of race could the Germans hope to rule the world, as they believed themselves functionally predestined to do. They were keen developers of Galton's eugenic ideas and supported the concept of "racial hygiene," the removal of "bad blood." A cult of the body beautiful grew up, nudism and exercise alternating with well-pressed folk costumes and shiny uniforms. (While ostensibly heterosexual, the amusingly camp undertones of all this are not lost on Tom of Finland fans.)

Heinrich Himmler reinterpreted the archaeological data for the European Upper Paleolithic in the light of the supposed connection between Semitic and Hamitic races outlined by Gobineau. Identifying the Venus figurines from Willendorf and Dolní Věstonice as displaying steatopygia of the sort seen among modern Bushman women, he branded Ice Age Europeans as mixed-race "Hottentot-Jews"—an inferior and impure stock that had been wiped out when the noble Nordic German farmers swept down from the north.

The Nazi party organized many neopagan rallies, fusing ancient religious symbols with Christian ones. They set up the notorious stud farms, where effectively polygamous sex was encouraged (perhaps *organized* is a better word) between girls of "good farming stock" and the elite of the party organization. Concentration camps were established, where, along with Jews and gypsies, homosexuals and transvestites were incarcerated as biologically dysfunctional, ex-members of human society. What the early German transvestite priests of Tacitus would have thought is hard to say, but they were not included in the Nazi myth. As the historian E. H. Hobsbawm so aptly put it, "getting one's history wrong is part of being a nation."

The Meaning of Race

The Nazi idea of racial purity still has currency in parts of the modern world, even if it flies in the face of every scientific argument. Archaeologists and physical anthropologists working in South Africa under the old apartheid regime came face-to-face with it, but they did not cave in. Philip Tobias, for example, the leading authority on the skeletal morphology of the Olduvai *Homo habilis* fossils, produced an influential pamphlet called *The Meaning of Race* that addressed the question head-on. Several things about race are now abundantly clear to biological anthropologists. First, each person's appearance is based on a unique combination of a vast number of genes and is further affected by the circumstances of birth, growth, diet, and disease. Second, there is much more genetic variation within any particular group of people than between the averages of groups, although the boundaries of groups cannot be easily drawn. A study by Walter F. Bodmer and Luca Cavalli-Sforza indicates that 85 percent of all variable genes are typically present within individual cultures, while there is an 8 percent variance between the average of different cultures, and a further 7 percent difference between races at the global level. The human species is thus "polytypic," and the idea of racial purity—based on the exclusive possession of some special essence ("blood")—is a complete fiction.

Intriguingly, however, the observed 7 percent interracial genetic variation is weighted toward visible characteristics—precisely those features upon which sexual selection would most likely work, and which may be altered most quickly. This explains the existence of more or less distinctive populations of people. When individuals from such distinctive populations interbreed, the children they produce are of "mixed" race. This does not mean that their genes are any more scrambled than anyone else's—they patently are not—but simply that they are, initially, not very numerous. The proper study of race, therefore, involves the observation of trends rather than the definition of sharp boundaries. Different classifications emerge, according to whether one looks at blood types, skin color, cranial morphology, dentition, or other genetically governed variables. Measurement and comparison of these variables have reality insofar as the trends do reflect something of the actual breeding choices that human populations have made in the past, and therefore they can help track our morphological development and geographical spread.

In 1924 the first true "missing link," the *Australopithecus africanus* skull from Taung in South Africa, was recognized, beginning a process that has vindicated Darwin's belief in an African origin for humanity (although he might have been surprised by the bewildering variety of hominids now known to have graced the last four million years). Today it is certain that one of our most important fossil ancestors, the Nariokotome boy, lived at a time—1.6 million years ago— when australopithecines were still plentiful (Chapter 1 and Figure 1.3) and the possibility of having sex with them was therefore real. By classifying the Nariokotome boy as *Homo*, scholars are making the claim that he belonged not only to a different species but to a different *genus* from the other bipedal hominids of his time, the australopithecines and paranthropines.

Some scholars, harking back to Pouchet, have argued that modern human racial diversity began when different groups of *Homo* (but not australopithecines) left Africa and colonized the four corners of the earth. There they slowly evolved into various distinct races, parallel to one another. Until quite recently some (European) scholars have argued that European humans were the most evolutionarily different, uniquely gifted people with the capacity to produce Upper Paleolithic cave art.

The Birth of Racism

Much of the debate about human evolution turns on how species, subspecies, and races are defined. Zoologists find such classifications difficult enough among living creatures; doing it for long-extinct populations of broken bones makes it infinitely harder. Dogs are remarkably varied in their skeletons, yet they constitute a single species (although they are capable of successful hybridization with wolf and coyote). Yet sheep and goats, which belong not just to different species but to different genuses, are a nightmare to distinguish from one another when their bones occur during excavations. The eighteen or so modern species of vervet monkey are indistinguishable skeletally, but they do not interbreed. German philosopher Immanuel Kant was one of the first to stress that species must be understood in terms of real breeding populations rather than in terms of the formal or apparent differences that taxonomists can measure. Herring gulls prove his point.

Scandinavian herring gulls show racial differences from herring gulls in Britain, which in turn show differences from those of Iceland. The differences have mainly to do with the predominant markings of the plumage, which are coded by a small number of genes. But each population interbreeds with the next during occasional forays into each other's home territories. Moving westward, right around the North Pole, seven interbreeding races of a single species are encountered; but the seventh race, in northern Russia, does not interbreed with the Scandinavian form at the point, over the White Sea, where the circle is closed. Although genetically they could breed, their mating behaviors are too different. Instead of mating with each other, they compete as separate groups in the constant battle for survival. The total pattern, of continuous racial variation in one direction and a species divide in the other, is termed a *Formenkreis*.

Such *Formenkreis* patterns must have characterized the evolution of hominids from four million years ago onward. John Baker's claim that "no normal human being of modern times would willingly copulate with any of the australopithecines" raises the question of what kept incipient robust paranthropines, protohabilines, and ancestral *Homo ergasters* apart effectively enough for them to become separate species. As part of the answer, imprinting should not be ruled out. Early hominids almost certainly had less mental flexibility than modern humans, and like vervet monkeys, they would have been more bound to their immediate subtypes. Nevertheless, this rule is not ironclad; as Robin Dunbar has shown, for example, different species of baboon will hybridize in the wild under certain conditions. The key to the emergence of subtypes of hominid, and their subsequent marked speciation, is probably isolation. Although early hominids inhabited the same grassland regions of eastern Africa, the ecological niches that they exploited kept them apart. Incipient paranthropines were moving toward specialization on heavy plant food, while incipient *Homo ergaster* was developing meat-scavenging and hunting strategies.

Such niche-specialization, which was almost trivial at first, inexorably created "bottleneck" effects, wherein opportunities for mating with members of another group became rarer, and within-group idiosyncrasies in appearance gave rise to distinctive canons of beauty. Sexual selection within groups, or between groups in the same niche, can rapidly change the outward appearance of a population. As Richard Dawkins strikingly puts it, "Nothing can stop the spread of DNA that has no beneficial effect other than making males beautiful to females"—and of course, vice versa. Add polygamy, and the process accelerates, as both males and females with a favored feature get better opportunities to breed—more choice in partners, and more partners. Disfavored appearances may simply have been excluded from the breeding pool, through infanticide or sexual avoidance. Today, cultural evaluations of skin shades can make people feel isolated, as Carrie Allen McCray's poem evokes: "In ugly tones they / called me 'Yaller Gal' / How lovely to have been / born black or brown / Pure substance the artist / could put his pen to / Not something in between— / diluted, undefined, unspecific." In prehistory, among small foraging bands, the fatal sanction for looking different might have been actual isolation. Even persistent minor discrimination in food sharing would have had a significant adverse effect on the survival chances of the disfavored and their offspring.

An even more distasteful mechanism may also have been in operation. In the late eighteenth century, English antiquarian John Frere first recognized that prehistoric flint artifacts were fashioned by humans. He called them "weapons of war." Our modern fashion for calling them all "tools" may be a little euphemistic. Throughout more recent prehistory, unambiguous weapons of war are ubiquitous in the archaeological record. We simply do not know how, say, the massive "Acheulian hand axes," which occur from 1.5 million to 150,000 years ago, were used. They could have been used for killing.

It now seems clear that several species or subspecies of human existed over the period between a million and 150,000 years ago, during which *Homo erectus/ergaster* gave way to "late archaic *sapiens.*" Transitional fossils, such as the skull from Bodo in Ethiopia (Figure 1.3, number 14), are attributed to "early archaic *sapiens*" and are found on sites where different types of "stone tools" were also found. The Bodo skull is covered with cut marks, and it appears to have been deliberately defleshed. Was the Bodo person a crossbreed—an unfortunate hybrid who perished at the hands of rival groups competing for survival and maintaining their distinctiveness by patrolling sexual boundaries? We do not know, but it is clear that warfare—the traces of which become ever more obvious as we move toward the present—always has some racial component. This is not such an extreme statement as it at first seems. A family that views itself as part of a larger racial group may find itself embroiled in a civil war, with members fighting on both sides. Although at the outset no tangible new physical differences can emerge between the two sides, the very fact of division sets up conditions that limit breeding opportunities across the battle line while tending to enhance them within each camp; ultimately, that is all races are—temporarily isolated gene pools. When conflict is prolonged, the reduction in breeding across the battle lines will cause—through the accumulation of genetic differences and the emergence of different cultural canons of beauty—a slow differentiation of the hostile groups.

The "multiregional hypothesis," currently promoted by Milford Wolpoff, a paleoanthropologist at the University of Michigan, develops an old line of argument. He postulates that racial difference emerged very early on, and that the shared status of the world's races as modern humans today came about only through a constant level of interracial breeding on the peripheries of racial blocs. This interbreeding ensured, according to Wolpoff, that all "advanced" features—such as a distinctively modern capacity for thought—became established among all groups. His theories have been especially eagerly received by the Chinese, who have their own nationalistic reasons for wanting to believe in a regional, 1.8-million-year-long, China-based evolution of modern Chinese from a local *Homo erectus* that had moved there from Africa.

While the multiregional hypothesis attracts some strong support, I believe, along with the majority of researchers, that anatomically modern humans emerged just once, in Africa, a mere 100,000 to 200,000 years ago. This out-of-Africa theory was initially based on controversial research carried out by Rebecca Cann and others on differences in mitochondrial DNA found in the placentas of women from different parts of the world. This evidence at first suggested that there was an "African Eve"—a modern human female who was ancestral to us all in that her children spread out of Africa, supplanting all previously established *erectus* populations.

According to this view, anatomically modern humans evolved in eastern Africa sometime after 150,000 years ago and swept outward, into the Near East by 100,000 years ago, and onward, replacing *erectus* populations. Using boats for deep-sea navigation, they became, by around 50,000 B.P., the first (and only) species of hominid to reach Australia. Were Wolpoff's multiregional hypothesis true, modern human populations would be unlikely to be as similar as they are. (Wolpoff maintains that processes such as "the exchange of women" between groups maintained our global species identity.) The out-of-Africa scenario suggests that modern humans must have had some very crucial advantage over previous human types in order to completely outcompete them. Some mixing of different late archaic and anatomically modern humans may be most likely, as detailed by Günther Bräuer of the University of Hamburg, who sees replacement as the major force, but also some absorption of more archaic groups by interbreeding and hybridization.

As for the spread of anatomically modern humans into Europe, some researchers claim that the more archaic inhabitants, the Neanderthals, were outcompeted by the new species with whom they could not breed. Others disagree. All taxonomists class Neanderthals in the same genus as us, *Homo*, but some see a species difference between *Homo sapiens* and *Homo neanderthalensis*. Still others see a less significant *subspecies* divide, which they indicate by adding an extra classificatory term between *Homo sapiens sapiens* and *Homo sapiens ne-anderthalensis*. Were the differences between them merely racial? If so, why did the Neanderthal population remain distinctive, rather than interbreeding with modern humans, right up to the point of extinction? Were there offspring of Neanderthal-modern liaisons? Were they discriminated against? The data is ambiguous, which means that the answers given to these questions often have a lot to do with the prejudices of individual researchers.

The Neanderthal situation in Europe may have been a little like that of the herring gull. The ancestors of the Neanderthals, originally a variation of late archaic *sapiens*, may have reached the Levant and subsequently Europe through a series of steps in which their appearance and cultural behavior became progressively more idiosyncratic. When they eventually met up with anatomically modern humans, who had evolved at the other end of the *Formenkreis*, their dissimilarities proved too great for any systematic interbreeding to occur.

But humans are not herring gulls. The gulls, experiments demonstrate, are imprinted in infancy with a fixed idea of what a potential mate should look like by reference to their immediate family. If researchers dye their parents pink, the grown gulls will respond sexually only to pink-dyed mates. (Sadly, it is doubtful that the researchers feel any continued obligation to confect these mates for them.) Humans, on the other hand, are more complex. To be sure, there is good evidence that sexual learning does involve some degree of imprinting. Males have been known to fetishize objects such as phone booths, cars, and safety pins to the point of excluding all other sexual relationships, and there is a case of a woman who was aroused by particular letters of the alphabet. But humans are ordinarily not so limited, and there is widespread evidence for sexual activities with other species—conducted not as exclusive fetishes but simply as curious variations.

Bestiality may well have been a part of Neolithic life (see Chapter 7), and it can still be widely documented today. In rural America high rates of sexual contact between male adolescents and farm animals have been reported. For city dwellers, inflatable substitutes are available; mail-order catalogs exhort potential buyers to "enjoy the

pleasures of country life without the smell." Dogs and cats are sometimes co-opted as sex partners; dogs are featured relatively often in
the erotic encounters that women reported to Nancy Friday. Nondo-
mesticated animals are also possibilities. To the prehistoric moose
pursued on skis (Figure 7.5) may be added a recent case of a man
with a male dolphin. Women (and sometimes men) insert snakes,
mice, and other small animals into different orifices, and in a wide variety of poorly documented but believable accounts, chickens (alive
and dead), fish, and moths are used sexually in ways best left to the
imagination. Sex with captive primates has also been reported.

Races Around the Globe

Hominid development over the last four million years was a veritable
evolutionary ferment. Types and species appeared and vanished at
such a rate that many more forms probably still await our discovery.
The rapid speciations, powered by sexual selection within possibly
polygamous communities, mirror the later emergence of races among
modern humans, for which similar mechanisms are implicated. It
seems doubtful that Owen Lovejoy's monogamy theory of human origins (see Chapter 1) could have genetically fixed the divergent trends
among modern humans quickly enough for the races to look as different as they do today. Of course, most of the variation could have
arisen during the most recent historical period, when we know that
monogamy was not the global norm. But this possibility is not supported by studies that compare degrees of racial similarity with the
timing of global colonization.

When modern humans started their global spread, probably out
from Africa, bottlenecks became more frequent and more effective at
bolstering emergent racial variations. Certain parts of the world, such
as the Americas, could have been colonized by nonseagoing people
only during the brief appearance of land bridges, such as the one that
linked the Bering Strait around 13,000 years ago. Access to a place,
followed by geographical isolation, would have created "founder effects." That is, all genetic variation that occurred in the Americas be-

tween the Bering crossing and European contact was set by the genetic potentialities of the pioneer groups. Some racial features are likely to have been naturally selected, emerging as suitable for particular climates, but the correlations between features and climate are not particularly consistent. Dark pigmentation is commoner in the tropics, where it offers some protection from solar radiation, whereas a pale complexion is more often found toward the poles, allowing more natural production of vitamin D in the skin. But such "adaptations" probably originated in fairly arbitrary cultural choices about what features were deemed attractive. People with very dark skin can be found in the Congo basin, where clouds let through only about three hours of direct sunlight each day (and not all of it gets past the trees), while people with genetically fair skin inhabit the Tibetan plateau, where solar radiation is particularly intense. Whereas animals adapt themselves to environments, humans adapt environments to themselves. With the aid of culture — bush hats, parkas, and shades — anyone can live anywhere.

One slightly more regular correlation with climatic factors is that between colder habitats and populations with broader skulls and higher faces. There is a noticeable division between European and American Indian skull shapes (cold climate), on the one hand, and Australo-Melanesian and African skull shapes (warm climate) on the other. That this difference resulted from a climatic adaptation is suggested because it cross-cuts other measures of similarity: the history of global colonization shows a different type of distinction between Europeans and Africans on the one hand, and Australians, American Indians, and Polynesians on the other.

The most detailed modern study of skull shape contradicts the multiregional hypothesis of the origin of modern human races and supports the idea of a single recent origin of anatomically modern humans. By using a statistical technique called *principal components analysis*, the study grouped a sample of more than three thousand skulls from different human populations, both ancient and modern, into clusters of most closely related types. The researchers found that Neanderthals, including those from La Ferrassie 1 and La Chapelle, dated to around 35,000 years ago, are closer to the archaic *Homo sapiens* group, such as skull number 5 from Skhūl cave in Israel, dated to around 90,000 years ago, than they are to modern humans. At the same time and in the same region, early anatomically modern humans, a distinctive group, overlapped with the archaics (as demonstrated by skeletons from Qafzeh, within 25 miles of Skhūl, dated to 92,000 B.P.). Yet they are nevertheless more closely linked to modern human populations than to the archaics and Neanderthals. These findings indicate that the separate-species definition of Neanderthals is probably correct, although with some possible later hybridization in Europe.

Although Neanderthal skeletons typically show high numbers of injuries, their eventual extinction was probably the result not so much of direct conflict with moderns as of competition for limited resources and differences in fertility. Neanderthals were physically bigger and heavier than moderns, and therefore they may have reproduced more slowly. Ezra Zubrow of the State University of New York at Buffalo has shown in a computer simulation that the Neanderthals would have needed only a slightly lower fertility for moderns to completely replace them in time.

Skeletal variability is greatest among peoples in the two regions—the Americas and Polynesia—that were colonized last. In other places, a slow process of intermingling has homogenized skeletal features, even if it has periodically emphasized particular skin colorings—the marks of ethnic affiliation and immediate ancestry. In North America skeletal features coincide with genetic, linguistic, and dental features in ways that suggest that people crossed the Bering Strait in a sequence of three migrations, forming the paleoindians, the Na-Dene of the northwestern coast, and the Eskimo-Aleuts. Archaeological evidence for the Plains Indians suggests that they represent a mix of several diverse groups, "suggesting that any common cranial and skeletal form is a late development."

Incest and Ownership

Fine-tuned local racial differences are created, maintained, and dissolved in different ways in different kinds of societies. The Plains Indians, for example, practiced outmarriage. Such exogamy is a typical pattern for hunter-gatherer or forager groups (as it is among primates), for whom survival depends on good communication and alliance networks. Agriculturalists, on the other hand, often have more endogamous or inmarrying systems, designed to keep clan property together. These systems sometimes lead to a high incidence of brother-sister marriage, as in historical times both in rural Norfolk and in Ireland.

As we saw in Chapter 6, farming was spread in Neolithic Europe primarily by movements of people, such as the LBK longhouse dwellers. The earliest knowledge of metal in central and western Europe may also be associated with the immigration of a group known as the Beaker Folk (although the skeletal data is ambiguous). With respect to Bronze Age cultures, an increasing focus on ethnicity, along with the elaborate marking of gender in burials, make it easier to determine probable mating patterns. In western Europe *Fremdfrauen* appear — "foreign women" — whose jewelry is clearly of more eastern origin. In the sixth-century-B.C. Iron Age multiple burial mound of the Magdalenenberg, near Villingen in Baden-Württemberg, a woman's grave contained a typically Spanish decorative belt plate, suggesting that she herself came from Spain. Of course, the belt plate could have been acquired by trade, but such traded items do not regularly appear in this period and they were essentially made to express association. That women within the richer sections of society sometimes married into faraway communities is supported by literary evidence. Herodotus records polygyny and diplomatic intermarriage among the Scythian and Thracian elites. In Roman times alliances among various Celtic tribes of western Europe were secured by intermarriage at the chiefly level, as recorded by Caesar, whose campaigns brought him into contact and confrontation with them.

Concerns about lineage and race came to the fore in the Iron Age. The perfection of animal management since the Neolithic meant that stockbreeding was deliberately carried out for particular features, especially in horses. It is not surprising that people should have applied breeding techniques to themselves as well. This practice has already been hinted at in the Scythians-and-Amazons story, where the Scythian men were attracted to the idea that the Amazon women would be able to bear them strong children. As I suggested in Chapter 8, more "masculine" genetic traits might have become quite rapidly fixed in the elite female population. Herodotus is clear that in Scythia polygamy was common, which would have sped up the effects of sexual selection. As endemic warfare and the export of slaves winnowed the existing Scythian population, polygamy would have provided the means for a rapid directional change that could establish new local or regional racial types.

This said, deliberate breeding may well have been used for purposes that were more social and hierarchical than regional. Its greatest impact would have been on martial elites who intermarried over wide distances to create alliances. Alexander the Great encouraged his generals to marry into the best aristocratic Asian families; by doing so he thought that they would produce a vigorous new generation with the best qualities of both peoples. Ideas of purity and hybridity are also reflected in the art of the time. The griffon was a composite beast, with eagle's wings and beak, lion's claws, and the scales of a fish or reptile, encompassing the armored and aggressive aspects of life on air, sea, and land. The griffon was joined in art by the centaur, the faun, and many other "half-and-half" creatures.

The activities of traders, slavers, mercenaries, nomads, and other itinerants created ever more multiethnic societies in Eurasia, and peoples went to great lengths to make themselves appear recognizably distinct. The skeletons of Huns buried in fifth-century A.D. Ukraine, for example, show remarkable cranial deformation, with the head elongated backward. We know from historical records that this was the result of binding the head from infancy onward. It could also, of course, have had a genetic component: in a society where longheadedness was deemed attractive, sexual selection could have begun to fix such a quality. But it seems much more likely that the binding was carried out to create a physical identity for an elite section of society, whose membership was elective and volatile and widely distributed and who would otherwise have had no shared physical characteristics to mark themselves as distinct. That is, the artificial deformation may have been used to hide natural variety rather than to enhance a stable racial trend.

In some places the actual reproductive choices that people made within particular communities are beginning to come into sharper focus, thanks to new techniques for extracting and analyzing ancient DNA from bone. Scott Woodward and Wilfred Griggs are currently excavating a cemetery of upward of one million individuals, around the Fayum oasis in Egypt. Over the years, as ever siltier mud is deposited there, the ground surface has thickened, so that the oldest burials are now deepest while the later, Christian burials are nearest the top. DNA analysis seems to demonstrate that the earlier burials are of people who were genetically all very similar to one another, while those buried later were genetically more diverse.

The preliminary results support the idea that the early Egyptians attempted to keep property in the family and, perhaps, to keep their racial identity "pure," through brother-sister marriage. Such practices were previously known only for the historically recorded ruling dynastic lines, in whom some scholars connect brother-sister marriage to an apparent increase in congenital illness. No one really knows what effect brother-sister marriage has on a human population *en masse*, but as with dogs, prolonged inbreeding can probably lead to reduced fitness in humans. The diversity of the later Fayum skeletons cannot be solely explained in terms of the significant immigration at the start of the Christian period; the Christian definition of brother-sister marriage as incestuous probably had as great an effect.

Intelligence or Knowledge?

Despite all the evidence for complex patterns of interbreeding, stretching back into deep prehistory, the idea of "pure races" has persisted. A white superiority myth still endures, maintained by a strange group of people who believe that the subtlety and beauty of human intelligence, manifested in the myriad cultures of the world, can best be expressed by a simple two- or three-figure number. Einstein was "148." This "intelligence quotient," or IQ, is the result of tests that their designers think measure innate intelligence—as a single straightforward and additive quality. Despite several decades of often deeply flawed statistics, some testers believe that they adequately demonstrate that men are genetically more intelligent than women, whites than blacks, rich than poor. In 1969 A. R. Jensen presented evidence that "Negroes" tested 15 IQ points lower than whites and drew the conclusion that "genetic factors" were "strongly implicated"; in 1994 Richard Herrnstein and Charles Murray presented similar evidence in *The Bell Curve*.

The IQ brigade display little understanding of the subtleties of personal motivation and cultural learning. As Philip Tobias has demonstrated, many of the original IQ tests conducted in South Africa were biased toward well-educated whites. The early, strongly culture-biased tests, with their divisive results, fostered resentment and suspicion and demotivated black people who were subjected to subsequent "intelligence" tests that were of a more abstract nature and that IQ testers promoted as fairer. Once a particular group realizes that tests "prove" them to be inferior, their respect for such tests goes down. If motivational issues could be compensated for (which is unlikely) *and* if it were possible to create tests unaffected by differences in cultural learning (which is unproven and also unlikely), then any gross differences that remained in the test results of different ethnic groups would still not prove the existence of a race-based genetic factor. This is because environment plays a much deeper role in the development of mental abilities than is usually appreciated.

Key experiments by Simon Biesheuvel and co-workers have shown that rats reared on protein-deficient diets score badly in rat intelligence tests, and that the effect is passed to their offspring, even when these have a proper diet. The detrimental effect is even passed on to the grandchildren. Both nutritional and emotional stress can interfere with animals' capacity for rational problem solving, and related effects may well be produced in humans in similar circumstances. The complex social histories of modern racial groups who, within three generations, may have jointly experienced war, starvation, malnutrition, pogroms, and migrations, may well adversely affect the results of IQ tests that people in power devise for them.

Most damningly, IQ believers cannot yet explain the most glaring anomaly in their own data—the Flynn effect. Scores on virtually every kind of IQ test, surveyed over twenty countries, show a continuous rise from 1920 onward, ranging from 10 points per generation in Sweden and Denmark to 20 points per generation in Israel and Belgium. Back-projecting the tests at the same rate would clearly drop Newton and Galileo off the bottom. Jensen believes that the effect is probably environmental, having to do with better nutrition. (People are also becoming taller.) But the effect's discoverer, James R. Flynn, thinks that it is ludicrous to imagine that each generation is cleverer than the last, and he remains "baffled."

I believe that IQ tests do not directly measure genetically innate intelligence at all. How could they, when so much about the way we think comes from our spoken language and our visual symbol systems, to which the developing brain molds itself *after* birth? IQ tests are as much a part of our cultural environment as any other symbol system. They thus test *knowledge*, not *intelligence*.

My younger daughter has a "Post the Shapes" box, a toy based on the same so-called abstract principles as many IQ shape tests. She may insert the differently shaped blocks through the matching holes; or she may deliberately try to force them through nonmatching holes to see if they will fit (some will); or she may slide the lid back and fill the box with shapes directly, avoiding the tedious holes; or she may ignore the box altogether and observe the behavior of her sister. What she "should" do with the box is a matter of cultural knowledge and choice, not innate intelligence. On the basis of their performance with "Post the Shapes," chimpanzees have been rated by humans as more intelligent than orangutans. Wild orangutans are capable of extraordinary feats of self-motivated learning, but they generally refuse to post shapes in the laboratory. This, it strikes me, is not because they are genetically stupid but because they are unwilling to slavishly copy their abductors.

The "Post the Shapes" box does, nevertheless, change the

worldview of every child who sees it. Whether or not I teach my daughter the "right" answer, playing with a shape-fitting IQ test will give her a cultural advantage over, say, a girl in a rural African community who has never seen such a box. My daughter's experience of digital clocks, car speedometers, and itemized cash register receipts will give her similar advantages in the mathematics IQ test. The rural African girl may be multilingual, proficient from the time she can talk in three or more languages; she may be able to classify hundreds of species of plant and animal and know what each is good for; and so on. But none of her cultural knowledge, born of natural human intelligence, will give her any advantage when she is presented in missionary school with a piece of paper printed with a sequence of apparently random numbers and the instruction, "Circle the odd one out."

I am not arguing intelligence has no genetic basis. I argued in Chapter 1 that our larger brains may be a direct result of sexual selection over the last four million years. But the process that led to the intelligence of anatomically modern humans involved the selection of very large numbers of genes for the many different areas of the brain and nervous system. By contrast, the subsequent creation of people of different appearances, as *Homo sapiens* spread around the world, is the result of the selection of a small number of highly visible genes, such as those for eye color, skin pigmentation, and various sizes of genitalia, selection that will not interfere with the body's higher functions and that can be easily fixed among local communities.

The prehistory of race indicates that gross innate differences in mental qualities among regionally distinctive populations (as between the sexes) are likely to be trivial. But in any case they can never be directly measured; humans do not exist biologically outside culture — nor do races. Race is a cultural creation that uses biological materials. But although breeding may enhance certain features and bring change quite quickly, fashion often demands still more rapid changes, as in the case of the Huns' long heads. Communities often enhance physical conformity before biology does. Skin can be stained or bleached. Soft-tissue areas like the genitalia can be cut and stretched, to a point where it is difficult to know which features are genetic and which are artificial. Genetic changes may typically follow artificial changes: Paraguayan men of Darwin's time did not need to shave, as they were beardless—a feature that presumably women of previous generations had consistently selected as attractive—but they did need to pluck their eyebrows and eyelashes. Those with the heaviest eyebrows would have needed more time to pluck them, time that they could have spent courting; or they could have been less than diligent and subsequently less lucky in love. Whatever the mechanism, it is clear that cultural fashion can influence opportunities for sexual contacts and thus foreshadow genetic change.

Racial prejudice, which is cultural, is one of the race-creating mechanisms. Regardless of whether a particular quality, such as "Nordicness," has any objective basis in genetics, it can still be used as a criterion for sexual selection, as stud farms and concentration camps illustrate. IQ test results are already being used as a criterion in sexual selection. Some British and American people meet their partners at Mensa, a club in which membership requires an IQ of at least 120, while in the United States it is possible to pay for artificial insemination with the sperm of a "high-IQ" donor. Whatever underlying genetic feature the IQ tests might actually test, it may become commoner in some communities in the future. We have the ability to choose, but the results may not always meet our expectations.

The Austrian women who apparently want to be inseminated with five-thousand-year-old Iceman sperm should perhaps be aware that according to the Flynn effect *and* Günther's racial assessment of Alpinids, the child of such an insemination should tend toward an IQ well into minus figures and a career characterized by "sneak thievery" and "sexual perversion." The child of the IQ fanatic may be genetically predisposed to behave more like a chimp in a laboratory than an orangutan in a rainforest. We simply do not know—but that their parents' culture will foster such behavior is certain.

Prehistoric fertility control and knowledge of plant-based contraception, outlined in Chapter 3, underscores everything that has been said here. Sex—even of the heterosexual intromissive variety—

need not lead to babies. In most cultures, people plan their offspring with greater care than their sexual liaisons.

Fascination with identity does not stop at appearance; it includes sexual behavior. In a global village that increasingly subscribes to an ideal of romantic love, of finding Plato's "perfect other half," sexual orientation produces labels similar to racial ones, involving the same sorts of cant and make-believe. Thus "homosexuals" and "heterosexuals," "lesbians" and "transvestites," are socially defined with all the finality of distinct species. Everyone is involved with such labeling, despite all the evidence that our shared underlying potentials are very malleable.

CHRISTOPHER ANTHONY MASTERS,
TH.D., Ph.D., J.D.
RANCHO SAN·DIEGO, CALIFORNIA

Conclusion

Beyond Culture

"Society is indeed a contract . . . it becomes a partnership not only between those who are living, but between those who are living, those who are dead, and those who are to be born."

EDMUND BURKE

We cannot revisit prehistory, nor even gain a full knowledge of it, given the limits of the surviving evidence. Much of the fine-grained detail of people's everyday lives and loves has been lost forever. Whole categories of sexual behavior, such as lesbianism—which is as common among our primate relatives as among modern humans—have left no discernible trace in the archaeological record. But there is much that we do know that I have had neither the space nor the special knowledge to do justice to, such as the sexual cultures of the prehistoric Americas and ancient India. I have said virtually nothing about China or Australia. Future research, such as the wider application of DNA sex-testing on skeletal remains, and the development of the theory of gender, will certainly shed more light on the sexual culture of the prehistoric communities described in this book.

Biology and culture are more closely entwined than we would like to believe. Codes of sexual morality that make appeals to some simple, universal "human nature" should be viewed with some skepticism: on the face of it, if what they advocate is truly natural, then enforcement should be unnecessary. But some people (such as the so-called "moral majority" in contemporary America) argue that, although there is a natural pattern of sexual morality, it needs additional support in order to survive in the face of increasing decadence; immorality is seen as a function of "bad" culture.

In biological versions of this argument, sexual immorality is imputed to other races. A Canadian psychologist has recently argued that "Negroids" are biologically prone to "low marital stability," despite the fact that one of the most eminent social anthropologists of the century, Edmund Leach, doubted that the English-language term "marriage" could be effectively used as a universal classification, so varied were the human institutions that it could in some sense be applied to. The idea that such variation arises from racial difference is idiotic, as marriage patterns are known to show marked historical change within the same communities (as has happened with the spread of Islam in Africa, for example).

Whose norms get accepted is a more complex issue now than it was when missionaries first went to Samoa to persuade the locals to do sex differently. Appreciation of cultural difference has grown, so that we feel less easy about branding others as wrong, yet the problem of sexual morality remains in many respects unresolved. Erotica that is thought in Britain to have the power to "deprave and corrupt" (to use the legal formulation) is freely available in continental Europe. Perhaps the British constitution is peculiarly vulnerable to depravity and corruption. As information technology develops, the battle to enforce particular versions of human sexuality as the global cultural norm will heat up, but networking will probably contribute to an ever greater cultural (or "subcultural") richness and variety.

While it is true that there are some beliefs about sexuality that can be found in nearly every human community around the world, by far the majority remain culturally specific. Sex between adults and children, incest (however defined), sex with the dead, and—perhaps

(Fig. 10.1) Trash—a New York drag king. Although Trash may look strange and "unnatural" to many people, the ambiguous appearance has a long prehistoric pedigree. Naked skin evolved alongside leather clothing, body paint, and material accessories. Photograph: Doris Kloster.

to a lesser extent—sex with animals all attract social and moral disapproval in widely separate communities worldwide. This may be part of a common, species inheritance, although one not necessarily shared with other primates (see Chapter 3). On the other hand, attitudes to some other types of behavior, such as male homosexuality, lesbianism, masturbation, group sex, oral sex, sex during menstruation, heterosexual anal sex, sexual displays, nudity, cross-dressing, and so on, are so different around the globe that no real norm exists (except that, approved or not, most of these things go on in most communities).

As I argued in Chapter 1, our nakedness is in itself not a purely natural condition, but came about bio-culturally through the exercise of choice in sexual selection, and evolved in tandem with the development of clothing. Thus to discard clothing, as nudists (or "naturists") do, is actually no more natural than to wear it. Wearing rubber, leather, silk, or anything else during sex is no more a cultural kink than wearing nothing at all. From a bio-cultural point of view, fetishists, nudists, and unassuming monogamous heterosexual folk (husband in striped pajamas, wife in pink nylon nightdress) are all equally normal. It is also bio-culturally normal for each of these three types to feel that the others are weird, and that only they themselves are doing the right thing. Defining one's own culture runs deep, and seems to have provided the necessary social cohesion by which human groups were able to colonize every global environment.

I started this book by going "beyond nature" because I wanted to challenge the sociobiologists. The variety of human sexual culture that I described cannot be explained by reference to a simple genetic imperative. Human cultures co-opt biology for their own immediate and short-term aims. But I end now by going "beyond culture," to stress the longer term biological backlash. We have no straightforward choice between "biology as destiny" and "culture as freedom." Boyd Eaton, of Emory University in Atlanta, is one of a small but growing number of doctors who promote "Darwinian medicine," based on the idea that our cultural solutions to disease and well-being must take into account the long-term legacy of biological evolution. As Roger Lewin reports, Eaton

> argues, for instance, that changes in reproductive patterns in western women mean that they have up to a hundred times increased risk of breast cancer and increased risk of endometrial and ovarian cancers compared with women who still have a hunter-gatherer lifestyle. The increased risk is a consequence of a combination of earlier menarche, later first birth, fewer births, and later menopause; in addition, modern women breast-feed for much shorter times. One consequence of these differences is that during their lifetime, hunter-gatherer women ovulate on average 158 times, while the average for modern affluent women is 451 times.

But this is just one of the implications of our current cultural organization.

Inventions such as the baby carriage appear to provide a benign and easier way of transporting children, but they have produced biological effects of dubious value. The sling, which our prehistoric ancestresses invented when nakedness and bipedalism made the "grip-on" method of infant transportation impossible, rapidly organizes the child's sense of balance, just as it would be organized in a clinging chimp, and thus assists in the child's physical, emotional, and social development. The recent sharp rise in osteoporosis—brittle bone disease—among Western women (and men) seems, at least in part, to be related to their reduced load bearing, coupled with alterations in the calcium balance of the body caused by the typically low level of breast-feeding in those modern communities that also typically use baby carriages.

These interactions between biology and culture present us with dilemmas. We cannot simply go back to hunting and gathering. But we could, for example, organize work and society in such a way that enabled women to breast-feed as long as they wished, rather than genetically engineer cows to produce milk that is "virtually human," as the Genpharm Company is currently attempting to do. The project, in any case, is doomed to failure, because even if the lactoferrin levels in engineered milk can be boosted to increase its nutritiousness, it will carry none of the profound immunological benefits that have recently prompted the World Health Organization and UNICEF to recommend breast-feeding to "two years and beyond." The attempt to produce artificial breast milk from dairy herds can be seen as a long-term extension of the controlling patriarchal value system of the Neolithic farmers.

The biological backlash affects men as well. The Scythians whose testicles, according to Hippocrates, were seriously functionally impaired by wearing pants and riding horses, may have a message for us today. Pants were invented by pastoralists and others who lived in cold climates, and they were shunned by people such as the Greeks and Romans who inhabited warmer climes. But they are now a global norm. Western men, who spend ever more time sitting in cars, have seen their sperm count drop off alarmingly in the last few decades, leading inevitably to an increase in fertility problems. (Estrogenic residues found in tap water and in agrochemically farmed vegetables are also implicated.) Part of the Darwinian solu-

tion might be found in the French fashion designer Jean-Paul
Gaultier's attempt to revive the kilt.

Over the last hundred years scientists have made a concerted effort to explain some of the mysteries of sex by uncovering its genetic
and behavioral bases. The most rigorous synthesis of the results is
currently being produced by biologists, but it is not complete. The biological synthesis omits the wild card—culture. Cultural intervention
(through contraception, abortion, IVF treatment and the use of
sperm banks) plays havoc with the rules of selection and evolution
that apply to the rest of the natural world.

Sociologist Anthony Giddens, in his book *The Transformation of
Intimacy*, has argued that in the modern period sex is characterized by
the emergence of "plastic sexuality." This phrase refers not to the
plethora of "well-made Japanese substitutes" now available, but to
what he claims is the almost complete detachment of sexual life from
any reproductive or biological imperative. The corollary of sex without reproduction is reproduction without sex. Richard Posner, too,
has drawn attention to some of the social and legal implications of the
new medical technology that enables reproduction "without sex,"
through IVF. Posner's views are based on a highly intercourse-
focused view of human sexuality: the semen for in vitro fertilization
has to come from somewhere—as far as I know, it is the result of a
man masturbating, which is nothing if not a sexual act (although no
erotic activity is required on the woman's part).

Although IVF is new, artificial insemination as such is suffi-
ciently low-tech (it can be done with a spoon) that it must have been
well within the reach of our prehistoric ancestors. Giddens's
thoughts, on the other hand, while provocative and well-considered,
are based on the idea that successful reproductive controls are a recent invention. (See Chapter 3.) Humans have lost control of their
fertility only when particular cultural circumstances have conspired
against good management.

Culture, in fact, can erode our basic physical capacities. For
most of human prehistory, as for many small-scale societies today,
the typical resting posture is the squat, a position that keeps the
pelvic floor muscles trim. The Celts were described as people who

squatted, and the powerful sexual aspects of related but more physically demanding poses were not lost on the steppe shamans and Indian practitioners of Tantra. But the women depicted on the bronze *situla* art described in Chapter 8 had sex on beds and chairs. These were high-status novelties in Europe at the time, but they became increasingly common during the Roman Empire and afterward. Today, sitting on chairs is becoming global. Because it requires little effort, it allows the pelvic floor muscles to become slack. And when this happens, sexual enjoyment is reduced—which led the sexologist Dr. Kegel to devise the therapeutic regime of pelvic muscle exercise that bears his name.

Doing "Kegels" may not only enhance (or normalize) sexual enjoyment, it may afford positive reproductive control. The powerful expulsion of semen by women who did not want to become pregnant, described by Hippocrates and the Trobriand Islands magistrate of Malinowski's time, could not have been achieved with slack musculature. Male practitioners of Tantra can also separate orgasm from ejaculation. (Some claim to be able to divert semen internally, so that it is ejaculated into the bladder rather than out the urethral opening.)

The natural body knowledge that has made us so successful at optimally timing reproduction and at intensively rearing small numbers of young has allowed for prolonged learning and the development of complex culture. But our culture has now developed to such a point that we are in danger of losing touch with our biology. We exert massive effort and resources to find cultural solutions for problems that need not exist in the first place.

The oral contraceptive pill, for example, has been a profound failure in most of the world. According to Gabrielle Palmer, in her classic *The Politics of Breastfeeding*, the Pill has actually been the single most important factor in recent global population *increases*. Because breast-feeding is incompatible with the combined Pill, it undermines natural lactational fertility control. Lured away from traditional ways and ancient herbal wisdom by the glamorous mirage of Western science, people switch to the Pill when it is promoted freely but subsequently cannot afford it regularly enough for it to work. (On the other hand, the Pill has been supremely successful in making some pharmaceutical companies very rich, along with the manufacturers of formula milk and the medicines that are standardly required in the Pill's wake.) This failure is a double whammy, in that it is felt most markedly in the tropical regions of the world. There a rapidly expanding population is involved in destroying the very natural pharmacopeia—the rainforest—that their ancestors used to keep their numbers in balance.

Looking back at the past four million years should make us humble in the face of the next four million. There is every possibility that our species will still be here at the end of that time, but whose great-great-grandchildren will be represented is anybody's guess. In the West, personal biological reproduction is no longer a cultural imperative. To maintain a sexual morality that is based on reproduction is nonsense and, at present world population levels, dangerous nonsense. The development and transmission of cultural knowledge offers our brightest hope for the future. It will be best served by a diverse array of minds, with heterodox experiences of the human condition. If we ignore our inherited flexibility, we may end up like the robust australopithecines sooner than we think.

But sooner or later, some end must come. When it does, a species as interesting as ours will deserve an epitaph. These words of Goethe should do:

What they did, what they tried,
No person knows! That they loved,
That we know . . .

Notes

This section stands between the main text and the bibliography and provides a guide to the sources I used, arranged by chapter and sub-theme. To avoid tedious repetition, the references here are abbreviated according to the "Harvard system" (an author's name, followed by a date and sometimes a page number; "f." after a page number means that page and those immediately following). The Harvard references relate to the full references in the alphabetical bibliography.

Many things are not amplified in these notes, indicating that the reference for what was said in the text can be found directly in the bibliography. For example, when I say in Chapter 1 that "Richard Leakey and Alan Walker have dated the Nariokotome skeleton to 1.6 million years ago," one should (after drawing an, I hope, only slightly irritating blank under "Leakey and Walker" in the bibliography) be able to unambiguously identify "Walker, A. and R. Leakey, eds. 1994. *The Nariokotome Homo Erectus Skeleton*. Berlin: Springer-Verlag," as the work that contains the details of the dating (mostly I've tried to get the author order right in the text, but this one caught me out).

Although I have tried to put in as much as possible of what is relevant, it is a wide field, and I know that I have missed much. The works cited have their own bibliographies that can provide further information for the curious or the skeptical.

INTRODUCTION

Beyond Nature

The opening quotation is from an English subtitle to words spoken by the actor Jean-Paul Belmondo in Jean-Luc Godard's film *Pierrot-Le-Fou*, released in 1965.

The Iceman.

The principal information about the Iceman came from Spindler's English-language book (Spindler 1994), from which the main quotations also came, including the reported views of Torstein Sjøvold; I also consulted Barfield 1994 and Egg et al. 1993. There is still some dispute over the precise date of the Iceman, as the carbon-14 analyses are not in tight enough agreement: 3300 B.C. is possible, but so is 200 years later. The *Lambda Nachrichten* quotation and some other elements of the "gay rumor" were reported and spread more widely in Wockner & Frings 1992. The report that Austrian women wanted to be inseminated with Ötzi's sperm was broadcast on the British news comedy quiz "Have I Got News for You"; the European paper from which the story purported to come was not identified, but I suppose it to have some degree of truth behind it. I expended many fascinating days tracking Ötzi rumors, usually drawing a blank; rumors, by their very nature, may have no identifiable source of truth or falsehood—in this case their existence is the interesting thing.

Darwin.

Darwin's evolutionary ideas were first presented in *On the Origin of Species* (Darwin 1859); he developed the idea of sexual selection and his theories of human evolution and the creation of racial diversity in *The Descent of Man, and Selection in Relation to Sex* in 1871; my source was the second edition (Darwin 1874).

Sociobiology.

There is a broad literature on sociobiology, supported by journals such as *Behavioral Ecology and Sociobiology;* I cite specific sources in various chapters, but a good overview from a sympathetic perspective can be found in Ridley 1993 (with a useful bibliography); see also Rasa et al. 1989.

Freud and matriarchy.

Freud's strange claim that "anatomy is destiny" can be found in Freud 1924–34, vol. 5, p. 210; his yet stranger belief that 1930s America was a matriarchy is recorded in Steinem 1994, p. 37, footnote 1. His prejudice against clitorises (motivated by envy perhaps) comes over best in German (Freud 1987: 165—"Der Minderwertigkeit der Klitoris"). Matriarchy was most influentially postulated by Bachofen in the early nineteenth century (see Bachofen 1973). I owe the insight that Victorian ethnographers probably viewed egality as matriarchy to my friend and colleague Yuri Lesman of the Hermitage Museum, St. Petersburg. Gimbutas's version of matriarchy, or matriliny as she often later termed it, can be found in a series of works, including Gimbutas 1981, 1982, 1989, and 1991. See Moore 1988 for an overview of gender issues in anthropology.

Culture.

The general formulation of "culture" that I have used comes from Ernest Gellner (Gellner 1989). Lamarck's idea that characteristics acquired during life would be passed on was replaced, for biology, by Darwinism and the development of genetics (Fisher 1930; Dobzhansky 1937), but remains a metaphor for *cultural* inheritance.

Various biologists have attempted to theorize culture: Lumsden & Wilson 1981 proposed the term *culturgens* to mean individual cultural traits or units with some genetic correspondence. Dawkins (1989: 192–201) has attempted to formulate a cultural counterpart to genes—memes; this idea has recently been popularized by Dennett 1995 among others. Neither sociocultural anthropologists nor archaeologists have found culturgens or memes particularly useful ideas. One reason is that the artifacts that constitute the principal evidence for early culture cannot really be dealt with like biological taxa; they are not "replicated" as genes are, and their classification is radically polythetic (see Clarke 1972 and Hodder 1986 for an appreciation of the symbolic dimension). More satisfactory formulations of the problem of initial cultural emergence can be found in Gibson & Ingold 1993.

Archaeology.

There are many good surveys of human cultural development as established by archaeology: Scarre 1988 and Fagan 1989 are both attractive and accessible. The ecofactual nature of the modern Greek landscape is described by Runnels 1995. *How* archaeology arrives at conclusions is well explained in Renfrew & Bahn 1991. For Rathje's "garbage project," see Rathje 1984 and a useful summary in D. H. Thomas 1989.

Anthropology and sex.

Anthropological approaches to sex were greatly influenced by the theories of Malinowski (1927, 1929). Foucault's *History of Sexuality* (1981) is accessibly introduced and discussed by Giddens (1992, especially Chapter 2); see also Halperin et al. 1990. For the European-inspired suppression of "alternative" sexuality among Native Americans, see Walter Williams's groundbreaking book 1986.

CHAPTER 1

Making the Beast with Two Backs:
The Evolution of Human Sexual Culture

The words from Shakespeare's *Othello* are spoken in Act 1, Scene 1.

Evolution.

The estimate that we share 98 percent of our genetic code with chimpanzees has, for me, almost the same epistemological status as an urban myth; the estimate clearly turns on how a gene is defined (no easy matter); Jared Diamond says 98.4 percent (reported in Ghazi 1993), while Daniel Dennett (1995: 112, footnote 7) says that human and chimpanzee DNA is "over 90 percent the same at every locus."

The two evolutionary sequence pictures discussed at the start of the chapter come from Wendt 1971 and Wood 1976, respectively.

One of the best general introductions to human evolution, covering both the historical development of thought and modern orthodoxies and controversies, is Jurmain & Nelson 1994. This well-illustrated book provides basic essential summaries of the major findspots, such as Laetoli and Olduvai, and individual fossil finds. Richards 1987 provides a very evenhanded treatment of rival arguments. The formal aspects of the fossil material are well presented in Aiello and Dean 1990, while a good recent summary of the taxonomic position has been provided by Wood 1992. Important issues of sexual dimorphism are covered by Zihlman 1993.

For molecular clock approaches to primate speciation events (i.e., the calculation of an eight-million-year separation of human and chimpanzee evolutionary lines), see Marks 1995; Rouhani 1989; for the Rift Valley topographic and climatic separation theory, see Coppens 1994.

Although literature in the field of human evolution goes out of date with startling rapidity, there are several popular accounts that capture the excitement of research and still contain much of value. Leakey & Lewin 1977 is a thoughtful overview; Leakey 1981 is wideranging and well illustrated; "Lucy" and related discoveries can be read about in Johanson & Edey 1981 and Johanson & Shreeve 1991. The Nariokotome skeleton is described and set in its place within current thinking in Walker & Leakey 1994, including Walker 1994 (they call it *Homo erectus*, in common with most scholars in the field, whereas I have followed Wood in calling it *Homo ergaster*; this has no implications for the points I am making).

Hunting and swimming.

Man-the-hunter theory can be found in Ardrey 1976 and Morris 1967; Hurcombe's quotation comes from her recent discussion of it (1995).

The aquatic theory was first postulated by Hardy 1960, and developed by Morgan 1982, 1984, 1985. Recently it has been supported by Morris 1994, while Richards gives it fair-minded, although to my mind overgenerous, treatment (1987: 193–204).

Walking, nakedness, and breasts.

Various debates concerning the development of human breasts are outlined in Gallup 1982 and N. W. Smith 1986.

On the general evolution of nakedness see Lunde 1984; Lunde & Grøttum 1984; Montagna 1983; Ebling 1985; the thermal argument that connects upright walking and nakedness has been well developed by Wheeler (1985, 1992), while quotations from Pete Wheeler and Russell Tuttle were taken verbatim from a television program ("Some Liked It Hot," *Horizon,* BBC2, 1994); the program also presented Dean Falk's "radiator" theory in some detail. Upright walking is also discussed by Lovejoy 1988. The throwing hypothesis is reviewed and supported by Knüsel 1992; for the Laetoli footprints, see Leakey and Harris 1987.

Sexual implications of upright walking are the subject of a stimulating discussion by Sheets-Johnstone 1990.

Sexual selection.

Darwin's idea of sexual selection is not universally popular; Darwin quotations are as follows: on page 26 from 1874: 857; page 34 on nakedness from 1874: 916; page 35 defining sexual selection, from 1874: 939. An edited volume to mark the centenary of the idea was produced by Bernard Campbell (1972); his introduction is of special interest, as are the chapters by Caspari, Crook, Fox, and Mayr. Nevertheless, writing in the nineties, Dennett, a strong defender of Darwinism, finds space only for a single reference to sexual selection (1995: 352). See also Ghiselin 1974; Low 1979. Marion Petric's work (reported in Ferry 1994) shows that the peacock example may not be as clear-cut as Darwin thought (cf. Dawkins 1995).

For the argument that human brains were sex-selected, see Wills 1993. Despite a close relationship with his wife, Darwin seems not to have considered motivational factors in his slight lifetime preponderance of backgammon wins over her (see Desmond & Moore 1991: 562, etc., for a description of the games, which sometimes drew spectators). The assumption of female inferiority in subsequent accounts of human evolution is reviewed by Erskine 1995; Hrdy 1981 represents a systematic challenge to the idea. See also Fedigan 1986; Lancaster 1991; Tanner & Zihlman 1976. The Specific Mate Recognition System (SMRS) has been advanced by Patterson (1985).

Sperm competition.

Sperm competition in animals is the subject of a useful edited volume by R. L. Smith (1984a), whose own paper (Smith 1984b) focuses on hominids. For modern humans, the recent work by Baker and Bellis is of great interest (Baker & Bellis 1993, 1995; Baker 1996). For primate penises, see Dixson 1987; Margulis & Sagan (1991) present some theories of their own.

Lucy's pelvis.

The controversy over the reconstruction of the obstetric pelvis of "Lucy" is difficult for a nonspecialist like me to follow. The initial formulation was Tague & Lovejoy 1986; I was swayed by arguments against Lucy being female, presented by Häusler & Schmid (1995), not having seen Ruff's clearly articulated objections until just before this book went to press (Ruff 1995). Overall, it is not possible to be certain about whether Lucy was female or male, but more specialists support the former. Karen Rosenberg's research on "the origins of the midwife" was summarized by Bunney (1993); her view, shared by Ruff, that the heads of australopithecine fetuses passed transversely through the pelvis seems, on balance, most likely.

Those interested in birth among Neanderthals, which I did not discuss in the book, should consult Trinkaus 1984; Rak & Arensburg 1987; Tompkins & Trinkaus 1987; Tague 1992. There is a suggestion that Neanderthals may have had a twelve-month gestation period, but how this could fit into a model of seasonally fluctuating food is unclear to say the least (for example, both the nine-month gestation in humans and the twenty-one-month gestation in elephants allows for pregnancy at the end of a three-month season of plenty, when nutrients are most easily available and body-fat reserves have been topped up, and birth at the beginning of another such season).

Biology, culture, and language.

For the interplay between biology and culture in human evolution, see Irons 1979; Ingold 1993a, 1993b; Wynn 1993. My idea of a flexible, gendered division of labor, rather than a rigid sexual one, among early hominids is in sympathy with Zihlman's view that "the overall behavioral flexibility of both sexes [was] a major contributing factor to early hominid survival" (1993: 34). One or two researchers have previously drawn attention to the potential importance of baby-carrying slings (see Bolen 1992: 54, with references to Zihlman and others), but the problem of lack of direct evidence may remain insuperable.

The debate about the emergence of human language, singing, and speech is complex and currently unresolvable (Falk 1987, 1989; Isaac 1989; Arensburg, Schepartz, et al. 1990). On the one hand, chimpanzees seem to be able to master some elements of language using signs (Gardner et al. 1989); on the other hand, some scholars doubt whether even Neanderthals could produce and understand rapidly spoken language (Noble and Davidson 1991; Milo & Quiatt 1993, with a useful collection of responses—both strongly critical and supportive—from other researchers). For the possibilities of speech at 1.6 million years ago, see MacLarnon 1994 and Walker 1994 (a thumbs-down).

Behind the technical debates I sense a problem with conceptualizing one or two million years of hominids with language but no "progress"; we find it hard to envisage our remote ancestors talking but not planning to build something. The conservatism of the surviving material cultural record—hundreds of thousands of years with the same sort of basic stone tools—is viewed as a result of lack of intelligence. I believe language started to emerge very early, and developed very slowly. I wonder whether bipedalism itself, emerging from four million years ago onward, was not an integral, bio-cultural element in the process that freed the abdominal cavity for ever more complex vocalization. That is, rather than seeing upright walking as a prerequisite (or "exaptation" in Gould & Vrba's 1981 terminology) for speech, the two features emerged in positive feedback. Both singing (Richman 1993) and "vocal grooming" (Aiello and Dunbar 1993) would have been good candidates for sexual selection. By "full language" (page 50), I mean a grammatical system that can be continuously extended.

If language and faking orgasm were connected, the process would not necessarily have been sex-selected; *She* magazine (Nov. 1995: 103) reports that in a survey of 2,000 men virtually all admitted to faking orgasm sometimes.

Chapter 2

Skull Sex and Brain Sex

The Greer quotations come from *The Female Eunuch,* first published in 1970 (1993: 35). The Sworn Virgins of Albania, who still exist, are best described by Edith Durham 1985 (original 1909).

Skeletal sex.

The sexing of human skeletons and genetic sexing is described in general terms in Jurmain and Nelson 1994; for sexual dimorphism see Richards 1987: 157; Crook 1972; Joan Silk in Miller, ed., 1993: 216 ff. Tim Ingold's observations on walking styles and skeletal development were made in a TAG (Theoretical Archaeology Group) conference session at the University of Durham in 1993. I owe most of my understanding of pelvic growth to Charlotte Roberts and Chris Knüsel.

Orgasm and spandrels.

Gould's view of the clitoris is in Gould 1995. The views of Sigmund Freud, Alfred Kinsey, and Sarah Blaffer Hrdy on vaginal versus clitoral orgasm are reprised in Gould 1995. The spandrel idea and the concept of exaptation (developed by Gould with Lewontin and Vrba, respectively) have recently been the subject of serious criticism by Dennett. Dennett says that "there will always be plenty of undesigned features in a system that is maximally well designed" (1995: 276); Gould argues that such features may be a later focus of evolution; starting as unselected "exaptive" by-products, they can become adapted. But Dennett does not agree, providing the following example (p. 280): "The Dadaist artist Marcel Duchamp . . . would not have been exapting a *spandrel* when he appropriated a urinal as his *objet trouvé* and called it a sculpture, since the urinal had a function in its earlier life." Nevertheless, to me this example—under a different interpretation—seems to prove Gould's point. Duchamp did not take a urinal and call it art simply by signing it "R. Mutt"; he exhibited it in an art gallery in a new orientation, so that the part normally mounted flush to the wall projected at right angles and formed a suspended base, and enabling the triangular array of urine drainage holes to be seen as part of the features of a face, while the pearlike curves of the whole suggested a female form, not unlike that of many prehistoric Venus figurines. Symbolically, Duchamp turned a receptacle for male fluid (urine) toward which a penis was pointed into a female form that might accept a penis and a different male fluid (semen). Duchamp thus developed latent associations and provided new visual "functions" for forms that had been produced for a different purpose (the original urinal being the product of necessary design decisions and their various subordinate formal implications—spandrels). My understanding of Gould and Vrba's idea of "exaptation" is broadly this. For a good bio-cultural example of exaptation, see notes to Chapter 8 on intersex individuals.

For lemur clitorises see Russell 1993; for hyena clitorises, and a good overview of recent advances in understanding animal sex, see Crews 1994.

Hippocratic gynecology.

Hippocratic gynecology was unfavorably reviewed by King 1988; the best introduction to the corpus, from which my quotations come, is Lloyd 1978. Modern data on female ejaculation, described in the Hippocratic corpus, comes from experiments by Perry & Whipple, reported in Hooper 1994: 76. My description of endometriosis comes from the Endometriosis Society's entry in Phillips and Rakusen 1989: 515–18; as far as I know, my interpretation of Hippocrates's "wandering womb" is novel.

Brain sex.

Matt Ridley (1993: 248) speculates that it "would be easy to engineer a society with no sex difference in attitude between men and women. Inject all pregnant women with the right dose of hormones and the result would be men and women with normal bodies, but identical feminine brains." In such a world, according to Ridley, "War, rape, boxing, motor racing, pornography, beer and hamburgers would soon be distant memories. A feminist paradise would have arrived." Aside from the fact that this ignores some level of documented involvement by women in everything on the list, this is a grotesque overstatement of brain differences.

For neuropsychological theories, see Newcombe & Ratcliff 1978, McGlone 1980, Edelman 1990, Kimura 1992, Short & Balaban 1994; for the cultural creation of sex roles, see O'Brien 1992; for the prospect of fuller bio-cultural explanations, see Begley 1995. For transsexual brains, see Tully 1992 for an overview (also Radford 1995); for a skeptical view, see Raymond 1979.

Genetic sex.

Maria Martinez Patino's reinstatement as a female competitor in international athletics is presumably a matter of record, but my information is informal insofar as I gleaned it from news reports on television for which I have no details. For Klinefelter's syndrome (XXY, but also XXXY and XXYY), mosaics, and other chromosomal abnormalities, see Warne et al. 1993, and Harry Brierley in Howells, ed., 1984: 75ff.; of Klinefelter's, Brierley says, "it is not clear why these cases are regarded as male with an extra X chromosome rather than female with a Y. . . . The Klinefelter has been quoted in older textbooks as sometimes transvestite, fetishistic and sometimes homosexual. Of course such sexual behaviours are likely to be sought out in the examination of individuals seen at the outset as having sexual problems and they merit no wide generalization." The transvestite and homosexual labels can be rendered meaningless according to how biological sex is described, but make sense if the gender choice of the genetic-sex-ambivalent individual is accorded priority. Actually XXY individuals can be functionally female: the female bodybuilder Bev Francis is on record as saying, "A Bulgarian woman was forced to retire because she had XXY—so she went home and had a baby. Who decides what a woman is?" (reported in Steinem 1994: 113f.).

Warne et al. 1993 describe a strongly hostile response to the prospect of medical treatment for an intersex condition in an Australian aboriginal community. The Mesopotamian *sag-ur-sag* are described in Leick 1994.

The one-per-thousand figure for clinically recognized intersex individuals is given by Glatzl (1987), who provides a useful overview of the various conditions. The relative prevalence of intersex individuals in any given community will depend on many factors. We should probably not assume that there is a standard congenital rate. It may be that intersex individuals are less prevalent under conditions of environmental stress, where the female body is less likely to "take a chance" on producing a child with a genetic coding defect: in one study of pregnancy and reproduction among 268 prisoners in the United States, 136 spontaneous abortions and stillbirths were recorded, against 373 live births with a zero incidence of birth defects, whereas, among the general population, an average of 27 birth defects would be expected (and correspondingly fewer abortions and stillbirths).

Childbirth and motherhood.

For Beit Shamesh, see Zias et al. 1993; for Worthy Park and other obstetric hazards documented through archaeology, see Wells 1975 and 1978. For childbirth as a critical component of gender systems, see Callaway 1978. For the Hua, see Peoples and Bailey 1994: 359–61.

The "gay gene."

Dick Swaab's research was reported in Radford 1994. The "gay gene" was postulated by teams led by LeVay and Hamer (LeVay and Hamer 1994); see response by Byne 1994. For Athenian sexuality, see Halperin et al. 1990. For male gender, see Gilmore 1990.

CHAPTER 3

Mysteries of the Organism

The Dawkins quotation is a compaction (representative, I hope) of three sentences in *The Selfish Gene* (second edition 1989: 201): "We, alone on earth, can rebel against the tyranny of selfish replicators" and the footnote to it (p. 331): "We, that is our brains, are separate and independent enough from our genes to rebel against them. As already noted, we do so in a small way every time we use contraception." My heuristic postulation of a "free will" gene (p. 85) can be seen to relate to Dawkins's belief (1982: 11) that "human nervous systems are so complex that in practice we can forget about determinism and behave as if we had free will."

The ground rules of British censorship of erotic imagery are unknown in a positive sense and can only be deduced from the recorded instances of past prosecution. The goalposts seem to shift from year to year; photographs of erect penises, and soft-focus, distance images of penetration, have recently avoided prosecution when presented within an explicitly sex-educational context.

The Soviet "glass of water" idea is well known to my Russian colleagues; it smacks of Lenin, but I'm not sure if it is his phrase.

Definitions of sex.

The ultrasound image of *in utero* masturbation was made in the Riverside Perinatal Clinic, Virginia; the estimate of the average age for the onset of masturbation in children (made defining masturbation broadly as digital genital manipulation, rather than necessary orgasm) was made by Gene Abel of the Behavioral Medicine Institute of Atlanta; my source for both was the Channel 4 television program, *Equinox*, "Beyond Love," (1995). From a bio-cultural perspective, I presume that the widespread use of diapers in the modern Western world must impact on emergent sexuality, as it insulates the genitals from such manipulation for much of infancy. This again suggests, as I have argued throughout, that there *is no* easy objective measure of "natural" human sexual response—culture plays a part from the very outset (see Ortner and Whitehead 1981).

Hewitt (1983: 151) quotes a description of the perfected yogin in the following terms: "for them an erotic relationship with the external world operates between that world and every single nerve ending. Their whole organism—physical, psychological and spiritual—is an erogenous zone. Their flow of love is not channelled as exclusively in the genital system as is most other people's." This finds some resonance in the West in some of the ideas of Reich (Rycroft 1971; Giddens 1992).

The Posner quotations come from Posner (1992: 91). For the history of sex studies in general, see also M. Diamond 1984, Hall 1994, Rusbridger 1986, Bullough 1995. Masters and Johnson 1966 is a milestone; Fricker 1994 has a useful update of facts and statistics. The field is a vast one and there is no space to provide a comprehensive guide to it here even were I competent.

Primate sexuality.

For the electric toothbrush experiment, see Burton 1971. The zoological statement on animal bisexual potential comes from page 240E of my 1948 edition of *Encyclopaedia Britannica*, volume 20, "Sexual Behaviour," by Frank A. Beach, then Chairman and Curator of the Department of Animal Behavior at the American Museum of Natural History.

The Jolly quotation came from Wavell 1995. Other bonobo data came from de Waal (1995) and "Monkey in the Mirror," *The Natural World*, BBC2 (1995). The most up-to-date summary of homosexual behavior in primates is Vasey 1995. See also Susman 1987.

Human sexuality.

I am grateful to Professor Bruce Trigger of McGill University for discussion of sexual license among North American Indian groups and its underrepresentation in ethnographic accounts. See also Williams 1986. The Liedloff quotation is as cited in Jackson 1989.

Robin Baker's figures for the lifetime tally of sexual partners for "most readers" is problematic. He cites a skewed male:female lifetime sexual partner ratio of 12:8 (Baker 1995: 273). This is clearly impossible as a *mean average* in a society with broadly equal numbers of men and women. On an imaginary island inhabited for fifty years by just twelve men and twelve women, each man would eventually have to have sex with every woman, but each woman would somehow have to have sex with only eight of the men! Baker suggests that *modal* differences —variations in the pattern —explain the figures. In my island example eleven of the men could total two sexual relationships each while eleven of the women could be monogamous; the remaining woman could eventually have sex with all twelve men, including the twelfth man, who would be monogamous with her; the mean average for men and women would even out, as it must (in this case to 1.9167 sexual partners each), but it would be true to say that most men had two partners while most women had one. Such considerations could technically explain Baker's figures if his sample was statistically biased such that, for example, each of his men had had four of their twelve sexual contacts with prostitutes and none of his female sample were themselves prostitutes. But I feel that reporting biases are far more likely to be at the root of most of the discrepancy, as I suggest.

Rape and its apologists.

The Baker quotation is 1996: 318.

Contraception.

Sir James Biment, an eminent British entomologist, made his remarks on a televised version of "Notes and Queries," hosted by Clive Anderson; I took down his words verbatim but do not have a record of the transmission date. The Pitt-Rivers quotation came from Himes 1970. Malthus's views about hunting groups were recorded in Gamble 1994. For Hippocrates, see Lloyd 1978. A good survey for more recent history is McLaren 1990. For ancient recipes and the reports of Skarzynski, Butenandt, and Jacobi, see Riddle 1992, Riddle et al. 1994. I relied heavily on these sources for the contraceptive plant detail. For the Melanesian magistrate's statement, see Himes 1970: 31.

Dastur 1962 lists contraceptives used in Ayurvedic medicine. My information on the Deni Indians and the Saami was from Gordon Hillman, a paleobotanist at the Institute of Archaeology, London. For estrogenic effects of hops, see Mabey 1989. I am very grateful to Paul Vasey for agreeing to go on record with his tentative hypothesis about the possibility of herbal abortifacient use among orangutans. Infanticide is discussed by Riddle, and by Hausfater and Hrdy (1984). See also Bernds and Barash 1979.

CHAPTER 4

Meet the Real Flintstones

The Nancy Friday quotation is from *Women on Top* (1991: 14).

Earliest art.

There has been some debate over whether the Berekhat Ram object (Goren-Inbar 1986) has been artistically worked; pending full publication of the site, Alex Marshack, who has examined the piece, is convinced that it has been (personal communication, Marshack 1990). Makapansgat is well illustrated in Morris 1994. For early ocher, see Knight, Power, and Watts 1995.

Menstruation and ovulation.

The detail of the sex strike theory is developed in Knight 1991, 1994a, 1994b, Knight and Maisels 1994 (from which I quote), Knight and Power 1994, Knight, Power, and Watts 1995, Power 1994. Dunbar's summary of Knight 1991 is in Dunbar 1992, from which the quotation is taken. Studies of menstrual synchrony and marginal fertility are reviewed in Shuttle and Redgrove 1994: 149f. and 183f. Fer-

tility awareness—ovulation pain, fertile mucus, etc.—is outlined by
Fiona McCloskey in Phillips and Rakusen 1989: 37. Frolov's proposed lunar calendar is outlined in Renfrew and Bahn 1991: 346. See
also Manson 1986.

It may appear inconsistent that I have recorded Hrdy's observation that concealed ovulation is not unique to humans when I claim
not to believe in concealed ovulation in humans. The problem is with
the terminology; it seems better to talk of a group of primates, including humans, in whom ovulation is not primarily visually signaled, but
among whom it is nonetheless signaled through changed behavior
and smell (for smell, see Stoddart 1990).

Shanidar, Doura, Skhūl.

Solecki's and subsequent work at Shanidar, and work at Skhūl, is
usefully summarized in Trinkaus 1983. I am grateful to Gordon Hillman for information on borage processing at Doura. For the con-
stituents of breast milk, see Palmer 1988 and Newman 1995.

Ice Age Eurasia.

Good summaries of the climatic and cultural background can be
found in Champion et al. 1984, Chapter 2, and Mellars 1994. I am
grateful to Chris Knüsel for the report of David Frayer's assessment
of the hip condition of the central figure in the Dolní Věstonice
triple burial.

CHAPTER 5

Venus in Furs

The Joan Bamberger quotation comes from her article "The Myth of
Matriarchy" (1974).

Ice Age art in Eurasia.

The best general introductions are Marshack 1972 and Bahn and Vertut 1988. The Venus figurines are given the fullest treatment in Delporte 1993. See also articles by Marshack; Gvozdover 1995 for eastern Venuses; and Neugebauer-Maresch 1993 for the context of Willendorf. For their distribution, see Mellars 1994: 72. I have only read one of Jean Auel's Ice Age novels (Auel 1990)—it is a ripping yarn despite Ayla's physique.

Opinions.

The views of Absolon (1949) are discussed in Delporte 1993; the quotations from Leroi-Gourhan and Guthrie, along with the reported views of Gobert, Jude, and Piette, can all be found in Delporte 1993 (in French; retranslating Guthrie has probably altered his phraseology somewhat, but his drift seems clear enough). Singh's work was reported in Horgan 1995: 150. See Grayson 1993 for the Donner Party disaster. Leroi-Gourhan's theories are well presented in Bahn and Vertut 1988. The Bahn quotation is from Bahn 1986; for the vulva debate, see Bahn 1986 and Lee 1986. Bahn warns me that there is a rumor to the effect that the Gorge d'Enfer double baton (Fig. 5.9) was a specially commissioned fake, and that there is also doubt about the antiquity of the red painting around the cave fissure at Niaux (p. 133); for Gorge d'Enfer at least, my view is that there has been so little made of the phallic nature of the batons that such a rumor is quite likely to stem from a prudish "protection" of Paleolithic reputations and concomitant unwillingness to discuss prehistoric sexuality openly. This is not to say that the possible sexual aspects of Ice Age art have not been discussed before, just that they have either been discussed in an extremely conventional manner (viewing the art essentially as pinups for male consumption) or as abstract and symbolic (Leroi-Gourhan's structural approach); feminist-inspired approaches have reacted against sexist naïveté by attempting to remove much of the art from a sexual realm, rather than postulating active female involvement in Ice Age sexual culture. The quotation from Clive Gamble came from McKie 1995.

CHAPTER 6

The Milk of the Vulture Goddess

The Winston Churchill quotation came from a radio broadcast of 21 March 1943, recorded in *Complete Speeches* (1974), volume 7, and abstracted in *The Concise Oxford Dictionary of Quotations* (expanded edition of 1993), page 99, number 21.

Scene setting.

For modern human global expansion, see Fagan 1989. For the European Mesolithic, see Mithen 1994, with details of the Skateholm burial and Lepenski Vir; Mithen is informative on health differences among various Mesolithic populations. See also Meiklejohn and Zvelebil 1991.

Neolithic economy.

The "squirrel" quotation came from Pearce (1994: 30) and is typical of many along the same lines. "Amazon-style felling" was the headline to an article by Keys 1989. General perspectives on Neolithic Europe are provided by Whittle 1994, Hodder 1990, and Gebauer and Price 1992. For a gradualist view of forest clearance and subsistence change in Britain, see J. Thomas 1991. The Gimbutas quotation (p. 148) comes from 1982: 11; her assertion that Neolithic cosmology was an extension of Paleolithic cosmology is developed more fully in 1989: xv–xxiii. The Meaden quotation is from Meaden 1991: 214. Childe's views and the site of Jericho are outlined in Fagan 1989.

Gender relations.

Data on Caddoan Mounds and Mississippi valley cultures' nutritional status can be found in Cohen 1993 (see Cohen 1989 for a classic overview of developing health problems among humans). For basic demographic issues, see Hassan 1981; see also Wailes 1984, R. B. Lee 1972. Lactational birth control is described in Palmer 1988; see also La Leche League International 1981: 316f. For women's role in early plant domestication, see articles in Gero and Conkey 1991.

The Mother Goddess theory.

The Gimbutas quotation relating to Çatal Hüyük (p. 156) is 1989: 107, caption to figure 177); that relating to Hağar Qim (p. 159) is 1989: 106, caption to figure 167. I made the suggestion that each female figurine might contain a seed because it might—as far as I know, no one has ever looked.

For variability in, and ways of calculating, the duration of full-term pregnancy in humans, see B. van der Kooy 1994.

Neolithic cultures in Europe.

In general see Whittle 1994. The Spanish evidence for violent death can be found in Campillo et al. 1993. Mithen (1994) summarized compatible evidence for the preceding Mesolithic period. The idea that permanent longhouses might have provided privacy was put to me during a seminar I gave on this chapter at the Department of Archaeology, University of Southampton; I believe it was attributed, but to whom I do not know. At the same seminar Michael Ryder kindly informed me of the rules of open-air sexual decorum among pastoral nomads. An isolated Inuit lovers' camp is described by Binford 1983.

CHAPTER 7

The Grave of the Golden Penis

The opening Milton quotation is from *Paradise Regained*, Book 4: 220. My opening words may appear to be an attempt to shoot myself in the foot after my disavowal of biological determinism and support for a fluid anthropological concept of gender in earlier chapters. I hope the meaning becomes clear: it is a gender distinction based on the cultural exploitation of biology in terms of an unprecedented reduction in birth spacing achieved by strict weaning regimes, producing demographic and emotional effects conducive to the strengthening of the martial element in society. Within such a system Stonehenge could, of course, have been ordered by a woman — one like Margaret Thatcher.

Secondary products.

For Talheim, see Spindler 1994: 251f. For secondary products, see Sherratt 1994; Peter Bogucki has argued that the use of bovine milk may have begun with the initial LBK cultures (Bogucki 1986). The ability to digest milk is not shared by all adult human populations; the development of dairy farming is connected to selection for lactose tolerance among early farming groups (see Jurmain and Nelson 1994: 153f.). Archaeological and osteological evidence for weaning was reviewed by Sholl (1995); see also Moogi-Cecchi et al. 1994, Fildes 1988, Stuart MacAdam and Dettwyler, forthcoming.

Rock art.

For the Val Camonica rock art, see Anati 1965. For Siberia, see Martynov 1991. The homosexual interpretation of one of the Bohuslan

Learned helplessness.

"Learned helplessness" (Seligman 1975; Peterson, Maier, and Seligman 1993) is a very specific theory that I have probably misrepresented here, firstly by being too brief in describing it and secondly in trying to impute it to a prehistoric situation where it cannot be tested (although the theory has been applied, with the approbation of its pioneers, to the personality of Saint Paul as deduced from his New Testament writings (Peterson, Maier, and Seligman 1993: 248–49). My "for instance" about weaning is not an example Seligman et al. use; rigid routine is not their prescription for curing learned helplessness, but figures as a potential ameliorating factor or strategy in some of the cases and results they describe. The Alison Sheridan quotation comes from Beaumont 1993.

Food, gender, and sex.

The connection between food and sexuality is investigated by Fiddes (1991) in a chapter on sex and meat; gender issues in contemporary food production are analyzed by Ferguson 1994.

CHAPTER 8

Shamans and Amazons

The RuPaul quotation is a catchphrase of his; my source was an interview in *Phase* magazine, issue 2, April 1994: 32.

Gender and metal.

For Lanhill, see J. Thomas 1991: 120 (all the caveats about sexing uncertainties must apply); Harrison 1980 and Sherratt 1994 outline the Beaker period. I am grateful to Bruce Albert at Durham for dis-

scenes was made by Tim Yates. For the historical development of the social aspects of human-animal relationships, see K. Thomas 1983.

Varna.

The most accessible source is Katinčarov, Mohen et al. 1989. The skull photograph from Grave 43 has a very protuberant chin that may be pathological; while the general stature and robusticity of the skeleton would normally indicate male sex, the ascription must remain uncertain. The possibility that the original burial was prone (facedown) is based on a published photograph (Georgiev 1979: 78); I am grateful to Chris Knüsel for sharing his thoughts on this with me. The Hazda myth of the woman with the zebra's penis was recorded by James Woodburn and recently discussed in Knight and Power 1994.

Divine masturbation.

Pyramid Utterance 527 is translated in Rundle Clark 1959. Additional information on Egypt came from Bruce Trigger. For Mesopotamia, see Leick 1994. The Zuñi "spring riding" is described in Fulton and Anderson 1992. The Larisa figurine is in Gimbutas 1989: 181, figure 281.

Megaliths.

For plow marks under British barrows, see Fowler and Evans 1967; compare Patzold 1960. The Sharp quotation is in Sharp 1989: 76. Newgrange solstice is described in Patrick 1974. For Kintraw, see Sharp 1989: 101f. John Barber's paper "Infanticide in prehistory" was presented at the autumn 1993 meeting of the Neolithic Studies Group at the British Museum on the theme "Women and Children in the Neolithic"; the Ian Kinnes quotation came from Beaumont 1993.

cussion of putative biological female Beaker graves with daggers. Assumptions about gender and metal in this period are discussed by Budd and Taylor (1995). The Reid and MacLean quotation is 1995: 149. For the development of metals in the East and the formation of a Eurasian cultural zone, see Chernykh 1992 and Taylor 1994.

Iron Age evidence.

For Pazyryk and Letnitsa, and an overview of Thracians, Scythians, etc., see Taylor 1994. This also deals with Amazons, for whom also see David 1976a and 1976b, Lloyd 1978, Rolle 1989 (with descriptions of Aul Stepan Zminda and Chertomlyk), Rolle et al. 1991, Weidegger 1986, Williams 1986 (for the naming of Amazonia). While some Soviet and former Soviet scholars have discussed shamanic transvestism among extant peoples of the Soviet/Russian empire (e.g., Basilov 1978), general sexual repression meant that sexual aspects of prehistory could not be easily theorized (one of the foremost Leningrad/St. Petersburg archaeologists has spent time in prison camp on a homosexuality charge: see Taylor 1993).

I am indebted to Alex Bursche for discussion of his work in progress on Roman brothel tokens. For *situla* art, see Kastelic 1965, Boardman 1971, Bonfante 1981 and 1985. For the background to Hochdorf, see Cunliffe 1994. For Greek and Roman erotica, see Johns 1982. For the origins and spread of syphilis, see Dutour et al. 1994.

Enarees.

For ethnographic descriptions of berdaches, see Fulton and Anderson 1992; Williams 1986. In narrow, biological evolutionary terms those intersex individuals who cannot (or otherwise do not) physically breed cannot be seen as adaptive. When given special cultural status, however, they can be considered exapted spandrels (see notes to Chapter 2). The interpretation of lines in Ovid's poetry was suggested by one of my students, Rhîan Evans, herself a postoperative

male-to-female transsexual; I had read Ovid before, but had made
nothing of the lines that now seem so significant. The quotations are
from Grene's translation. For the Sokolova "priestess," see Kovpanenko 1991. For the Gundestrup cauldron, see Klindt-Jensen 1979,
Kaul 1991, Bergquist and Taylor 1987, Taylor 1992. For Cernunnos,
also see Bober 1951.

Sex and death.

For Harald Bluetooth, and the possible rape victim at Worthy Park,
see Hawkes and Wells 1975, from which the quotations from Tacitus
(p. 219) and Wulfstan come. My colleague Charlotte Roberts, who
now heads the Calvin Wells Laboratory at Bradford, believes that
Hawkes and Wells were too firm in their diagnosis of rape, and suggests that many other events could have caused similar trauma. Yet
the historical evidence and the lack of grave goods suggest to me that
the Hawkes and Wells interpretation remains the most likely. For
bog bodies in general, see Glob 1969, Brothwell 1986.

　　Don Brothwell informs me that a forensic test for semen has
never been part of the analytical procedure with ancient preserved
bodies; when mummified or freeze-dried, semen preserves very
well (A. Gallop in Radford 1994), yet freeze-dried bodies have not
been tested (e.g., Harthansen et al. 1991). For those that remain
skeptical that sex and death may be culturally conjoined in later
prehistoric and early medieval Europe, Sass (1995) provides a useful translation of the tenth-century A.D. Arab diplomat Ibn
Fadlan's account of chiefly burial among the Rus, in which a ser-
vant girl is required to have sexual intercourse with seven men
before being ritually killed.

Rituals and clothing.

For Germanic religious transvestism, see Knüsel and Ripley (forthcoming). I am indebted to the Rev. Dr. Anders Bergquist for infor-

mation on later medieval baptism ceremonies. My information on Cerne Abbas came from Cooper 1994. The cross-dressed (cross-wrapped?) Egyptian mummy is British Museum Cat. No. BM6704, and is illustrated in Putnam 1993: 49. Scyles's Greek dress is described by Herodotus (see Herodotus 1987: 4.78–80). The Vix burial and controversy is outlined in Arnold 1991.

CHAPTER 9

The Return of the Beast with Two Backs:
Sex and the Prehistory of Race

The Baker quotation is in Baker 1974: 96.

The history of race.

Baker's typological view of race was already becoming outmoded in 1974, but his book contains a wealth of historical detail; see also Coon 1962 and Cole 1965. The last gasp of this way of thinking is, according to Moore (1995), epitomized in Cavalli-Sforza and Cavalli-Sforza 1995. For a different perspective, see Dobzhansky 1972 and most recently Brace 1995. Darwin's information on human-subtype-specific lice came from the surgeon of a whaling ship (Desmond and Moore 1991: 155). Information on the last of the Tasmanians can also be found in Baker.

Bruce Trigger (1989) provides a thorough introduction to issues of race in archaeology that I used as a source for Peyrère, Rousseau, "psychic unity," etc. For Gobineau, Pouchet, and Vogt, see Baker 1974. The *Times* report on Romanes was cited in Desmond and Moore 1991: 633.

For the history of research on Neanderthals, see Richards 1987, Jurmain and Nelson 1994, Shreeve 1995. Wills (1993: 56) considers the possibility of a frozen Neanderthal "Ötzi" being found and resolving the species debate by yielding analyzable mitochondrial

DNA. For Piltdown, see Gould 1981. The Orce conference is not yet published: see Denison 1995a for a report.

Chosen ones.

The Vogt quotation (p. 234) is given in Baker 1974. The Darwin and Galton quotations (p. 236) come from Desmond and Moore (1991: 521 and 557) along with the account of Galton's lagomorph-blood transfusion experiments. All Günther quotations can be found in Günther 1927. Trigger 1989 provides a good outline of Kossinna's career and references to Eliot Smith. Tom of Finland was a noted homoerotic artist; the Tom of Finland Foundation is in Los Angeles; an example of his work is reproduced in Muthesius et al. 1993: 27. Himmler's interpretation of Ice Age Venuses was discussed by Pete Stone in an article in the *World Archaeology Congress* newsletter/magazine around 1988. My reference for the Hobsbawm quotation is even worse, as I cannot remember where I read it, but my notes are verbatim, so if the source was correct then the quotation is. On eugenics today, see Horgan 1993.

Race, *Formenkreis*, species.

Kant's thoughts on species and the herring gull example come from Baker 1974. Carrie Allen McCray's poem was reproduced in Steinem 1994: 277. John Frere's words are recorded in Daniel 1967. For Bodo, see Jurmain and Nelson 1994: 437f.; for overviews, see W. Howells 1976 and Foley 1989.

   For Rebecca Cann's work, see Stoneking and Cann 1989. For a lucid discussion of skin pigmentation and the problem with adaptationist arguments for human racial diversity, see Kingdon 1993. The most detailed modern study of skull shape is W. Howells 1989.

   I am grateful to Clive Gamble for information on the date of the latest Neanderthals in Spain.

   The Dawkins quotation is 1995: 65.

Inflatable sheep and pigs are obtainable from Hollywood International in Torquay.

Marriage patterns.

I am grateful to Richard Harrison for sight of an English-language version of his paper (1994) dealing in part with marriage patterns among the Beaker complex cultures on the basis of physical anthropology. For the Magdalenenberg, see Spindler et al. 1976. For diplomatic marriages among barbarian tribes in western Europe on the eve of the Roman conquest, see Fitzpatrick 1989. For cranial deformation among Huns, see Rolle et al. 1991: 431. Scott Woodward's DNA studies at Fayum were reported on television ("Secrets of the Pharaohs," *Encounters*, Channel 4, 1995).

Intelligence or knowledge.

The quotations from Jensen 1969 were taken from Tobias 1972, who also reports Biesheuvel's work; the rat experiment was published in Cowley and Griesel 1966. The Flynn effect was described by John Horgan in the editorial section of *Scientific American*, "Science and the Citizen" (1995, vol. 273(5): 10–11), from which the "baffled" statement came. Recent and complementary criticisms of IQ theories are presented in Goleman 1995. See Wills 1993: 184–85 on lack of success of eugenic sperm banks. For orangutan intelligence, see Schwartz 1987; for chimpanzee language, see Gardner et al. 1989.

CONCLUSION

Beyond Culture

The Burke quotation came from *The Concise Oxford Dictionary of Quotations* (1993 edition, p. 80, no. 17) and is referenced as from *Reflections on the Revolution in France*, 1790: 234.

Issues of sexual morality.

The Canadian psychologist is J. Phillippe Rushton and the terms are taken from Rushton 1990. Edmund Leach's questioning of "marriage" as an unproblematic cross-cultural term was something I was made aware of as an undergraduate student by the anthropologist Gilbert Lewis; I could not find the reference when completing these notes, but the issues are accessibly summarized in Ferraro et al. 1994: 376f.; they cite the famous example of Nayar "marriage" in southern India, characterized by a ceremony that results in no necessary subsequent sexual activity or fidelity, cohabitation, or expectation of permanency — indeed the bride may never see her groom again afterward (but, as there is no divorce in such a system, "marital stability" would have to be rated "high").

Doris Kloster (1995: 11) prefaces her recent photograph album with a thought about the natural selective advantages of sexual dressing: "At a time when exchange of body fluids is perilous, donning insulating apparel such as rubber clothing and gas masks for sex may not be that excessive."

Osteoporosis and milk.

The causes of osteoporosis are not yet fully understood, but the connection to decreased load-bearing seems strong according to Professor Don Ortner of the Smithsonian Institution who took the time to discuss it with me. I gleaned the information about Genpharm from a television report. The UNICEF recommendation on breast-feeding is cited in Newman 1995. I am emphatically *not* advocating a return to the values of "women at home, men at work"; the current problem, as I see it, is with Western men's and women's work culture, not with breast-feeding itself (see Shuttleworth 1994 and Small 1995).

Plastic sexuality and Kegels.

The oblique reference to prosthetic devices comes from a line in the song "Dicks Don't Grow on Trees" (written by a Canadian lesbian chanteuse of the mid-eighties called Robin whose second name escapes me): "Well I know that we could root-toot-toot with a well-made Japanese substitute" — Giddens's idea of "plastic sexuality" always reminds me of this song.

Kegels are also commonly known as pelvic floor exercises and involve flexing of the two *levator ani* muscles (Balaskas and Gordon 1987: 40; Phillips and Rakusen 1989: 347 — both descriptions of women) and related muscles such as the *bulbo-spongiosus* in women and the *transversus pevinei* in men (Hewitt 1983: 148f.). Before Kegel, the idea was already well developed in sexual yoga: Hewitt (1969, 1983) describes yogic and Tantric abdominal and pelvic flexes *(mudras)* and muscle locks *(bandhas)* that can enhance sexual pleasure.

Sex and population growth.

A sexual morality based on reproduction is most familiar in the West in the Catholic Church's interdictions on abortion, contraception, and homosexuality, but it is equally strongly present in scientific thinking. Darwin, for example, wrote (1874: 945) that "our natural rate of increase, though leading to many and obvious evils, must not be greatly diminished by any means . . . the most able should not be prevented by laws or customs from succeeding best and rearing the largest number of offspring." This carries the implication that those of "lesser ability" (however they might be defined) should perhaps be so prevented (an idea Darwin was not averse to); Galton's and Stopes's views follow from this, even though their belief that poor, uneducated, feckless people should not be allowed to swamp the "best" by weight of numbers ignores the fact that those who breed most *are* by definition the fittest and the best on the strict interpretation of Darwin's scheme. This point seems also to have escaped Herrnstein and Murray in their polemic, *The Bell Curve* (1994).

The words of Goethe at the end come from a poem called "Noch ein Paar" ("Another Couple") in the "Uschk Nameh — Buch der Liebe" section of *West östlicher Divan*, composed between 1814 and 1819. The German reads: "Was sie getan, was sie geübt, / Das weiß kein Mensch! Daß sie geliebt, / Das wissen wir . . ." I ended with this not just because it is about humanity's finest capacity, love, but also because of its admission and acceptance of ignorance beyond a certain point.

Bibliography

Absolon, K. 1949. "The diluvial anthropomorphic statuettes and drawings, especially the so-called Venus statuettes discovered in Moravia." *Artibus Asiae* 12(3): 201–20.

Aiello, L. and C. Dean. 1990. *Human Evolutionary Anatomy*. San Diego: Academic Press.

Aiello, L. and R. Dunbar. 1993. "Neocortex size, group size, and the evolution of language." *Current Anthropology* 34: 184–93.

Alexander, R. D. and K. M. Noonan. 1975. "Concealment of ovulation, parental care, and human social evolution." In N. Chagnon and W. Irons, eds. *Evolutionary Biology and Human Social Behaviour:* 436–53. North Scituate, MA: Duxbury Press.

Anati, E. 1965. *Camonica Valley* (Translated by L. Asher). London: Readers Union/Jonathan Cape.

Anderson, E. F. 1993. *Plants and People of the Golden Triangle: Ethnobotany of the Hill Tribes of Northern Thailand*. Portland, Oregon: Dioscorides Press.

Ardener, E. 1975. "Belief and the problem of women: the problem revisited." In S. Ardener, ed. *Perceiving Women:* 1–28. New York: Wiley.

Ardener, S., ed. 1978. *Defining Females: the Nature of Women in Society*. London: Croom Helm.

Ardrey, R. 1976. *The Hunting Hypothesis*. New York: Athenaeum.

Arensburg, B., L. Schepartz, *et al.*, 1990. "A reappraisal of the anatomical basis for speech in Middle Paleolithic hominids." *American Journal of Physical Anthropology* 83(2): 137–46.

Arnold, B. 1991. "The deposed princess of Vix: the need for an engendered European prehistory." In D. Walde and N. Willows, eds. *The Archaeology of Gender: Proceedings of the 22nd Annual Chacmool Conference:* 366–74. Calgary: Archaeological Association of the University of Calgary.

Arrian. 1971. *The Campaigns of Alexander* (Translated by A. deSélincourt). Harmondsworth: Penguin.

Auel, J. M. 1990. *The Plains of Passage*. London: Coronet.

Bachofen, J. J. 1973. *Myth, Religion and Mother Right*. Princeton: Princeton University Press.

Bagemihl, B. 1997. forthcoming. *Lesbian Gulls and Gay Giraffes: the Natural History of Homosexuality*. San Francisco: HarperCollins.

Bahn, P. 1986. "No sex, please, we're Aurignacians." *Rock Art Research* 3(2): 99–120.

Bahn, P. and J. Vertut. 1988. *Images of the Ice Age*. Leicester: Windward.

Baker, R. 1974. *Race*. London: Oxford University Press.

———. 1996. *Sperm Wars: Infidelity, Sexual Conflict and Other Bedroom Battles*. London: Fourth Estate.

Baker, R. and M. Bellis. 1993. "Human sperm competition: ejaculate adjustment by males and the function of masturbation." *Animal Behaviour* 46: 861–85.

———. 1995. *Human Sperm Competition: Copulation, Masturbation and Infidelity*. London: Chapman and Hall.

Balaskas, J. and Y. Gordon. 1987. *The Encyclopedia of Pregnancy and Birth* (with photographs by A. Sieveking). London: MacDonald.

Bamberger, J. 1974. "The myth of matriarchy: why men rule in primitive society." In M. Rosaldo and L. Lamphere, eds. *Women, Culture and Society:* 263–80. Cambridge: Stamford University Press.

Barber, E. W. 1995. *Women's Work, the First 20,000 Years: Women, Cloth and Society in Early Times.* London: W. W. Norton.

Barfield, L. 1994. "The Iceman reviewed." *Antiquity* 68: 10–26.

Barkow, J. 1991. "Précis of *Darwin, sex and status: Biological approaches to mind and culture.*" *Behavioral and Brain Sciences* 14: 295–334.

Barkow, J., L. Cosmides, and J. Tooby, eds. 1992. *The Adapted Mind: Evolutionary Psychology and the Generation of Culture.* New York: Oxford University Press.

Basilov, V. N. 1978. "Vestiges of transvestism in Central-Asian shamanism." In V. Diòszegi and M. Hoppál, eds. *Shamanism in Siberia* (Translated by S. Simon): 281–89. Budapest: Akadémiai Kiado.

Bates, D. G. and S. H. Lees, 1979. "The myth of population regulation." In N. Chagnon and W. Irons, eds. *Evolutionary Biology and Human Social Behaviour:* 436–53. North Scituate, MA: Duxbury Press.

Beaumont, P. 1993. "Grisly rituals cast light on henges." *Observer*, Sunday 20th June 1993: 64.

Begley, S. 1995. "Nature plus nurture: searching for how experiences influence sexuality." *Newsweek*, November 13, 1995.

Begun, D. and A. Walker, 1993. "The Endocast." In Walker, A. and R. Leakey, eds. *The Nariokotome Homo Erectus Skeleton.* Berlin: Springer-Verlag.

Bergquist, A. and T. Taylor. 1987. "The origin of the Gundestrup Cauldron." *Antiquity* 61: 10–24.

Bernds, W. P. and D. P. Barash. 1979. "Early termination of parental investment in mammals, including humans." In N. Chagnon and W. Irons, eds. *Evolutionary Biology and Human Social Behaviour:* 436–53. North Scituate, MA: Duxbury Press.

Binford, L. 1983. *In Pursuit of the Past*. London: Thames and Hudson.

Black, J. and A. Green. 1992. *Gods, Demons and Symbols of Ancient Mesopotamia: an Illustrated Dictionary*. London: British Museum Press.

Blakely, R. 1989. "Bone strontium in pregnant and lactating females from archaeological samples." *American Journal of Physical Anthropology* 80: 173–85.

Boardman, J. 1971. "A southern view of Situla art." In J. Boardman, M. A. Brown, and T. G. E. Powell, eds. *From Bronze to Iron Age: A Sequel to a Sequel. The European Community in Later Prehistory: Studies in Honour of C. F. C. Hawkes:* 123–40. London: Routledge and Kegan Paul.

Bober, P. F. 1951. "Cernunnos: origin and transformation of a Celtic divinity." *American Journal of Archaeology* 55: 13–51.

Bodmer, W. and L.L. Cavalli-Sforza. 1976. *Genetics, Evolution, and Man*. San Francisco: W.H. Freeman.

Bogucki, P. 1986. "The antiquity of dairying in temperate Europe." *Expedition* 28(2): 51–58.

Bolen, K. 1992. "Prehistoric construction of mothering." In C. Claassen, ed. 1992. *Exploring Gender through Archaeology: Selected Papers from the 1991 Boone Conference* (Monographs in World Archaeology Vol. 11): 49–62. Madison: Prehistory Press.

Bonfante, L. 1981. "Etruscan couples and their aristocratic society." In
H. Foley, ed. *Reflections on Women in Antiquity:* 323–41. London:
Gordon Breach.

——. 1985. "Amber, women, and Situla art." *Journal of Baltic Studies*
16(3): 276–91.

Bosinski, G. 1991. "The representation of female figures in the
Rhineland Magdalenian." *Proceedings of the Prehistoric Society* 57:
51–64.

Bower, B. 1995. "Pruning the family tree: a controversial study sends
many species packing." *Science* 148: 154–55.

Brace, C. L. 1995. "Region does not mean 'race'—reality versus convention in Forensic Anthropology." *Journal of Forensic Sciences* 40(2):
171–75.

Bräuer, G. 1989. "The evolution of modern humans: a comparison of the
African and non-African evidence." In P. Mellars and C. Stringer,
eds. *The Human Revolution: Behavioural and Biological Perspectives on the
Origin of Modern Humans:* 123–54. Edinburgh: Edinburgh University Press.

Brothwell, D. 1986. *The Bog Man and the Archaeology of People.* London:
British Museum Publications.

Brown, P. and L. J. Jordanova. 1982. "Oppressive dichotomies: the na-
ture/culture debate." In The Cambridge Women's Studies Group,
ed. *Women in Society:* 224–41. London: Virago.

Brüning, H. 1908. *Geschichte der Methodik der künstlichen Säuglingser-
nahrung.* Stuttgart: Enke.

Budd, P. and T. Taylor. 1995. "The faerie smith meets the bronze industry: magic versus science in the interpretation of prehistoric metal-
making." *World Archaeology* 27(1): 133–43.

Bullough, V. L. 1995. *Science in the Bedroom: a History of Sex Research*. New York: Basic Books.

Bunney, S. 1993. "On the origins of the midwife." *New Scientist* 22nd May 1993: 18.

Burkill, I. H. 1966. *A Dictionary of the Economic Products of the Malay Penin-sular* (Two volumes). Kualar Lumpur: Ministry of Agriculture and Co-operatives.

Burley, N. 1979. "The evolution of concealed ovulation." *The American Naturalist* 144: 835–58.

Burton, F. 1971. "Sexual climax in female *Macaca mulatta*." *Proceedings of the Third International Congress of Primatology* 3: 180–91.

Buss, D., *et al*. 1990. "International preferences in selecting mates." *Journal of Cross-Cultural Psychology* 21: 5–47.

Butler, J. 1993. *Bodies that Matter*. London: Routledge.

Byne, W. 1994. "The biological evidence challenged." *Scientific American* 270(5): 19–25.

Callaway, H. 1978. "The most essentially female function of all: giving birth." In S. Ardener, ed. *Defining Females: the Nature of Women in Society*: 163–85. London: Croom Helm.

Campbell, B., ed. 1972. *Sexual Selection and the Descent of Man 1871–1971*. London: Heinemann.

Campbell, J. 1976. *The Masks of God: Primitive Mythology*. Harmonds-worth: Penguin.

Campillo, D., O. Mercadal and R-M. Blanch. 1993. "A mortal wound caused by a flint arrowhead in individual MF-18 of the neolithic period exhumed at Sant Quirze del Valles." *International Journal of Osteology* 3: 145–50.

Cant, J. 1981. "Hypothesis for the evolution of human breasts and buttocks." *American Naturalist* 117: 199–204.

Carter, C. S. and L. L. Getz. 1993. "Monogamy and the prairie vole." *Scientific American* 268(6): 70–76.

Caspari, E. 1972. "Sexual selection in human evolution." In B. Campbell, ed. *Sexual Selection and the Descent of Man 1871–1971*: 332–57. London: Heinemann.

Cavalli-Sforza, L. L. and F. Cavalli-Sforza. 1995. *The Great Human Diasporas: the History of Diversity and Evolution* (Translated by Sarah Thorne). Reading, MA: Addison-Wesley.

Chagnon, N. and W. Irons, eds. 1979. *Evolutionary Biology and Human Social Behaviour*. North Scituate (MA): Duxbury Press.

Champion, T., C. Gamble, S. Shennan, and A. Whittle, 1984. *Prehistoric Europe*. London: Academic Press.

Chernykh, E. N. 1992. *Ancient Metallurgy in the USSR: the Early Metal Age* (Translated by S. Wright). Cambridge: Cambridge University Press.

Claassen, C., ed. 1992. *Exploring Gender through Archaeology: Selected Papers from the 1991 Boone Conference* (Monographs in World Archaeology Vol. 11). Madison: Prehistory Press.

Clarke, D. 1972. *Analytical Archaeology* (Second edition, edited by Bob Chapman). London: Methuen.

Cohen, M. N. 1989. *Health and the Rise of Civilisation*. New York: Yale University Press.

———. 1993. "Skeletal evidence for sex roles and gender hierarchies in prehistory." In B. Miller, ed. *Sex and Gender Hierarchies:* 273–96. New York: Cambridge University Press.

Cole, S. 1965. *Races of Man* (Second edition). London: Trustees of the British Museum (Natural History).

Coon, C. 1962. *The Origin of Races*. New York: Knopf.

Cooper, L. no date [on sale 1994]. *The Rude Man of Cerne Abbas and Other Wessex Landscape Oddities*. Lyme Regis: Nigel J. Clarke Publications.

Coppens, Y. 1994. "East side story: the origin of humankind." *Scientific American* 270(5): 62–96.

Cowley, J. and R. Griesel. 1966. "The effect of rehabilitating first and second generation low protein rats on growth and behaviour." *Animal Behaviour* 14: 506–17.

Crews, D. 1994. "Animal sexuality." *Scientific American* 270(1): 96–103.

Crook, J. H. 1972. "Sexual selection, dimorphism, and social organisation in the primates." In B. Campbell, ed. *Sexual Selection and the Descent of Man 1871–1971:* 231–81. London: Heinemann.

Cucchiari, S. 1981. "The gender revolution and the transition from bisexual horde to patrilocal band: the origins of gender hierarchy." In S. Ortner and H. Whitehead, eds. *Sexual Meanings:* 31–79. Cambridge: Cambridge University Press.

Cunliffe, B. 1994. "Iron Age societies in western Europe and beyond, 800–140 B.C." In B. Cunliffe, ed. *The Oxford Illustrated Prehistory of Europe:* 336–72. Oxford: Oxford University Press.

Daly, M. and M. Wilson. 1983. *Sex, Evolution and Behaviour* (Second edition). Boston: Willard Grant Press.

Daniel, G. 1967. *The Origins and Growth of Archaeology.* Harmondsworth: Pelican.

Darwin, C. 1859. *On the Origin of Species by Means of Natural Selection.* London: John Murray.

———. 1874. *The Descent of Man, and Selection in Relation to Sex* (Second edition; 1922 reprint). London: John Murray.

Dastur, J. 1962. *Medicinal Plants of India and Pakistan.* Bombay: D. B. Taraporevala Sons & Co. Private.

David, R., ed. 1978. *Mysteries of the Mummies: the Story of the Manchester University Investigation.* London: Book Club Associates.

David, T. 1976a. "La position de la femme en Asie Centrale." *Dialogues D'Histoire Ancienne*: 129–62.

———. 1976 b. "Amazones et femmes de nomades: à propos de quelques représentations de l'iconographie antique." *Arts Asiatiques* 32: 214–21.

Dawkins, R. 1982. *The Extended Phenotype: the Gene as the Unit of Selection.* Oxford: Freeman.

———. 1989. *The Selfish Gene* (Second edition). Oxford: Oxford University Press.

———. 1995. "God's utility function." *Scientific American* 273(5): 62–67.

Dawkins, R. and J. R. Krebs. 1979. "Arms races between and within species." *Proceedings of the Royal Society of London B* 205: 489–511.

de Beauvoir, S. 1983. *The Second Sex.* Harmondsworth: Penguin.

de Waal, F. B. M. 1995. "Bonobo sex and society." *Scientific American* 272(3): 58–64.

Delporte, H. 1993. *L'Image de la Femme dans l'Art Préhistorique*. Paris: Picard.

Denison, S. 1995a. "1.8 million-year-old human presence claimed in Spain." *British Archaeology*, 7, September 1995.

———. 1995b. "From modern apes to human origins." *British Archaeology*, 8, October 1995.

Dennett, D. 1995. *Darwin's Dangerous Idea: Evolution and the Meanings of Life*. London: The Penguin Press.

Desmond, A. and J. Moore. 1991. *Darwin*. London: Michael Joseph.

di Leonardo, M. 1991. *Gender at the Crossroads of Knowledge: Feminist Anthropology in the Postmodern Era*. Berkeley: University of California Press.

Diamond, J. 1992. *The Third Chimpanzee: the Evolution and Future of the Human Animal*. New York: HarperCollins.

Diamond, M. 1984. *Sexwatching: Looking into the World of Sexual Behaviour*. London: Macdonald Orbis.

Didsbury, P. 1992. "An Anglo-Saxon mammiform pottery vessel from Barton-upon-Humber." In L. Blackmore and M. Redknap, eds. *Medieval Ceramics*: 66–67. Medieval Pottery Research Group.

Dixson, A. F. 1987. "Observations on the evolution of the genitalia and copulatory behaviour in male primates." *The Journal of the Zoological Society of London* 213, 423–43.

Dobzhansky, T. 1937. *Genetics and the Origin of Species*. New York: Columbia University Press.

———. 1972. "Genetics and the races of man." In B. Campbell, ed. *Sexual Selection and the Descent of Man 1871–1971*: 59–87. London, Heinemann.

Duhard, J-P. 1991. "The shape of Pleistocene women." *Antiquity* 65: 552–61.

Dunbar, R. 1988. *Primate Social Systems*. London: Croom Holm.

———. 1992. "Feasting and sexual licence." (Review of *Blood Relations: Menstruation and the Origins of Culture* by C. Knight.) *The Times Higher Education Supplement*. 31st January 1992.

Durham, E. 1985. *High Albania*. London: Virago.

Dutour, O., G. Pálfi, J. Berato, and J. P. Brun, eds. 1994. *L'origine de la syphilis en Europe: avant ou après 1493?* Paris: Centre archéologique du Var-Éditions Errance.

Ebling, J. 1985. "The mythological evolution of nudity." *Journal of Human Evolution* 14: 33–41.

Edelman, G. 1990. *The Remembered Present: a Biological Theory of Consciousness*. New York: Basic Books.

Egg, M., R. Goedecker-Ciolek, W. Groenman-Van Waateringe, and K. Spindler. 1993. *Die Gletschermumie von Ende der Steinzeit aus den Ötztaler Alpen* (Jahrbuch des Römisch-Germanischen Zentralmuseums 39 [1992]). Mainz: RGZM.

Ehrenberg, M. 1989. *Women in Prehistory*. London: British Museum Publications.

Ellis, H. 1947. *The Psychology of Sex*. (Eleventh impression.) London: Heinemann.

Ellis, P. 1994. "Sexual metaphors in the Neolithic." (Paper delivered to the "Sexuality, Society and Archaeology" session, TAG 94. *Programme and Abstracts for the Sixteenth Annual Conference of the Theoreti-*

cal Archaeology Group: 21. Bradford: University of Bradford, Department of Archaeological Sciences.

Engels, F. 1972. *The Origin of the Family, Private Property and the State* (Reprint of English edition of 1891). New York: Pathfinder Press.

Erskine, F. 1995. "The origin of species and the science of female inferiority." In D. Amigoni and J. Wallace, eds. *Charles Darwin's The Origin of Species: New Interdisciplinary Essays:* 95–121. Manchester: Manchester University Press.

Fagan, B. 1989. *People of the Earth: an Introduction to World Prehistory* (Sixth edition). Glenview, Ill: Scott, Foresman.

Falk, D. 1987. "Brain lateralization in primates and its evolution in hominids." *Yearbook of Physical Anthropology* 30: 107–25.

——. 1989. "Comments." *Current Anthropology* 30: 141.

——. 1993. "Sex differences in visuospatial skills: implications for hominid evolution." In K. R. Gibson and T. Ingold, eds. *Tools, Language and Cognition in Human Evolution:* 216–29. Cambridge: Cambridge University Press.

Fedigan, L. M. 1986. "The changing role of women in models of human evolution." *Annual Review of Anthropology* 15: 25–66.

Ferguson, A. E. 1994. "Gendered science: a critique of agricultural development." *American Anthropologist* 96: 540–52.

Ferraro, G., W. Trevathan, and J. Levy. 1994. *Anthropology: an Applied Perspective.* Minneapolis/St. Paul: West Publishing Company.

Ferry, G. 1994. "Flash dads make fitter kids." *New Scientist* 22nd October 1994: 81.

Fiddes, N. 1991. *Meat: A Natural Symbol*. London: Routledge.

Fildes, V. 1988. *Wet Nursing: a History from Antiquity to the Present*. Oxford: Basil Blackwell.

Fisher, H. 1986. Review of "Signs of the Flesh" by D. Rancour-Laferrière. *Journal of Human Evolution* 15: 413–18.

Fisher, R. A. 1930. *The Genetical Theory of Natural Selection*. Oxford: Clarendon Press.

Fitzpatrick, A. P. 1989. "The uses of Roman imperialism by the Celtic barbarians in the Later Republic." In J. Barrett, P. Fitzpatrick, and L. Macinnes, eds. *Barbarians and Romans in North-West Europe: from the Later Republic to Late Antiquity* (British Archaeological Reports, International Series Vol. 471): 27–54. Oxford: BAR.

Foley, R. 1989. "The ecological conditions of speciation: a comparative approach to the origins of anatomically-modern humans." In P. Mellars and C. Stringer, eds. *The Human Revolution: Behavioural and Biological Perspectives on the Origin of Modern Humans*: 298–317. Edinburgh: Edinburgh University Press.

Foucault, M. 1981. *The History of Sexuality: Vol. 1: An Introduction*. Harmondsworth: Pelican.

Fowler, P. J. and J. G. Evans. 1967. "Plough-marks, lynchets and early fields." *Antiquity* 41: 289–99.

Fox, F. 1972. "Alliance and constraint, sexual selection and the evolution of human kinship systems." In B. Campbell, ed. *Sexual Selection and the Descent of Man 1871–1971*: 282–332. London: Heinemann.

Freud, S. 1924–34. *Gesammelte Schriften* (12 volumes). Vienna.

———. 1975. *Three Essays on the Theory of Sexuality* (Translated and revised by James Strachey; introduction by Steven Marcus). New York: Basic Books.

———. 1987. *Drei Abhandlungen zur Sexualtheorie, und verwandte Schriften* (Edited, with an afterword, by Alexander Mitscherlich). Frankfurt a. M: Fischer.

———. 1995. *Five Lectures on Psycho-analysis* (Translated, with notes, by James Strachey). London: Penguin.

Fricker, J. 1994. "Mysteries of the orgasm." *Focus*, February 1994: 20–24.

Friday, N. 1991. *Women on Top*. London: Hutchinson.

Friedl, E. 1994. "Sex the invisible." *American Anthropologist* 96(4): 833–44.

Fulton, R. and S. W. Anderson. 1992. "The Amerindian 'man-woman': gender, liminality, and cultural continuity." *Current Anthropology* 33(5): 603–10.

Gallup, G. G. 1982. "Permanent breast enlargement in human females: a sociobiological analysis." *Journal of Human Evolution* 11: 597–601.

Gamble, C. 1994. *Timewalkers: The Prehistory of Global Colonization*. Cambridge, MA: Harvard University Press.

Gardner, R., B. Gardner, and T. Van Cantfort, eds. 1989. *Teaching Sign Language to Chimpanzees*. Albany: State University of New York Press.

Gaulin, S. J. C. and J. S. Bostner. 1992. "Human marriage systems and sexual dimorphism in stature." *American Journal of Physical Anthropology* 89: 467–75.

Gebauer, A. B. and T. D. Price, eds. 1992. *Transitions to Agriculture in Prehistory* (Monographs in World Archaeology Vol. 4). Madison: Prehistory Press.

Gellner, E. 1989. "Culture, constraint and community: semantic and coercive conpensations for the genetic under-determination of Homo sapiens sapiens." In P. Mellars and C. Stringer, eds. *The Human Revolution: Behavioural and Biological Perspectives on the Origin of Modern Humans:* 514–25. Edinburgh: Edinburgh University Press.

Georgiev, G. I. 1979. "Utvurzhdavane na purvobitnoobshtinniya stroi i nachenki na negovoto razlagane." In D. Kosev, *et al.*, eds. 1979. *Istoriya na Bulgariya* Vol. 1 (edited by V. Velkov): *Purvobitnoobshchinen i robovladelski stroi. Traki:* 77–80. Sofia: Izdatelstvo na Bulgarskata Akademiya na Naukite.

Gerhardie, W. 1987. *The Polyglots.* (First published 1925.) Oxford: Oxford University Press.

Gero, J. and M. Conkey, eds. 1991. *Engendering Archaeology: Women and Prehistory.* Oxford: Basil Blackwell.

Ghazi, P. 1993. "Tribute to 'humanity' of apes." *Observer,* June 20, p. 64.

Ghiselin, M. 1974. *The Economy of Nature and the Evolution of Sex.* Los Angeles: University of California Press.

Gibson, K. 1993. "Animal minds, human minds." In K. Gibson and T. Ingold, eds. *Tools, Language and Cognition in Human Evolution:* 3–19. Cambridge: Cambridge University Press.

Gibson, K. and T. Ingold. 1993, *Tools, Language and Cognition in Human Evolution.* Cambridge: Cambridge University Press.

Giddens, A. 1992. *The Transformation of Intimacy: Sexuality, Love and Eroticism in Modern Societies*. Cambridge: Polity Press.

Gilmore, D. 1990. *Manhood in the Making: Cultural Concepts of Masculinity*. New Haven: Yale University Press.

Gimbutas, M. 1981. "Vulvas, breasts, and buttocks of the Goddess Creatress." In G. Buccellati and C. Speroni, eds. *The Shape of the Past: Studies in Honor of Franklin D. Murphy:* 15–43. Los Angeles: UCLA Institute of Archaeology.

———. 1982. *The Goddesses and Gods of Old Europe: Myths and Cult Images*. London: Thames and Hudson.

———. 1989. *The Language of the Goddess*. London: Thames and Hudson.

———. 1991. *The Civilization of the Goddess*. San Francisco: HarperCollins.

Glatzl, J. 1987. "Intersexformen im Kindesalter (Pathogenese-Klinik-Diagnose-Therapie)." *Wiener Klinische Wochenschrift* 99(9): 295–306.

Glob, P. V. 1969. *The Bog People*. London: Faber.

Goleman, D. 1995. *Emotional Intelligence: Why it Can Matter More than IQ*. New York: Bantam.

Goodall, J. 1986. *The Chimpanzees of Gombe*. Cambridge, MA: Harvard University Press.

Goren-Inbar, N. 1986. "A figurine from the Acheulian site of Berekhat Ram." *Mi Tekufat Ha Even* 19: 7–11.

Gould, S. J. 1981. *The Mismeasure of Man*. New York: Norton.

——. 1995. "Male nipples and clitoral ripples." In S. J. Gould, *Adam's Navel* (A short selection of essays): 41–58. London: Penguin.

Gould, S. J. and R. Lewontin. 1979. "The spandrels of San Marco and the Panglossian paradigm: a critique of the adaptionist programme." *Proceedings of the Royal Society of London B* 205: 581–98.

Gould, S. J. and E. Vrba. 1981. "Exaptation: a missing term in the science of form." *Paleobiology* 8: 4–15.

Grayson, D. K. 1993. "Differential mortality and the Donner Party disaster." *Evolutionary Anthropology* 1993: 151–59.

Greer, G. 1993. *The Female Eunuch*. London: Flamingo.

Günther, H. 1927. *The Racial Elements of European History* (Translated from the second German edition by G. Wheeler). London: Methuen.

Gvozdover, M. 1995. *Art of the Mammoth Hunters: The Finds from Avdeevo* (Edited by Paul Bahn). Oxford: Oxbow.

Hall, L. 1994. "Havelock's heirs: the history of sexuality today." *Social History of Medicine* 7(1): 135–42.

Halperin, D., J. Winkler, and F. Zeitlin, eds. 1990. *Before Sexuality: The Construction of Erotic Experience in the Ancient Greek World*. Princeton: Princeton University Press.

Hardy, A. 1960. "Was man more aquatic in the past?" *The New Scientist* 17: 642–45.

Harrison, J. 1921. *Epilegomena to the Study of Greek Religion*. Cambridge: Cambridge University Press.

Harrison, R. 1980. *The Beaker Folk: Copper Age Archaeology in Western Europe*. London: Thames and Hudson.

———. 1994. "La cultura dei vasi campaniformi: 2600–1900 a. C." In J. Guilaine and S. Settis, eds. *Storia d'Europa, Vol.* 2(1): *Preistoria e Antichita:* 333–53. Turin: Einaudo.

Harthansen, J., J. Meldgaard, and J. Nordqvist. 1991. *The Greenland Mummies*. London: British Museum Press.

Harvey, P. H. and A. H. Harcourt. 1984. "Sperm competition, testes size, and breeding systems in primates." In R. L. Smith, ed. *Sperm Competition and the Evolution of Animal Mating Systems:* 590–99. London: Academic Press.

Hassan, F. 1981. *Demographic Archaeology*. New York: Academic Press.

Hastrup, K. 1978. "The nature of women in society." In S. Ardener, ed. *Defining Females: the Nature of Women in Society:* 49–65. London: Croom Helm.

Hausfater, G. and S. B. Hrdy. 1984. *Infanticide: Comparative and Evolutionary Perspectives*. New York: Aldine de Gruyter.

Häusler, M. and P. Schmid. 1995. "Comparison of the pelves of Sts 14 and AL 288-1: implications for birth and sexual dimorphism in Australopithecines." *Journal of Human Evolution* 29: 263–83.

Hawkes, S. C. and C. Wells. 1975. "An Anglo-Saxon obstetric calamity from Kingsworthy, Hants." *Medical and Biological Illustration* 25: 47–51.

———. 1975. "Crime and punishment in an Anglo-Saxon cemetery." *Antiquity* 49: 118–23.

Herodotus. 1987. *The History* (Translated by David Grene). Chicago: University of Chicago Press.

Herrnstein, R. and C. Murray. 1994. *The Bell Curve: Intelligence and Class Structure in American Life*. New York: Free Press.

Hewitt, J. 1969. *Techniques of Sexual Fitness*. New York: Universal.

———. 1983. *The Complete Yoga Book* (Second edition). London: Rider.

Himes, N. 1970. *A Medical History of Contraception*. (First published 1936.) New York: Schocken.

Hodder, I. 1986. *Reading the Past: Current Approaches to Interpretation in Archaeology*. Cambridge: Cambridge University Press.

———. 1990. *The Domestication of Europe*. Oxford: Basil Blackwell.

Holloway, R. 1981. "Culture, symbols and human brain evolution: a synthesis." *Dialectical Anthropology* 5: 287–303.

Hooper, A. 1994. *Anne Hooper's Ultimate Sex Guide*. London: Dorling Kindersley.

Horgan, J. 1993. "Eugenics revisited." *Scientific American* 268(6): 92–100.

———. 1995. "The new Social Darwinists." *Scientific American* 273(4): 150–57.

Howells, K., ed. 1984. *The Psychology of Sexual Diversity*. Oxford: Basil Blackwell.

Howells, W. 1976. "Explaining modern man: evolutionists versus migrationists." *Journal of Human Evolution* 5: 477–95.

———. 1989. *Skull Shapes and the Map*. Cambridge, MA: Harvard University Press.

Hrdy, S. B. 1981. *The Woman That Never Evolved.* Cambridge, MA: Harvard University Press.

Humphrey, N. 1986. *The Inner Eye.* London: Faber.

Hurcombe, L. 1995. "Our own engendered species." *Antiquity* 69: 87–100.

Hutton, R. 1991. *The Pagan Religions of the Ancient British Isles: their Nature and Legacy.* Oxford: Basil Blackwell.

Ingold, T. 1993a. "Tool-use, sociality and intelligence." In K. Gibson and T. Ingold, eds. *Tools, Language and Cognition in Human Evolution:* 429–45. Cambridge: Cambridge University Press.

———. 1993b. "Technology, language, intelligence: a reconsideration of basic concepts." In K. Gibson and T. Ingold, eds. *Tools, Language and Cognition in Human Evolution:* 449–72. Cambridge: Cambridge University Press.

Irons, W. 1979. "Cultural and biological success." In N. Chagnon and W. Irons, eds. *Evolutionary Biology and Human Social Behavior:* 436–53. North Scituate, MA: Duxbury Press.

Isaac, G. 1989. *The Archaeology of Human Origins* (Collected papers, edited by Barbara Isaac). Cambridge: Cambridge University Press.

Jackson, D. 1989. *Three in a Bed: Why You Should Sleep With Your Baby.* London: Bloomsbury.

Jensen, A. 1969. "How much can we boost IQ and scholastic achievement?" *Harvard Educational Review* 39(1): 1–123.

Johanson, D. C. and M. A. Edey. 1981. *Lucy: the Beginnings of Humankind.* London: Book Club Associates.

Johanson, D. and J. Shreeve. 1991. *Lucy's Child: the Discovery of a Human Ancestor*. London: Penguin.

Johns, C. 1982. *Sex or Symbol: Erotic Images of Greece and Rome*. London: British Museum Publications.

Jurmain, R. and H. Nelson. 1994. *Introduction to Physical Anthropology* (Sixth edition). Minneapolis/St. Paul: West Publishing Company.

Kastelic, J. 1965. *Situla Art*. London: Thames and Hudson.

Katinčarov, R., J.-P. Mohen, *et al.* 1989. *Le Premier Or de l'Humanité en Bulgarie, 5e Millénaire*. Paris: Réunion des musées nationaux.

Katz, S. H. 1972. "Biological factors in population control." In B. Spooner, ed. *Population Growth: Anthropological Implications*: 351–69. Cambridge, MA: MIT Press.

Kaul, F. 1991. *Gundestrupkedlen: Baggrund og Billedverden*. Copenhagen: Nyt Nordisk Forlag Arnold Busck.

Keys, D. 1989. "Amazon-style felling of ancient oaks." *The Independent*, Saturday 18th November 1989: 3.

Kimura, D. 1992. "Sex differences in the brain." *Scientific American* 267(3): 80–87.

King, H. 1988. "Hippocratic gynaecology made simple." *Omnibus* 15: 4–5.

Kingdon, J. 1993. *Self-Made Man and His Undoing*. London: Simon and Schuster.

Klima, B. 1988. "A triple burial from the Upper Paleolithic of Dolní Věstonice, Czechoslovakia." *Journal of Human Evolution* 16: 831–35.

Klindt-Jensen, A. O. 1979. *Gundestrupkedelen*. Copenhagen: National-museet.

Kloster, D. 1995. *Doris Kloster*. Cologne: Taschen.

Knight, C. 1991. *Blood Relations: Menstruation and the Origins of Culture*. Cambridge, MA: Yale University Press.

———. 1994a. *The Emergence of Language*. London: Department of Sociology, University of East London.

———. 1994b. *An Instinct for Revolution*. London: Department of Sociology, University of East London.

Knight, C. and C. Maisels. 1994. "Fertility rights." *The Times Higher Education Supplement*. September 1994: 20.

Knight, C. and C. Power. 1994. *Ritual and the Origins of Symbolism*. London: Department of Sociology, University of East London.

Knight, C., C. Power, and I. Watts. 1995. "The human symbolic revolution: a Darwinian account." *Cambridge Archaeological Journal* 5(1): 75–114.

Knüsel, C. 1992. "The throwing hypothesis and hominid origins." *Human Evolution* 7(1): 1–7.

Knüsel, C. J. and K. M. Ripley, forthcoming. "The berdache or man-woman in Anglo-Saxon England and Post-Roman Europe." In A. Tyrell and B. Frazer, eds., *Social Identity in Early Medieval Britain*.

Knussmann, R., K. Christiansen, and J. Kannmacher. 1992. "Relations between sex hormone level and characters of hair and skin in healthy young men." *American Journal of Physical Anthropology* 88: 59–67.

Kooy, B. van der. 1994. "Calculating expected date of delivery—its accuracy and relevance." *Next Generation Digest,* September 1994: 2–5.

Kovpanenko, G. T. 1991. "Die sarmatische 'Priesterin' aus der Sokolova Mogila." In R. Rolle, M. Müller-Wille, and K. Schietzel, eds. *Gold der Steppe: Archäologie der Ukraine*: 221–26. Neumünster: Karl Wachholtz Verlag.

La Leche League International. 1981. *The Womanly Art of Breastfeeding,* Illinois: La Leche League International.

Lancaster, J. B. 1991. "A feminist and evolutionary biologist looks at women." *Yearbook of Physical Anthropology* 34: 1–11.

Leakey, M. D. and J. Harris, eds. 1987. *Laetoli: a Pliocene Site in Northern Tanzania.* New York: Oxford University Press.

Leakey, R. 1981. *The Making of Mankind.* London: Book Club Associates.

Leakey, R. and R. Lewin. 1977. *Origins: What New Discoveries Reveal About the Emergence of Our Species and Its Possible Future.* London: MacDonald and Jane's.

Lee, G. 1986. " 'No sex, please, we're Aurignacians': further comment." *Rock Art Research* 4(1): 51–55.

Lee, R. B. 1972. "Population growth and the beginnings of sedentary life amongst the !Kung Bushmen." In B. Spooner, ed. *Population Growth: Anthropological Implications*: 329–42. Cambridge, MA: MIT Press.

Leick, G. 1994. *Sex and Eroticism in Mesopotamian Literature.* London: Routledge.

LeVay, S., and D. H. Hamer. 1994. "Evidence for a biological influence in male homosexuality." *Scientific American* 270: 19–25.

Lewin, R. 1993. "Shock of the past for modern medicine." *New Scientist* 23 October, 1993: 28–32.

Lloyd, G. E. R., ed. 1978. *Hippocratic Writings*. Harmondsworth: Pelican.

Lovejoy, C. O. 1981. "The origin of man." *Science* 211: 341–50.

——. 1988. "Evolution of human walking." *Scientific American* 259(11): 82–89.

Low, B. S. 1979. "Sexual selection and human ornamentation." In N. Chagnon and W. Irons, eds. *Evolutionary Biology and Human Social Behavior:* 436–53. North Scituate, MA: Duxbury Press.

Lumsden, C. and E. O. Wilson. 1981. *Genes, Mind, and Culture: The Coevolutionary Process*. Cambridge, MA: Harvard University Press.

Lunde, O. 1984. "A study of body hair density and distribution in normal women." *American Journal of Physical Anthropology* 64: 179 –84.

Lunde, O. and P. Grøttum. 1984. "Body hair growth in women: normal or hirsute." *American Journal of Physical Anthropology* 64: 307–13.

Mabey, R. 1989. *Food for Free*. London: HarperCollins.

MacLarnon, A. 1994. "The vertebral canal." In Walker, A. and R. Leakey, eds. *The Nariokotome Homo Erectus Skeleton:* 359–90. Berlin: Springer-Verlag.

Malinowski, B. 1927. *Sex and Repression in Savage Society* (First published 1924). London: Kegan Paul, Trench, Trubner.

——. 1929. *The Sexual Life of Savages in North-Western Melanesia*. New York: Harcourt, Brace and World.

Manson, W. C. 1986. "Sexual cyclicity and concealed ovulation." *Journal of Human Evolution* 15: 21–30.

Margulis, L. and D. Sagan. 1991. *Mystery Dance: On the Evolution of Human Sexuality*. London: Simon and Schuster.

Marks, J. 1995. "Molecular genetics supplies new links." *Anthropology Newsletter,* October 1995.

Marshack, A. 1972. *The Roots of Civilization*. New York: McGraw-Hill.

———. 1986. "Une figurine de Grimaldi 'redécouverte': analyse et discussion." *L'Anthropologie* 90(4): 807–14.

———. 1990. "Early hominid symbols and evolution of the human capacity." In P. Mellars, ed. *The Emergence of Modern Humans:* 457–99. Edinburgh: Edinburgh University Press.

———. 1996 forthcoming. "Figuring the figurines" (Comment on L. McDermott, "Self-representation in Pavlovian, Kostenkian and Gravetian Female Figures during the European Upper Palaeolithic"). *Current Anthropology* 17(2).

Martynov, A. I. 1991. *The Ancient Art of Northern Asia* (Translated by D. B. Shimkin and E. M. Shimkin). Urbana and Chicago: University of Illinois Press.

Masters, W. H. and V. E. Johnson. 1966. *Human Sexual Response*. Boston: Little, Brown.

Matthews, K. 1995. "Archaeological data, subcultures and social dynamics." *Antiquity* 69: 586–94.

Mayr, E. 1972. "Sexual selection and natural selection." In B. Campbell, ed. *Sexual Selection and the Descent of Man 1871–1971:* 87–104. London: Heinemann.

Mays, S. 1993. "Infanticide in Roman Britain." *Antiquity* 67: 883–88.

McDermott, L. 1985. *Self-Generated Information and Representation of the Human Figure During the European Upper Palaeolithic.* Unpublished Ph. D. Thesis, University of Kansas.

McEvilley, T. 1981. "An archaeology of yoga." *Res* 1: 44–77.

McGlone, J. 1980. "Sex differences in human brain asymmetry: a critical survey." *The Behavioral and Brain Sciences* 3: 215–63.

McKie, R. 1995. "The dawning of humanity." *Observer*, January 22: 23.

McLaren, A. 1990. *A History of Contraception: From Antiquity to the Present Day.* Oxford: Basil Blackwell.

Mead, M. 1973. *Coming of Age in Samoa: a Psychological Study of Primitive Youth for Western Civilization.* American Museum of Natural History.

Meaden, G. T. 1991. *The Goddess of the Stones: the Language of the Megaliths* (foreword by M. Gimbutas). London: Souvenir Press.

Meiklejohn, C. and M. Zvelebil. 1991. "Health status of European populations at the agricultural transition and the implications for the adoption of farming." In H. Bush and M. Zvelebil, eds. *Health in Past Societies. Biocultural Interpretations of Human Skeletal Remains in Archaeological Contexts* (British Archaeological Reports, International Series 567): 129–45. Oxford: BAR.

Mellars, P. 1994. "The Upper Palaeolithic revolution." In B. Cunliffe, ed. *The Oxford Illustrated Prehistory of Europe:* 42–78. Oxford: Oxford University Press.

Meskell, L. 1995. "Goddesses, Gimbutas and 'New Age' archaeology." *Antiquity* 69: 74–86.

Mies, M., V. Bennholdt-Thomsen, and C. von Werlhof. 1988. *Women: the Last Colony*. London: Zed Books.

Miller, B. D., ed. 1993. *Sex and Gender Hierarchies*. Cambridge: Cambridge University Press.

Milo, R. and D. Quiatt. 1993. "Glottogenesis and anatomically modern *Homo sapiens*: the evidence for and implications of a late origin of vocal language." *Current Anthropology* 34: 569–98.

Mithen, S. 1994. "The Mesolithic age." In B. Cunliffe, ed. *The Oxford Illustrated Prehistory of Europe:* 79–135. Oxford: Oxford University Press.

Molleson, T. 1994. "The eloquent bones of Abu Hureyra." *Scientific American* 271(2): 60–65.

Montagna, W. 1983. "The evolution of human skin." *Journal of Human Evolution* 14: 3–22.

Moogi-Cecchi, J., E. Pacciani, and J. Pintoi-Cisternas. 1994. "Enamel hypoplasia and age at weaning in 19th-century Florence, Italy." *American Journal of Physical Anthropology* 93: 299–306.

Moore, H. 1988. *Feminism and Anthropology*. Cambridge: Polity Press.

Moore, J. H. 1995. "The end of a paradigm." *Current Anthropology* 36(3): 530–31.

Morgan, E. 1982. *The Aquatic Ape: A Theory of Human Evolution*. London: Souvenir Press.

———. 1984. "The Aquatic Hypothesis." *New Scientist* 1045: 11–13.

———. 1985. *The Descent of Woman* (Revised edition). London: Souvenir Press.

Morgan, L. H. 1964. *Ancient Society* (Edited, with an introduction, by L. White). Cambridge, MA: Belknap Press of Harvard University Press.

Morris, D. 1967. *The Naked Ape*. London: Jonathan Cape.

———. 1994. *The Human Animal: a Personal View of the Human Species*. London: BBC Books.

Muthesius, A., B. Riemschneider, and G. Néret. 1993. *Erotic Art*. Cologne: Taschen.

Napier, J. R. and J. H. Napier. 1985. *The Natural History of the Primates*. London: British Museum (Natural History).

Nelson, S. M. 1990. "Diversity of the Upper Paleolithic 'Venus' figurines and archaeological mythology." In S. Nelson and A. Kehoe, eds. *Powers of Observation: Alternative Views in Archaeology* (Archaeological Papers of the American Anthropological Association, Vol. 2): 11–22. American Anthropological Association.

Neugebauer-Maresch, C. 1993. *Altsteinzeit im osten Österreichs*. St. Pölten and Vienna: Niederösterreiches Pressehaus.

Newcombe, F. and G. Ratcliff. 1978. "The female brain: a neuropsychological viewpoint." In S. Ardener, ed. *Defining Females: the Nature of Women in Society:* 186–99. London: Croom Helm.

Newman, J. 1995. "How breast milk protects newborns." *Scientific American* 273: 58–61.

Noble, W. and I. Davidson. 1991. "The evolutionary emergence of modern human behaviour: language and its archaeology." *Man* 26: 223–53.

O'Brien, M. 1992. "Gender identity and sex roles." In V. B. van Hassalt and M. Hersen, eds. *Handbook of Social Development: a Lifespan Perspective:* 325–45. New York and London: Plenum.

O'Connell, S. 1994. "Why sex may be all in the mind." *Guardian*, Thursday, March 10th.

Odent, M. 1992. *The Nature of Birth and Breastfeeding*. London: Bergin and Garvey.

———. 1993. "Birth, sexuality and orgasm." *Body Politic* 4: 14–16.

Ortner, S. 1974. "Is female to male as nature is to culture?" In M. Rosaldo and L. Lamphere, eds. *Woman, Culture and Society*: 67–88. Stanford, CA: Stanford University Press.

Ortner, S. and H. Whitehead, eds. 1981. *Sexual Meanings: the Cultural Construction of Gender and Sexuality*. Cambridge: Cambridge University Press.

Ovid. 1982. *The Erotic Poems* (Translated by P. Green). Harmondsworth: Penguin.

Palmer, G. 1988. *The Politics of Breastfeeding*. London: Pandora.

Patterson, H. 1985. "The recognition concept of species." In E. Vrba, ed. *Species and Speciation* (Transvaal Museum Monograph 4); 21–29. Pretoria: Transvaal Museum.

Patrick, J. 1974. "Midwinter sunrise at Newgrange." *Nature* 249: 517–19.

Patzold, J. 1960. "Rituelles Pflugen beim vorgeschichtlichen Totenkult." *Prähistorische Zeitschrift* 38: 189–239.

Pearce, F. 1994. "Greening the heart of England." *New Scientist* 143(1944): 30–35.

Peoples, J. and G. Bailey. 1994. *Humanity: an Introduction to Cultural Anthropology* (Third edition). Saint Paul: West Publishing Company.

Peterson, C., S. Maier, and M. E. P. Seligman. 1993. *Learned Helplessness: a Theory for the Age of Personal Control*. New York: Oxford University Press.

Pfeiffer, J. 1979. *The Emergence of Society: A Prehistory of the Establishment*. New York: McGraw-Hill.

Phillips, A. and J. Rakusen, 1989. *The New Our Bodies, Ourselves: a Health Book by and for Women* (British edition). London: Penguin.

Pinker, S. 1994. *The Language Instinct*. London: Penguin.

Piotrovsky, B., L. Galanina and N. Grach. 1987. *Scythian Art*. Oxford: Phaidon.

Piotrovsky, B. B., M. P. Zavitukhina, and L. L. Barkova. 1978. *Frozen Tombs: the Culture and Art of the Ancient Tribes of Siberia*. London: British Museum Publications.

Plato. 1995. *The Symposium* (Translated by W. Hamilton). London: Penguin.

Posner, R. 1992. *Sex and Reason*. Cambridge, MA: Harvard University Press.

Power, C. 1994. "Lip service and confusing the male over menstrual cycles." *The Times Higher Education Supplement.* 21st October 1994.

Putnam, J. 1993. *Mummies*. London: Eyewitness Guides in Association with the British Museum.

Radford, T. 1994. "Tell-tale fragments hold crucial clues to lost identity." *The Guardian,* Tuesday, 8th March 1994.

———. 1995. "Transsexuals 'have female brain structure.' " *The Guardian,* 2nd November 1995.

Rak, Y. and B. Arensburg. 1987. "Kebara 2 Neandertal pelvis: first look at a complete inlet." *American Journal of Physical Anthropology* 73(2): 227–32.

Rasa, A. E., C. Vogel, and E. Voland, eds. 1989. *The Sociobiology of Sexual and Reproductive Strategies*. London: Chapman and Hall.

Rathje, W. L. 1984. "The Garbage Decade." *American Behavioral Scientist* 28(1): 9–29.

Raymond, J. G. 1979. *The Transsexual Empire*. London: The Women's Press.

Reid, A. and R. MacLean. 1995. "Symbolism and the social contexts of iron production in Karagwe." *World Archaeology* 27(1): 144–61.

Renfrew, C. and P. Bahn. 1991. *Archaeology: Theories, Methods, and Practice*. London: Thames and Hudson.

Rice, P. 1981. "Prehistoric Venuses: symbols of motherhood or womanhood?" *Journal of Anthropological Research* 37: 402–14.

Richards, G. 1987. *Human Evolution: an Introduction for the Behavioural Sciences*. London: Routledge & Kegan Paul.

Richman, B. 1993. "On the evolution of speech: singing as the middle term." *Current Anthropology* 34: 721–22.

Riddle, J. 1992. *Contraception and Abortion from the Ancient World to the Renaissance*. Cambridge, MA: Harvard University Press.

Riddle, J., J. Worth Estes, and J. Russell. 1994. "Ever since Eve . . . birth control in the Ancient World." *Archaeology* 47(2): 29–35.

Ridley, M. 1993. *The Red Queen: Sex and the Evolution of Human Nature*. London: Viking Penguin.

Roberts, N. 1993. *Whores in History: Prostitution in Western Society*. London: HarperCollins.

Rolle, R. 1989. *The World of the Scythians* (Translated by Gayna Walls). London: Batsford.

Rolle, R., M. Müller-Wille, and K. Schietzel, eds. 1991. *Gold der Steppe: Archäologie der Ukraine*. Neumünster: Karl Wachholtz Verlag.

Rosaldo, M. and L. Lamphere, eds. 1974. *Women, Culture and Society*. Stanford, CA: Stanford University Press.

Rouhani, S. 1989. "Molecular genetics and the pattern of human evolution: plausible and implausible models." In P. Mellars and C. Stringer, eds. *The Human Revolution: Behavioural and Biological Perspectives on the Origin of Modern Humans*: 47–61. Edinburgh: Edinburgh University Press.

Rowley-Conwy, P. 1994. "Mesolithic settlement patterns: new zooarchaeological evidence from the Vale of Pickering, Yorkshire." *Archaeological Reports 1994*: 1–6. Durham: University of Durham and University of Newcastle-upon-Tyne.

Ruff, C. B. 1995. "Biomechanics of the hip and birth in early *Homo*." *American Journal of Physical Anthropology* 98: 527–74.

Rundle Clark, R. T. 1959. *Myth and Symbol in Ancient Egypt*. London: Thames and Hudson.

Runnels, C. 1995. "Environmental degradation in Ancient Greece." *Scientific American* 272(3): 72–75.

Rusbridger, A. 1986. *A Concise History of the Sex Manual*. London: Faber and Faber.

Rushton, J. P. 1990. "Race differences, r/K theory, and a reply to Flynn." *The Psychologist* 3: 195–98.

Russell, R. 1993. *The Lemur's Legacy: the Evolution of Power, Sex and Love*. New York: Putnam.

Rycroft, C. 1971. *Reich*. Glasgow: Fontana.

Sandars, N. 1968. *Prehistoric Art in Europe*. Harmondsworth: Penguin.

Sanday, P. R. and R. Goodenough, eds. 1990. *Beyond the Second Sex: New Directions in the Anthropology of Gender*. Philadelphia: University of Pennsylvania Press.

Sass, T. 1995. Translation of Ibn Fadlan 87–92, "The Funeral of the Rus-Chief." In O. Crumlin-Pedersen and B. M. Thye, eds. *The Ship as Symbol in Prehistoric and Medieval Scandinavia* (PNM Studies in Archaeology and History, Vol. 1): 136–37. Copenhagen: National Museum of Denmark.

Scarre, C. ed. 1988. *Past Worlds: the Times Atlas of Archaeology*. London: Times Books.

Schwartz, J. H. 1987. *The Red Ape: Orang-utans and Human Origins*. Boston: Houghton Mifflin Company.

Seers, W. 1995. *Wearing Your Baby: The Art and Science of Wearing Your Baby*. Lake Arrowhead, CA: Parenting Concepts.

Seligman, M. E. P. 1975. *Helplessness: on Depression, Development, and Death*. San Francisco: Freeman.

Sharp, M. 1989. *A Land of Gods and Giants* (introduced by C. Chippindale). Gloucester: Alan Sutton.

Sheets-Johnstone, M. 1990. *The Roots of Thinking*. Philadelphia: Temple University Press.

Sherratt, A. 1994. "The transformation of early agrarian Europe: the later Neolithic and Copper Ages." In B. Cunliffe, ed. *The Oxford Illustrated Prehistory of Europe:* 167–201. Oxford: Oxford University Press.

Sholl, R. 1995. *Review of Literature and Metrical Studies of Dental Crowding and Mandible Development in Relation to Potential Changes in the Diet in Infant Weaning Regimes at the Mesolithic/Neolithic Boundary*. Unpublished undergraduate dissertation, Department of Archaeological Sciences, University of Bradford.

Short, R. V. and E. Balaban, eds. 1994. *The Differences Between the Sexes*. Cambridge: Cambridge University Press.

Shreeve, J. 1995. *The Neandertal Enigma*. New York: William Morrow.

Shuttle, P. and P. Redgrove. 1994. *The Wise Wound: Menstruation and Everywoman*. London: HarperCollins.

Shuttleworth, S. 1993. "A mother's place is in the wrong." *New Scientist*, 25 Dec 94–1 Jan 95: 38–40.

Sjöö, M. and B. Mor. 1981. *The Ancient Religion of the Great Cosmic Mother of All*. Trondheim, Norway.

———. 1987. *The Great Cosmic Mother: Rediscovering the Religion of the Earth*. San Francisco: Harper & Row.

Small, M. 1993. *Female Choices: Sexual Behavior of Female Primates*. Ithaca, NY: Cornell University Press.

———. 1994. "When Mr. Right is too much effort." *New Scientist* 143(1934): 30–33.

———. 1995. "Bringing up baby." *New Scientist,* 24 June 95: 36–39.

Smith, N. W. 1986. "Psychology and evolution of breasts." *Human Evolution* 1(3): 285–86.

Smith, R. L., ed. 1984a. *Sperm Competition and the Evolution of Animal Mating Systems.* London: Academic Press.

Smith, R. L. 1984b. "Comparative hominid reproductive and social biology." In R. L. Smith, ed. *Sperm Competition and the Evolution of Animal Mating Systems:* 618–59. London: Academic Press.

Spindler, K. 1994. *The Man in the Ice.* London: Weidenfeld and Nicholson.

Spindler, K., with contributions by E. Hollstein and E. Neuffer. 1976. *Der Magdalenenberg bei Villingen: ein Fürstengrabhügel des 6. vorchristlichen Jahrhunderts (Führer zu vor- und frühgeschichtlichen Denkmälern in Baden-Württemberg 5).* Stuttgart: Konrad Theiss.

Spring, D. B., et al. 1989. "The radiographic preauricular groove: its nonrelationship to past parity." *American Journal of Physical Anthropology* 79: 247–52.

Steinem, G. 1994. *Moving Beyond Words.* London: Bloomsbury.

Stoddart, D. M. 1990. *The Scented Ape: The Biology and Culture of Human Odour.* Cambridge: Cambridge University Press.

Stoneking, M. and R. Cann. 1989. "African origin of human mitochondrial DNA." In P. Mellars and C. Stringer, eds. *The Human Revolution: Behavioural and Biological Perspectives on the Origin of Modern Humans:* 17–30. Edinburgh: Edinburgh University Press.

Stringer, C. 1989. "The origin of early modern humans: a comparison of the European and non-European evidence." In P. Mellars and C.

Stringer, eds. *The Human Revolution: Behavioural and Biological Perspectives on the Origin of Modern Humans*: 232–43. Edinburgh: Edinburgh University Press.

Stringer, C. and C. Gamble. 1993. *In Search of the Neanderthals.* London: Thames and Hudson.

Stuart MacAdam, P. and K. A. Dettwyler, eds. forthcoming. *Breastfeeding: Biocultural Perspectives.* New York: Aldine de Gruyter.

"Support" editorial. 1994. "Premarin: does it alleviate or cause suffering?" *Support* (The magazine of CHANGE) 3(2): 1–3. London: Change.

Susman, R. L. 1987. "Chimpanzees: pigmy chimpanzees and common chimpanzees: models for the behavioral ecology of the earliest hominids." In W. Kinzey, ed. *The Evolution of Human Behaviour: Primate Models.* Albany: State University of New York.

Tague, R. 1992. "Sexual dimorphism in the human bony pelvis, with a consideration of the Neandertal pelvis from Kebara Cave, Israel." *American Journal of Physical Anthropology* 88: 1–21.

Tague, R. and C. O. Lovejoy. 1986. "The obstetric pelvis of A.L. 288–1 (Lucy)." *Journal of Human Evolution* 15: 237–55.

Tannahill, R. 1980. *Sex in History.* London: Hamish Hamilton.

Tanner, N. and A. Zihlman. 1976. "Women in evolution. Part I: Innovation and selection in human origins." *Signs: Journal of Women in Culture and Society* 1(3): 585–608.

Taylor, T. 1992. "The Gundestrup Cauldron," *Scientific American* 266(3): 84–89.

———. 1993. "Conversations with Leo Klejn." *Current Anthropology* 34: 723–35.

———. 1994. "Thracians, Scythians, and Dacians, 800 BC–AD 300." In B. Cunliffe, ed. *The Oxford Illustrated Prehistory of Europe:* 373–410. Oxford: Oxford University Press.

———. 1995. Review of Gwendolyn Leick, "Sex and Eroticism in Mesopotamian Literature." *Antiquity* 69: 632–33.

Thomas, D. H. 1989. *Archaeology* (Second edition). Fort Worth: Holt, Rinehart and Winston.

Thomas, J. 1991. *Re-Thinking the Neolithic*. Cambridge: Cambridge University Press.

Thomas, K. 1983. *Man and the Natural World: Changing Attitudes in England 1500–1800*. Harmondsworth: Penguin.

Tobias, P. V. 1972. *The Meaning of Race* (Second edition). Johannesburg: South African Institute of Race Relations.

Tompkins, R. L. and E. Trinkaus. 1987. "La Ferrasie 6: the development of Neandertal pubic morphology." *American Journal of Physical Anthropology* 73(2): 233–40.

Trigger, B. 1989. *A History of Archaeological Thought*. Cambridge: Cambridge University Press.

Trinkaus, E. 1983. *The Shanidar Neandertals*. New York: Academic Press.

———. 1984. "Neandertal pubic morphology and gestation length." *Current Anthropology* 25: 509–14.

Trivers, R. L. 1972. "Parental investment and sexual selection." In B. Campbell, ed. *Sexual Selection and the Descent of Man 1871–1971:* 36–79. London: Heinemann.

Tully, B. 1992. *Accounting for Transsexualism and Transhomosexuality*. London: Whiting & Birch.

van Gennep, A. 1979. *The Rites of Passage* (First French publication 1908; 1960 translation by M. Vizedom and G. Caffee). London: Routledge & Kegan Paul.

Vasey, P. L. 1995. "Homosexual behaviour in primates: A review of evidence and theory." *International Journal of Primatology* 16(2): 173–204.

Wailes, B. 1984. "Plow and population in temperate Europe." In R. L. Smith, ed. *Sperm Competition and the Evolution of Animal Mating Systems:* 154–79. London: Academic Press.

Walker, A. 1994. "Perspectives on the Nariokotome discovery." In A. Walker and R. Leakey, eds. *The Nariokotome Homo Erectus Skeleton*: 411–30. Berlin: Springer-Verlag.

Walker, A. and R. Leakey, eds. 1994. *The Nariokotome Homo Erectus Skeleton*. Berlin: Springer-Verlag.

Walker, B. 1977. *Body Magic: an Encyclopaedia of Esoteric Man*. London: Routledge & Kegan Paul.

Warne, G., H. MacLean, and J. Zajac. 1993. "Genetic disorders of human sex differentiation." In K. Reed and J. Graves. *Sex Chromosomes and Sex-Determining Genes* (Edited reports of the Australian Academy of Science 1992 Boden Research Conference on Mammalian Sex Chromosomes and Sex Determining Genes: Their differentiation, autonomy and interactions in gonad differentiation and function): 57–67. Chur, Switzerland: Harwood Academic Publishers.

Wavell, S. 1995. "No place for monkey business." *The Sunday Times*, 12th February 1995: 12–13.

Weidegger, P. 1986. *History's Mistress: a New Interpretation of a Nineteenth-Century Ethnographic Classic.* Harmondsworth: Penguin.

Weitz, S. 1977. *Sex Roles: Biological, Physiological, and Social Foundations.* New York: Oxford University Press.

Wells, C. 1975. "Ancient obstetric hazards and female mortality." *Bulletin of the New York Academy of Medicine* 51(11): 1235–49.

———. 1978. "A Medieval burial of a pregnant woman." *History of Medicine* 221: 442–44.

Wendt, H. 1971. *From Ape to Adam: the Search for the Ancestry of Man* (Translated by S. Cupitt). London: Thames and Hudson.

Wheeler, P. 1985. "The loss of functional body hair in man: the influence of thermal environment, body form and bipedality." *Journal of Human Evolution* 14: 14–28.

———. 1992. "The influence of the loss of functional body hair on the water budgets of early hominids." *Journal of Human Evolution* 21: 379–88.

Wheelwright, J. 1989. *Amazons and Military Maids: Women Who Dressed as Men in the Pursuit of Life, Liberty and Happiness.* London: Pandora.

Whittle, A. 1994. "The First Farmers." In B. Cunliffe, ed. *The Oxford Illustrated Prehistory of Europe*: 136–66. Oxford: Oxford University Press.

Williams, W. 1986. *The Spirit and the Flesh: Sexual Diversity in American Indian Culture.* Boston: Beacon Press.

Wills, C. 1993. *The Runaway Brain: the Evolution of Human Uniqueness.* London: HarperCollins.

Winkler, E-M. and K. Christiansen. 1993. "Sex Hormone Levels and Body Hair Growth in !Kung San and Kavango Men From Namibia." *American Journal of Physical Anthropology* 92: 155–64.

Wockner, R. and B. Frings. 1992. "Stone Age Leatherman Found in the Alps." *Capital Gay,* Summer 1992.

Wolpoff, M. 1989. "Multiregional evolution: the fossil alternative to Eden." In P. Mellars and C. Stringer, eds. *The Human Revolution: Behavioural and Biological Perspectives on the Origin of Modern Humans*: 62–99. Edinburgh: Edinburgh University Press.

Wood, B. 1976. *The Evolution of Early Man* (with illustrations by Giovanni Caselli). London: Peter Lowe.

——. 1992. "Origin and Evolution of the genus *Homo.*" *Nature* 355: 783–90.

Wylie, A. 1991. "Gender theory and the archaeological record: why is there no archaeology of gender?" In J. Gero and M. Conkey, eds. 1991. *Engendering Archaeology: Women and Prehistory:* 31–54. Oxford: Basil Blackwell.

Wynn, T. 1993. "Layers of Thinking in Tool Behaviour." In K. Gibson and T. Ingold, eds. *Tools, Language and Cognition in Human Evolution:* 389–406. Cambridge: Cambridge University Press.

Zias, J., H. Start, J. Seligman, R. Levy, E. Werker, A. Breuer, and R. Mechoulam. 1993. "Early medical use of Cannabis." *Nature* 363: 215.

Zihlman, A. 1993. "Sex differences and gender hierarchies among primates: an evolutionary perspective." In B. D. Miller, ed. *Sex and Gender Hierarchies:* 32–79. Cambridge: Cambridge University Press.

——. 1994. "Myths of Gender: a review of 'Female Choices: Sexual Behaviour of Female Primates' by M. Small." *Nature* 364: 585.

Index

ABOUT THE AUTHOR

TIMOTHY TAYLOR, PH.D., is a lecturer in archaeology at the University of Bradford in
the United Kingdom. He has presented his
work on *Down to Earth* in an episode that
won the British Archaeological Award for
best popular archaeology on television in
1991–92. He has contributed articles to *Scientific American, Antiquity,* and *The Oxford Illustrated Prehistory of Europe.*